CW01021061

Against the odds
AN AUTOBIOGRAPHY

JAMES
dyson

Against the odds
AN AUTOBIOGRAPHY

ORION
BUSINESS
BOOKS

Copyright © 1997 Giles Coren, 1998 James Dyson

All rights reserved

The right of Giles Coren to be identified as the author
of this work has been asserted by him in accordance
with the Copyright, Designs and Patents Act 1988

Hardback edition first published in Great Britain in 1997
This paperback edition first published in Great Britain in 1998 by
Orion Business
An imprint of The Orion Publishing Group Ltd
Orion House, 5 Upper St Martin's Lane, London WC2H 9EA

A CIP catalogue record for this book
is available from the British Library

ISBN 0-75281-383-8

Typeset by Selwood Systems, Midsomer Norton
Printed in Great Britain by
Butler & Tanner Ltd, Frome and London

contents

acknowledgements

Giles Coren and I first met when he did an interview for *The Times* in 1995. The resulting article was brilliantly structured. He is breathtakingly erudite. So I was flattered when he agreed to collaborate on this book. His clear synthesis of my long hours of rambling is nothing short of miraculous.

My success has been due to the unique spirit and extraordinary effort of everyone at Dyson. For me this has made the adventure exciting and a constant reminder of how wonderful human nature and talent can be. Thank you all (see pages 293 to 295) so much.

My wife Deirdre has admitted to enjoying my manic diatribes daily for the last twenty-seven years. But I think she has been stoic in the extreme. She is an artist and creator of her own beautiful works and has had to bring up our children at many times on her own. Emily, Jacob and Sam are a wonderful tribute to her wisdom and love. This book is dedicated to Deirdre.

preface

It must have been some time in 1979 that I first heard the words, 'But, James, if there were a better kind of vacuum cleaner Hoover or Electrolux would have invented it.' That was when I left the first company I had set up – gave up security, income, and respectability – and persuaded an old friend to come in with me on a project I was developing in the pigsties behind my house.

My experience was of a new kind of wheelbarrow, a high-speed launch craft, and a couple of castles in the air. For twelve years I laboured under heavier and heavier debt. I tried and failed to interest the major manufacturing companies in my product. I fought terrible legal battles to protect my vacuum cleaner. And in 1992 I went into production, on my own, as sole owner of the machine I had conceived, designed, built and tested alone.

After hundreds of prototypes, thousands of modifications, and millions of tests, I was in terrible debt, but in love with the Dual Cyclone. By 1997 I had a company turning over £100 million in the UK, and had generated sales of more than £1 billion worldwide. The Dyson was the biggest-selling vacuum cleaner in Britain. Bigger than Electrolux, bigger than Phillips, bigger than Hoover. In 1996 my company became the first British manufacturer of domestic electrical goods to export to Japan.

This is the story of how I did it.

Introduction

The funny thing about the story of the Dyson Dual Cyclone is that I knew it would turn out like this from the very beginning. Despite all the setbacks, the lawsuits and cash crises, the interminable patenting processes, the ridicule, bad feeling and doubt, the rippers-off and the clingers-on (outnumbered, sadly, by the rippers), I always knew, deep down, that everything would come up smelling of ... well, of something better than Shake 'n' Vac.

It isn't a pretty thing, writing a book about oneself, one's achievements, money, success and all the rest. So this is really a book about the things I have made: the products, the companies, the decisions, the enemies, sometimes, and the mistakes, often. The point, of course, is the vacuum cleaner, the Dyson Dual Cyclone, and since the object – like the company – bears my name, it is also, I am afraid, a book about me.

My desire to write a book was born of a number of half-related things. Unusually, I think, in the case of men who decide that the time has come to tell the story of their life, the secret of their success, my motivation never had anything to do with a need to see my name on a book.

I am a creator of products, a builder of things, and my name appears on them. That is how I make a living and they are what have made my name at least familiar in a million homes. I lay no claim to the epithet 'household word', though I harbour a secret dream of synonymity, and occasionally imagine a time, years from today, when 'dyson' replaces 'hoover', pulls that cunning stunt – like biro, tarmac, sellotape – and becomes a noun, a verb, out there on its own and detached from me to such an extent that most people will have no idea that there ever was a man called Dyson. I like the idea of a child in the twenty-first century telling his friends he can't come out for a bit because, 'Mum wants me to dyson my room', long after my bones have crumbled and I am no more than a potential clogging irritant for lesser machines. That, prosaic as it may sound, is how I have made my play for immortality. The book is not supposed to make me richer or more famous or more respected or more loved. Which doesn't leave much.

Part of it has to do with all the correspondence I receive from other inventors, which tends to come in great flurries of paper in the days after a newspaper article or television programme about me. And when I say inventors, I do not mean men with workshops and science degrees and designs registered at the patent office (although there are quite a few of them, too). I mean ordinary people who have had an idea. Believe me, there are a lot of them around. They ask for advice on developing their ideas, on finding out how feasible they are, on whether anything like that already exists, on marketing the product, and marketing themselves, and how to keep control of their idea, and make themselves, rather than some blood-sniffing corporate shark, rich.

I can't offer real advice to all those people individually, so, to an extent, this book represents my attempt to enter a dialogue, and answer the questions that are put to me so often. I do not pretend to offer a 'how-to' manual, for many of those exist already. I hope rather to lead by example.

This is also the exposition of a business philosophy, which is very different from anything you might have encountered before. And while there is always a limit to how exciting a business philosophy can be (it cannot actually be exciting at all – business is a revolting word, and is to do with nothing but the process of making money) the thing about this one is that it wasn't conceived by a businessman. And it has worked.

To use a Hollywood cliché, it is said that to be an overnight success takes years of effort. So it has proved with me. There were twenty years of debt, personal overdraft liabilities, at times, of millions of pounds. Four years ago I came out of the dark, and now I head a company turning over £100 million. Most bizarrely, it has all happened rather without anyone noticing. There have been no massive advertising campaigns (not from me at any rate, though there have been campaigns from the big boys designed to damage me, or at least to limit the damage I have done to them) and I have not taken over the market with a barrage of free offers, bombastic rhetoric, and gilded promotions. There have been no free air tickets with the Dual Cyclone. It has all happened, I really believe, because of the intrinsic excellence of the machine; because it is a better vacuum cleaner than anything that has gone before; and because it looks better than anything like it has ever looked.

Like little Dorothy in *The Wizard of Oz*, the vacuum cleaner discovered what life was really about only after the cyclone arrived. For a hundred years it had remained essentially unchanged, since the first prototype stopped sucking after ten minutes and just pushed the dirt around the room, and the first bag burst on a carpet.

The brand name Hoover became synonymous with this machine, and countless other industrial giants got rich on it. If anyone was going to step in and shake this global farrago up a bit, it was very unlikely to be me, an Englishman, who wasn't a qualified engineer, without even a physics O Level to my name, riding on the crest of one moment of Edisonian illumination.

And yet that was how it turned out. The bag was discarded for ever and replaced with a little typhoon that spun at the speed of sound, in a chamber that couldn't clog. And the vacuum cleaner was in total control of its own awesome potential. It was ready to clean up the planet, and ready for a new century. I own it exclusively, and with it, you might say, the key to every household in the developed world.

Launched in 1993, the Dyson Dual Cyclone is already the biggest-selling vacuum cleaner in Britain, and that despite costing, at £200, more than most competing Hoovers and Electroluxes. Dyson products have made over £100 million, and Dyson, the company, has become the fastest-growing manufacturing company in the country – and all in a couple of years, quite quietly, from a forty-something former art student who didn't know a ball-bearing from a Barings Bank.

If the Dual Cyclone is not yet an instantly recognisable object of desire, my first coup has got pretty close. The Ballbarrow, the wheelbarrow-shaped object with a pneumatic balloon in place of a wheel, became the market leader within three years of coming off the drawing board. It seems fairly straightforward: if you want a wheelbarrow that doesn't dig furrows in a soft lawn, doesn't sink in heavy mud, and maintains its balance regardless of the load, then you just replace a wheel with a ball. Easy. But not surprising that the thing was so useless for so long. After all, the man who invented the wheel was designing for a very different market – and he had something of a monopoly.

Such reverence has been accorded to the miserable wheel that perhaps that alone can account for the fact that it was never improved. Perhaps millions of people, in the last few thousand years, have had ideas for improving it. All I did was take things a little further than just having the idea.

And ideas are something we all have. Just as the old truism runs that everyone believes they have a novel in them, so most of us have at one time or another thought of an invention that would change the world. Whether it is a board game, or a bottle opener, a hat-stand or a harpsichord-holder, it never seems to get beyond the 'wouldn't-that-be-useful' stage. Some of this has to do with our own apathy, some of it is because British industry is so notoriously unwilling to put money into new ideas but, most of all, it is because we don't have the first idea how to go about making a daydream into a marketable object. My story, with a bit of luck, will give hope to anyone who has ever felt his dreams slipping away under pressure from the blind and powerful.

The first thing to forget is any notion that you have to be a qualified engineer to make an impact on engineering. I studied only art subjects at school and slipped into the Royal College of Art through a back door. I fiddled with wood for a while and then – when it was still looked upon as a barbarian at the gate – got into plastic, and drifted into product design. Convinced that engineering was no more than a state of mind, and determined to develop the products I was designing technologically, as well as visually, I began to moonlight as a professional.

The look of the product, the intangible style that sets one thing apart from another, is still closest to my heart. The Dual Cyclone is the only domestic appliance in the Twentieth Century Gallery at the V&A, and is uniquely on permanent view at both the Science Museum and the Design Museum. But it is only by remaining as close as possible to the pure function of the object that beauty can be achieved. My greatest hero was always Isambard Kingdom Brunel, whose inverted catenary curve was crucial to the structure of his bridges, and gave them the distinct stylistic power that still wows onlookers today.

An invention, if it is to woo the luddite minds of industry, and the more promiscuous hearts of the consumer, must look, as they say, 'the business'; in Brunel the purity of the engineering gives the design a special glow that no flippant sensationalist like Philippe Starck could dream of.

My own success has been in observing objects in daily use which, it was always assumed, could not be improved. By lateral thinking – the 'Edisonian approach' – it is possible to arrive, empirically, at an advance. Anyone can become an expert in anything in six months, whether it is hydrodynamics for boats or cyclonic systems for vacuum cleaners. After the idea, there is plenty of time to learn the technology. My first cyclonic vacuum cleaner was built out of cereal packets and masking tape (like some grotesque *Blue Peter* spaceship), long before I understood how it worked. After that initial 'Eureka!' it was a long haul to the Dual Cyclone – so called because an outer cyclone rotating at 200 m.p.h. removes large debris and most of the dust, while an inner cyclone rotating at 924 m.p.h. creates huge gravitational force and drives the finest dust, even particles of cigarette smoke, out of the air.

But the greatest lesson for aspiring inventors was yet to come. The actual making of money. Paper stuff in thick wads which they finally give to you because you have done something good.

Despite the success of the Ballbarrow (whose patent I foolishly assigned to the company rather than myself, and whose ubiquitousness has profited me not a bean), I could find no one at home to back my efforts with cash, a perennial problem for British inventors, which sees so many of our technological innovations being produced overseas. To raise the money I needed first for research, and then for production, I tried to sell licences to America and Japan. This time, by retaining the patent, I retained control.

In Japan, home of the high-tech appliance, the Dual Cyclone was an unprecedented success. Known as the 'G Force' and produced in pastel pink, it won the 1991 International Design Fair prize in Tokyo. So impressed were the Japanese that the 'G Force' became a luxury status symbol and, at a staggering price of £1,200 per machine, is currently making sales of £12 million a year. I really did get rich taking coal to Newcastle.

In America the story was less happy. After a licence agreement with them was terminated, a gargantuan manufacturer began making and selling a cyclonic vacuum cleaner under its own name. Just to keep the story ticking over, to reinforce the theme of one man taking on the world, I filed a lawsuit against the giant and fought it for five years.

The moral of some of this, which is more – and less – than mere trumpet blowing, is that British industry is just not doing enough to look after its own, and is suffering financial ruin as a result. Our attitude to development and designers is blighted by short-termism. You have to show a quick turnaround and immediate profit.

Engineering and design is not about that; it is a long-term way of regenerating a company and, by extension, a country. If the City fatcats and the banks, the monsters the Thatcher revolution made into prime movers, demand an instant return, we just sell our products better. We don't improve them. Advertising is the British answer to everything. But that is the way to a fast buck, not real money.

The best kind of business is one where you can sell a product at a high price with a good margin, and in enormous volumes. For that you have to develop a product that works better and looks better than existing ones. That type of investment is long term, high risk, and not very British.

Or at least, it looks like a high-risk policy. In the longer view, it is not half so likely to prove hazardous to one's financial health as simply following the herd. Difference for the sake of it. In everything. Because it must be better. From the moment the idea strikes, to the running of the business. Difference, and retention of total control.

This is not a glib guide to instant wealth or effective management by Californian-style happy-talk and company outings to assault courses. This is not even a business book. It is, if anything, a book against business, against the principles that have filled the world with ugly, useless objects, unhappy people, and brought the country to its economic knees.

We all want to make our mark. We all want to make beautiful things and a little money. We all have our own ideas about how to do it. What follows just happens to be my way.

1

Swallows and amazons, sand dunes and bassoons

Rural idyll. Death of my father. I am an underdog. Sent away to school. The bassoon. Running from the front. A painting in The Eagle. *My academic failures and the iniquities of the British education system. Faltering awakenings of an engineer, and attempts to swim. Why programmes should be flat. I do not become an estate agent or a doctor, but I nearly become an actor. Britain in the 1950s. Art school in London and a brave new world.*

Though writing an autobiography, I am not so terminally afflicted by solipsism as to think you will want much of my parents, birth, and what J.D. Salinger called 'all that David Copperfield kind of crap'.

I have been a misfit throughout my professional life, and that seems to have worked to my advantage. While it is that professional life that will be the true subject of this book, however, it seems only right – and in the tradition of these things – to begin, so to speak, *ab ovo*. Misfits are not born or made; they make themselves. And a stubborn opinionated child, desperate to be different and to be right, encounters only smaller refractions of the problems he will always experience. And he carries the weight of that dislocation for ever.

My father was a classics master at Greshams, a big old public school in Norfolk, and we lived in a huge Victorian house adjacent to the playing fields. It was divided into three parts – like Ancient Gaul under Caesar, as my father always used to say – and there was one other teacher's family, and Mrs Ransome, who owned the house and lived there with her daughter. Mrs Ransome was quite a frightening old woman and after seeing the Alec Guinness/James Mason *Great*

Expectations I came to think of her and her daughter as Miss Havisham and Estella, and me as poor old befuddled Pip.

It was all pretty idyllic, from a physical point of view. Norfolk then was all cobbled houses and red pantiles, unchanged for centuries. There were vast marshlands spotted with medieval churches, and wild countryside that spread for miles under dramatic, wide open skies. Both naturally and architecturally it was an aesthetically wonderful place to grow up and made a bit of a Brontë out of me.

I used to cycle to the village school early in the mornings when the mist always hung very low around the playing fields so that you couldn't see the school buildings. And in the school holidays we had the run of the place. We would play football on the school pitches with the other teachers' children and run amok in the school itself, playing murder in the dark at night in the empty dormitories and invading the music room to bash hell out of the drums. Then there were the great sand dunes which we used to explore, and we used to sail dinghies all over the place, indulging in the sort of Swallows and Amazons childhood that these days people think Arthur Ransome was romanticising, inventing even. But it was all there. Even Blakeney Point, which is a terrible tourist trap nowadays, was just bleak and isolated, and we used to swim naked with the terns and the seals.

Having all that, and particularly the school to myself, gave me very early on a feeling of difference from the other children. But that feeling, which was only a very vague sensation at first, really took hold when my father died of cancer in 1956. I was only nine at the time, my brother Tom was eleven, and my sister Shanie, fourteen. His death put me at a great disadvantage compared to the other boys. It made me feel like an underdog, someone who was always going to have things taken away from him. It made me feel that I was alone in the world – which inevitably, in better moments, will also make a small boy feel special.

I had no one to help me through my boyish problems, and no one to cite his own youthful experiences as an example to me when I thought I might be troubled by something that no one else had ever been through before. Life became something I had to make up as I went along, and I had to work everything out for myself. In crass, psychoanalytic terms, I suppose it made me a fighter.

Everyone in the house – my mother, my brother, my sister and all the other children – was older than I, so that when we played games like bulldog and lurky I was always up against people who were bigger and stronger than I was. It raised my standards – in that I was not prepared to lose everything all the time just because I was the youngest – and taught me that I could take on something much bigger than I was, and win. Combined with the loss of my father, this made me very competitive, and in the wider picture there is really not so great a difference between a rampaging industrial giant trying to sue you out of business, and a hulking great fifteen-year-old trying to knock you off a rock or duck you in the sea.

The other main formative aspect of my father's death was very different. He had been very ill for most of my life, and had been in hospital since I was six. All I remember is that he was quite a small man, and that he was a keen amateur actor and director and used to produce the school plays. (He must also have been something of a craftsman, for I have some frog puppets at home that he made for a production of Aristophanes' *The Frogs*.) At the time of his death he had been about to join BBC television, which was just starting up. But his move to change careers came too late.

Seeing him thwarted by death in that way, having done something else for so long, made me determined that that should never happen to me: I would not to be dragged into something I didn't want to do. It was always assumed I would be a classicist like he had been, and like my brother, and there was a certain shock when I left Latin and Greek behind me. But it was the very career that my father, however much he may have loved it once, was trying to escape from when he died, and that tarnished it for me for ever.

As far as I can gather, there was no real pension available to my mother from the school, but the headmaster, Logie Bruce-Lockhart, arranged for half my school fees, and those of my brother, to be paid by the school. And for that I remain eternally grateful.

So, at the tender age of nine, I was sent away to boarding school. It never occurred to me that the family should stay together at a time like that, or that our mother might have needed us – I know that I always want to have my own kids around me, no matter what, and there has never been any question of sending them away to school. But at that time, just after the war, there was a huge emphasis on education in Britain, and the pressure on middle-class children to go to private school was greater than it is now. My mother had left school at seventeen to join Bomber Command, where she spent the war moving flags around table maps with long sticks in one of those tactical headquarters you always see in black-and-white war films. She eventually went up to Cambridge to read English when she was fifty years old, which meant that she was a student at the same time as I was, so I had no one to go to for money. Even a little thing like that has had a profound effect on my career, because it was the lack of cash back then that got me involved with an engineering company and my first commercial commission – the Rotork Sea Truck.

To take things back, though, for I am in danger of leaping straight in to my inventing life at the first opportunity, I should go through a few little epiphanies in my childhood that might have contributed to my story – which is ultimately about how I took on the big boys at their own game, made them look very silly, just by being true to myself. I do not plan to give you the whole biography; I am not quite so involved in my own self-importance that I imagine a day-by-day account of my life will hold your attention very long. Still, I think there is the odd thing in my growing up which might be illuminating.

In terms of sheer pigheadedness and determination to take on things that were way beyond me, nothing so illuminates the sort of idiot child I was as my decision to take up the bassoon. I was about ten years old, and by no means a musical child. I was still spending most of my time in the fields and rivers around my house, collecting tadpoles in jam jars and doing the sorts of things that little boys who are left alone tend to do. Then one morning, after assembly, the headmaster made an announcement to the effect that there were vacancies in the school orchestra, a body of which I had never had even the vaguest intention of being a part.

The headmaster – a former Scottish rugby international who took school prayers with his face covered in bits of cotton wool which grew redder, as the prayers went on, with the blood of that morning's multiple shaving wounds – drew himself up to his full width at the lectern before 200 boys and said: 'Boys will be needed to play the oboe, the clarinet, the violin, the viola . . . and the bassoon.' I remember that that was the only one I had never heard of; none of us had. Everyone looked a bit puzzled. I mouthed the word over under my breath: 'bassoon, bassoooon, basssoooooooon', and I thought it sounded intriguing, not to say different and unusual. So I put up my hand.

I really think that was a watershed for me, because it was a complete leap in the dark. I must have felt that life was trundling along far too easily and that it was time to chuck something hefty in its way, an exhausting instinct whose constant reiterations in my life I have been suffering from ever since.

When I saw the instrument I was horrified. It was eight feet of pipe with millions of keys and was introduced to me as 'the most difficult instrument in the orchestra'. It was so difficult that even the 82-year-old woman who was appointed as my teacher didn't know how to play it.

So I beavered away at the double reed, and began complaining about it all the time because I had read in a book that bassoonists always complain about their reeds. And I mastered it pretty well. Along the way the old woman would just sit there, so silently sometimes that I occasionally panicked, thinking that she might be dead. And then she would suddenly rouse herself and say, 'Put some spunk into it boy,' which, if you are a ten-year-old boy, only makes you laugh and makes it even harder to play.

I had merely been obtuse. I had tried to be different on a whim, momentarily regretted it, and now here I was on this adventure. It was a lesson I never forgot, and in whimsical moments it even occurs to me to reflect on the similarity between a bassoon and a vacuum cleaner. I simply moved from a clumsy great piece of pipe that blows air out, to a clumsy great piece of pipe that sucks air in.

Adamantine stubbornness, and a certain amount of indolence, put paid to my nascent career as a bassoonist in the end. I had turned out to be reasonably good at it, and set about working through the grade system – that absurd series of examinations that says everything about the limitations of English education and its need to rationalise, quantify and ultimately dull any subject into insufferable boringness.

Up to grade five all had gone swimmingly and then my (by now 83-year-old) teacher entered me for grade eight, the highest level of all. To pass the exam you had to learn a lot of tricky scales, and labour through fingering exercises of Daedelusian complexity. Much as I loved playing the actual music, I really couldn't be bothered.

On examination day I played my prescribed pieces and the chap said they were marvellous. Then he said, 'Now, let's just hear a few scales, and it'll all be over.'

'I'm sorry,' I told him. 'I don't do scales.'

His crest rather fell. 'Oh, come on,' he said. 'You must know some. Any old thing will do.' He was really trying to help, but it was no good. I had a dusty memory of a B-flat scale I had once learned, and ground it out as well as I could remember. As I played it, I glanced across at him, and saw that he looked genuinely miserable.

He gave me two out of twenty for my scales, which I still think was generous, and as a result I failed. Disillusioned with the musical bureaucracy's determination to deny expression its true freedom, I hung up my bassoon and waved goodbye to my dreams of the Festival Hall.

These days I return to my bassoon only rarely, when a memory of childhood comes upon me out of the blue as I am sitting at a drawing board, or dozing on a Sunday afternoon, and I pull it down from the top of the wardrobe, blow the dust off the case, and try a few scales.

Another thing that happened about that time was that I discovered I was good at running; but just when I started to win some long-distance races puberty took a grip of my fellows, and they all got huge. I was a very late developer and so suddenly I was crap again.

Back to the ignominy of second-rate academic performance, few friends, and no dad.

The first race I entered after my own balls had dropped was a revelation. I was fourteen years old, a terribly mopey adolescent, and went into it expecting to come last. But as the race went on, over about three miles, all the other chaps started to slow down. This puzzled me a bit because I had just been jogging along thinking about this and that, rather enjoying the running, and wasn't tired at all. I had the impression that they were all running backwards, and suddenly the leading pack was only a few yards in front. I gritted my teeth and ground out every last bit of energy I had to battle past them before we got to the line.

This success delighted me no end. I was not doing very well at school and suddenly I had something in which I could kick people's asses occasionally. I entered more and more races and won them all quite easily.

Just as it had been with the bassoon, there was no one to teach me how to run. There was no dad to tell me how great I was, and it became a very introverted kind of obsession with me. Herb Elliot was a big name at the time, so I read a few books about him and discovered that his coach had told him that the way to develop stamina and strengthen the leg muscles was to run up and down sand dunes. This suited me fine, because if I had nothing else in darkest Norfolk, I certainly had sand dunes.

I would get up at six in the morning and run off into the wilds of Norfolk for hours, or put on my running kit at ten o'clock at night and not reappear until after midnight. Out there alone on the dunes I got a terrific buzz from knowing that I was doing something that no one else was – they were all tucked up in bed at school. I felt like a pioneer or an astronaut, or whatever kind of lone adventure felt right at the time, and I knew that I was training myself to do something better than anyone else would be able to do.

Running is a wonderful thing. It isn't like a team sport where you depend on other people, or they depend on you, and there is no question of your performance being judged. You either run faster than everyone else or you do not. In running your performance is absolute. I was out there learning how to do something, and getting a visible result. I experienced, in that sense, a very similar set of responses to the ones that made me move out of the arts later on and into a technical field, where my drawings would not be better or worse than other people's according to some spurious set of subjective criteria, but simply right or wrong.

The act of running itself was not something I enjoyed. The best you could say for it was that it was lonely and painful. But as I started to win by greater and greater margins I did it more and more, because I knew the reason for my success was that out on the sand dunes I was doing something that no one else was doing. Apart from me and Herb, no one knew. They were all running round and round the track like a herd of sheep and not getting any quicker. Difference itself was making me come first.

In so many ways it taught me the most significant lessons in all my youth. I was learning about the physical and psychological strength that keeps you competitive. I was learning about obstinacy. I was learning how to overcome nerves, and as I grew more and more neurotic about being caught from behind, I trained harder to stay in front. It is a horribly laboured analogy – and it is flavoured with the fickle seasoning of hindsight – but to this day it is the fear of failure, more than anything else, which makes me keep working at success.

'He runs,' you say, 'and he plays the bassoon, but what does this tell us? It is cod psychology, but it teaches us nothing of vacuum cleaners or building companies.' Fair enough. But I'm getting there. It is getting more relevant. You see, I also painted.

The smell of oil paints, linseed and turps is what I most remember about 1956. Painting at that age, about eight or nine, is visual expression at its most free. You are totally without inhibition, without pretension, and without shame. You are allowed to do whatever you want, and in my case that really did mean 'whatever' – because while the art master, one Stuart Webster, was a lovely, charming man and a very good watercolourist, he was also an alcoholic, and tended to conduct lessons from a semiconscious reclining position in a corner of the art room floor.

It was through painting that, at the age of nine, I first achieved national and international recognition. It was a painting of Blakeney Lagoon in north Norfolk, and it romped home to win first prize in the 1957 *Eagle* painting competition. I won a huge transistor radio – quite a highly desired object in those days – and found that the taste of success agreed with me very nicely. But there were darker hours to come. Over the next four years I began to paint more and more as I felt I ought to paint, and to follow the directions – however inebriated – of the art master. I was entirely without personality at the ages of eleven, twelve, thirteen. I was very inactive, did very badly at school, and went through the negative period that most boys do at that age, before they start to argue and question and become interesting (it is a pattern I have seen in my own children and one, incidentally, pointed out by Sean Connery, as Harrison Ford's father, in *Indiana Jones and The Last Crusade*). It was not until I started to become my own person again, at about fifteen, that I stopped loafing around and went back to the art room.

By then, what with the bassoon and the running, I had rediscovered the confidence and the stupidity to start doing things differently. I would smear shit-coloured paint all over a canvas, and then scratch away at the brown to draw out the light, trying to suggest the image of a cave, or a shoulder, or whatever seemed to be scratching its way into life. It was all very daft and Munsch-like, and I knew it, but at least I was creating the style for myself, and learning to do it my own way. My pictures were universally hated for a long time, and then gradually they started to grow on people. I got better at doing them, and I started to win art prizes. My mother was the only one who supported me in my artistic endeavours, and the way in which others eventually came round to an appreciation of my efforts was a reassuring precedent for future struggles.

Art, in those days, was not something that commanded much respect. I was expected to be a classicist, or at the very least an academic. My grandfather had been a mathematics scholar at Cambridge, my father was an Exhibitionist there, and my brother a classics scholar.

Things had not started terribly well, with me scraping only seven poor passes in my O Levels – not a good record for the school at that time. But the classics were foisted upon me anyway, because of the memory of my father and brother, and I was put down for Latin, Greek and ancient history.

I failed them largely because I used to sleep through the lessons. A typical day involved waking at 6.00 a.m. to go for a six-mile run before breakfast and rugger practice. I went to some lessons, then played rugger all afternoon, slept through prep, and then went out at 10 o'clock for another six-mile run. I think I would have slept through a lesson in anything, but there is nothing more boring or pointless than classics, and I saw it as no more than my duty to sleep, and to snore as loudly as I could. Back in my study, I would make a pretence at catching up, but always, having put on a Vivaldi or a Beethoven record, pass immediately, and deliciously, into sleep.

My anti-classics campaign is one that persists to this day. I recently went back to Greshams to give a lecture and when the headmaster, John Arkell, asked, publicly, if Latin had been a help to me I rather too quickly said, 'Not at all.' He looked horrified – not unreasonably, considering the uphill battle teachers fight to persuade boys of the importance of Latin – and I may even have been wrong: in the translations I did I only ever knew half the words, and having to make do with logic and imagination to fill the gaps might have prepared me for engineering, but it tickled not a neuron back in 1963.

I admit that occasional manifestations of classical sexual activity, in stories like Plutarch's life of the corrupt and bisexual statesman Alcibiades, sometimes woke me up. But tales of priapic Olympians raping nubile peasant girls while disguised as donkeys could glamorise the subject only so far in the face of more frequent demands to conjugate moribund verbs and translate *Radio Times* editorials in the manner of Pliny. But I passed ancient history because I couldn't help being excited by the gods and monsters that were so much larger than the little life I knew. And I passed art because I loved it.

At least, I had grown to love it, but rather in spite of the education system than because of it. Art should be studied for its own sake. I felt it as strongly then as I do now. But at O Level it had been the victim of a snobbery that tried to pull academic rigour into everything, in a miserable effort to dignify the discipline.

God, but it was pointless. We had to study a book about the churches of England and be able to say, under exam conditions, whether a certain church at Long Melford or Frogbourne-on-Squelch was early English, perpendicular, or mock Gothic. How stupid can they be? What on earth is the point of that to a spotty youth who only got into art because chucking glue around distracted him from the misery of growing fluff in unseemly places? (What does it serve to remember, by dint of rote learning, the *name* of a particular church? Far better to appreciate its strength and its statement.) The only benefit to me has been that whenever I arrive in a new town, I know what the church is going to look like before I get there. When the kids were younger, they would duck down in the back of the car and cover their ears whenever we approached, say, Long Melford, dreading a lecture on the architectural properties of its church.

Attempts to make art an 'academic' subject by involving the use of memory, rather than treating it as the figurative thing it really is, were part of the same kind of snobbery that would bugger about with woodwork, turning it into a miserable uncreative subject. None the less, it was probably the only course at school that taught me anything of any use.

At the time, the classical bits of my family made me suspicious of it. Woodwork, I had been led to believe, was something done by thickos in a shed. There was, and I believe still is, a pride taken by academics in not knowing how to make things with their hands, though why ignorance of anything should be cause for celebration I really don't know.

I was an arts man, and I was not supposed to be interested in how a car or a television worked. So the technological revolution that was changing the world was allowed to pass me by, leaving me in the reverie of my dream world in rural Norfolk. The closest I came to engineering, or to doing anything at all with my hands, was the two weeks I spent every year staying with a friend in Tonbridge by the name of Michael Brown. His father Tony was a printer, or at least owned a printing works, and was a very practical man. The sort of father, I suppose, that you would expect me to have had. He and his son used to make petrol engines and small steam engines in a workshop at the back of the house, the kind of crackpot paradise that I later had at my own home when I was developing the Dual Cyclone. But the Browns did not make vacuum cleaners, they made trains, and boats and aeroplanes with little engines that flew on two wires connecting them to you on the ground.

I was interested, but felt somehow that I shouldn't be. I had always been told that I would be no good at it, and when I tried to join in with Michael Brown, I felt rather inadequate. I didn't know how to work a lathe, I had never had anyone to show me how to play this game, and here was this kid whose dad had taught him how. I have since been able to give my own children that sort of guidance, but I just had to do it my own cack-handed way, and sometimes it worked, sometimes not.

I would try to build things when I got back home to Norfolk. For a couple of weeks I would labour away, once making a floodlighting system for the garden that achieved little more than to electrocute me and some of my friends. But without the encouragement of a mechanically-minded father, the enthusiasm would dull towards the end of the summer holidays, as the memory of late July in Somerset faded and I was left alone with the innards of whatever machine I had taken to pieces. I tried to remember the things Tony Brown had explained, about dynamos, and electrical connections, but I dissected with the detached fascination of an artist, not the method of an engineer and, having drawn every bolt and sprung every spring, never managed to breathe new life into the metal monsters I had slain.

So my only hope was the woodwork teacher. But that was usually some ex-army bloke who had no notion of design, and eschewed artistry to teach endless generations of pupils how to make wonky matchbox holders. And if you didn't make them his way, you got a clip round the ear. (I should point out that this is no longer the way with woodwork. It is now called Craft, Design and Technology – CDT – and schools are taking the biggest steps forward, with regard to design than anyone in the country.) In those days you had to choose between art and woodwork, just to ensure that no one with half an interest in aesthetics would get their hands on the tools to reproduce that enthusiasm in three dimensions. So I chose art over woodwork, in the same offhand way that I had faced that other major choice: humanities or sciences.

It is the roaring iniquity of our education system that children face this decision at such a feckless age. I went for humanities because I couldn't see the point of all those formulae you got in science – and I have spent the rest of my life not only attempting to turn the woolly headed artist who left Greshams into a scientist, but cursing the wrongheadedness of a system that forces students into such choices. It was quite simply a case of, 'Right, you can spell so you're an artist. You've got glasses so you will be going to science lessons. And you, matey, can go and do woodwork because you're thick.' Well that is not how Leonardo da Vinci looked at it, or Francis Bacon, or Thomas Browne, or Hobbes, or Michelangelo. But no one, these days, can be arsed with the intellectual open-mindedness it takes for a Renaissance.

So, stymied from the very outset in any effort to express my indi-viduality academically, I was forced to do it elsewhere. Thus, I am afraid, one or two more little episodes follow in which Dyson, young as he is, does it his own way.

Fired by my successes on the running track, I couldn't help scenting the whiff of glory when the annual swimming races came around. They were not a popular event, Norfolk being a place of extra-ordinarily low temperatures, and the pool being outside. This was a chance, in the absence of opposition, to triumph again. But I would not merely hoof into the water like a frog and hare up and down with arms and legs flailing, displacing water like an Archimedean nightmare, getting water up my nose and running out of puff halfway through the thousand-metre race. Oh no. I would do side stroke –

what they used to call 'English crawl' – and I would do it from a water-bound start. The logic was simple: a calm, still body gliding over the water, enjoying a constant level of submersion, rather than a splashing, frenetic body bobbing in and out, would encounter less resistance from air and water, and use less energy.

In practice, only two of my precepts held true: I did not get water up my nose, and I did not run out of puff. In terms of results, measured by placement at the finishing line, the experiment was a failure. I was still in the water, gliding up and down in my lane, for some hours after the other races had finished and everybody had dried off and gone in for tea. So I hung up my trunks, and became an actor (and it was through acting, ultimately, that I came to the decision that has put me where I am today). The creak of the boards! The smell of the greasepaint! Shakespeare. Marlowe. Molière. I gave my Trinculo, and I gave my Dangle, the inept but savage theatre critic in Sheridan's *The Critic*. It was an activity ideally suited to my rather perverse nature – and nicely indicative of the point I have been labouring these ten pages or so.

There is no obvious way of doing it – should you play Othello like Laurence Olivier, or like Orson Welles or like Laurence Fishburne? Facile questions, for there is no 'should' about it, or about anything – you cannot depend upon someone teaching you. You have to find your own way. You cannot stand up in a pair of tights and try to imitate Olivier; you will look a fool, because you are not Olivier. I began by overacting, just as I have begun everything by overdoing it, and then, as in all things subsequently, I realised that it was a more subtle beast than I had thought.

But it was as a stage designer that I found my youthful creative impulses challenged in the most serious way.

The house play of 1964 was to be Sheridan's *The Critic*, and I had taken charge of the design, as I had for every other play in which I had been involved. I was looking around for something to give the production a bit of an edge on the usual predictable run of school plays. And I lit upon the programmes.

They were always printed at the local press on folded A4 sheets and were extremely dull and nasty. I thought it would be more appropriate, in the context of the late eighteenth century, Augustan revival and all that, to have them done as scrolls on nice, aged vellum-effect paper. I planned out how they should look, italic script, full of archaisms, and scooted off into town on my bike to give the printers their instructions, terribly excited about the buzz of opening night, and the appropriateness of all these boys in old-fashioned uniform, and dressed-up parents, holding their scrolls and watching the play in the pukka manner Richard Brinsley would have had in mind. He was, after all, the great showman, and indeed salesman, of eighteenth-century theatre.

Two days before the first night, the boxes of scrolls were delivered. My housemaster, Paul Colombé, called me into his study and leered at me over his half-moons, his face full of blood and rage.

'This is absolutely ridiculous,' he boomed. 'How dare you insult the great tradition of drama at this school with this, this . . . folly.'

It was the most offensive word he could find to describe it, I suppose. I defended myself.

'But I thought it was rather suitable, and in the flavour of the period.'

'Programmes, Dyson,' he told me, 'should be flat.'

And he charged off to the printers to demand his money back and the expeditious reprinting of the programmes on folded A4 paper, in sans-serif Roman script, in conventional language, and with the addition of the usual paeans to the teachers and governors who had made it possible.

This was not one of those occasions when you realise, after the expression of youthful exuberance, that in fact the adult was right all along. I was doing what I felt to be logical, current, original, unusual, and in the spirit of the production, and here was this bloody maths teacher telling me that I was wrong for no better reason than that 'programmes should be flat'. I felt I was right, and that he was wrong. And I feel that still. It was an early artistic rebuff by a bean-counter, and in the years since then I have developed a little more resistance to reactionaries who put down whatever is new and unfamiliar.

But I was majorly miffed at the time and so turned my attention to a little public speaking. Where I was shot down again. Asked to give a reading from the Ten Commandments on speech day, I had a little thought that might enliven a text which was rolled out on a thrice-termly basis. I was seventeen and learning to drive, and had noticed the strong similarities between the decalogue and the Highway Code. So I decided to read out sections from the latter, in the manner of the former, in order to introduce the question of rules and their comparative relevance to the societies that make them. I assumed everyone would enjoy the analogy.

Same housemaster. Same expression on face. 'We did not think that was very funny, Dyson.' And my assault on the discipline of Tully ended in ignominy, and the stigma of blasphemy.

My school career was drawing to an end in a storm of sedition. It was not long after that that I was thrown out of the CCF for wearing a T-shirt underneath my horsehair tunic because I had got sunburnt running on the dunes the day before. Despite being the only boy to pass cert. A and quite a competent little soldier (my main asset being that I always finished the assault course first, which would probably not have been all that useful in the kind of global thermonuclear Armageddon that looked imminent in the mid-sixties), I was told by this sergeant major whose only role in life seemed to be to scream at small boys as they stomped around a parade ground, that I was a ''orrible little man and obviously didn't give a damn for the British Army'.

It was in this context, with potential careers being nipped in the bud at every turn, that I found myself eventually in front of the careers officer. He had a handlebar moustache, just like the sergeant major, so I knew our meeting was going to be productive.

'I see from your questionnaire that you like the outdoors,' he said, observing the running, sailing and rugby aspect of my 'other interests'. 'I think you should be an estate agent.'

So I went off to see some estate agents. There was one in Norfolk who said that it was a terribly interesting job, so I thought 'this sounds OK' – as feckless youths have a way of doing.

Then I went to see one in Cambridge. I chatted to the man who ran the company for a while, and he asked me what my paintings were like. I said that I thought they were pretty good and, with the wonderfully simplistic outlook that only that profession can achieve, he told me that I ought to be a painter. He was a man who sold houses and office space for a living, and yet he was the first person who ever told me I should go and be an artist.

This did not go down well with the handlebar moustache. He explained that unless one went to university one was considered a failure, and I did not want to be considered a failure did I? Even bearing in mind that I was a 'orrible little man. If I was dead set against it, he said, it was acceptable to go to medical school instead.

The idea of cutting people up seemed interesting, so I thought I would be a surgeon. In those days it didn't much matter what A Levels you had done when choosing a career, it was more about what contribution you could make to the hospital rugger team. But when I went for my interview at St Mary and St George's they did look a little perplexed when I told them I was doing English, ancient history, art, Latin, and Greek. Still, they offered me a place for some bizarre reason – but one of the doctors took me aside and said that if I enjoyed art, then I should pursue it, because I might find it more fun than surgery. Whether he did it out of concern for the art world or the medical profession, I have never been sure. But I knew he was right.

Unsure of how to square this with my family or with the school, for whom anything less than a classics degree would be a blot on my future prospects tantamount to the mark of Cain, I was finally steeled by one of those epiphanies that do not come often, but which, as Shakespeare would have said, 'When they seldom come, they wished for come'. And indeed it was Shakespeare who was the author of that epiphany.

At least, he was the author of *The Tempest*, and it was as Trinculo in that play that I was spotted by one of the Bolting brothers, who had come up to see the school play for a reason that remains a mystery to this day. After the performance he came backstage and told me that he was making a film which was, I gathered, a *Lord of the Flies* sort of affair, and invited me up to London to audition.

You have to remember that I was a country bumpkin then, a clueless Norfolk yokel who had always lived in a very remote area, and had been pretty detached from modern life. I had been down to London a couple of times on shopping trips with my mother in the late fifties, but only to be dragged round a shop for outsized women called Tall Girls – hardly the place to foster youthful metropolitan dreams. This was my first trip to the capital alone. It was 1964.

I caught the train up to London and alighted on a wonderful sunny day at Liverpool Street station. I walked all the way to the West End, gawping at miniskirts, Morris minors, men in winkle-pickers and shops full of televisions and fancy clothes. I stopped off in Carnaby Street on the way to the audition and bought a pair of elephant cord trousers, then went into a pub in Soho to buy a pint of beer, which I drank standing outside in the sunshine.

The audition itself was a disaster. Drunk with the excitement of London, and dreaming of being a film star, I stood in a small room in Harrington Place, SW7, and projected my voice as if I were speaking at the Albert Hall without a microphone. They kept telling me to relax and talk more quietly, but I was just staring at this tall, beautiful blonde girl with long brown legs. I can still remember her white boots and short skirt, and as I stood there, declaiming away at the top of my voice, I knew at last that I was never going to make an actor, and that this place, London, at this moment, was the world for me.

Back in Norfolk I had only to inform people of my decision. While everyone else was going off to university, or to do VSO and teach the natives a thing or two – things that seemed to me to belong to an old world order, and the maintenance of extinct empires – I would be going to art school.

'Which art school?' my headmaster asked.

'An art school in London,' I told him.

Not long after that, my mother got a letter from him, dated 5 May 1965:

Dear Mary

    We shall be sorry to part with James. I cannot believe that he is not really quite intelligent, and I expect it will be brought out somehow somewhere.

    Yours sincerely Logie BL.

I wrote back, thanking him for his encouragement, and he replied, in a letter dated 24 September, as follows:

Dear James

    It was very civil of you to offer your thanks for the little we have done. The academic side, although we have to pretend it is important, matters comparatively little. You will do all the better for not having masses of tiresome degrees full of booklearning hanging round your neck. Good luck at Art School.

    Yours sincerely, Logie Bruce Lockhart.

I just didn't have the heart to tell him that in this Brave New World, two hundred miles from Greshams, there were men in smocks and berets at the Royal College of Art, calling themselves professors and giving out masters degrees for painting.

This, then, was the world in which I grew up. A world where Britain still sat comfortably on the top of the pile. At least, that was how it felt to us then. For in the superficial things that make up the imaginative world of a young boy, who is just beginning to understand the radio and television news, there seemed no end to the success stories.

    There was a coronation. We conquered Everest. We regained the Ashes and beat all-comers in test matches. We broke the four-minute mile. There was the Festival of Britain, and Morris Minors being exported all over the world. The message to a child seemed to be that Britain was the centre of the universe, and that you, as an individual, could conquer the world. Anyone born now would grow up with the impression that the British cannot really do anything.

    And then there was the war, which we had not had to experience but whose effects on the national psyche infused everything. Everything became suddenly possible. Children were prized because so many had been killed, and money was poured into education. We felt needed, important, protected, and at the centre of the world.

The comics I read and the films I saw were obsessed with the endless reproduction of British victory. We bashed the Bosch and we blasted the Japs. Now, I am no warmonger and do not vaunt the imperial arrogance and racism of those images. But the effect on my mindset, when it comes to taking on the world leaders in industry – Germany and Japan – must surely be subconsciously steeled by the childhood certainty that it was they, not we, who were the weak ones. I do not, at least, suffer from the terrible defeatism that makes British industry shirk the battle because of apparently impossible odds or seek to copy their methods just because they have worked before.

By the time I left this world to travel to London and make my fortune – Dick Whittington on a Honda 50 – it was 1966. I was innocent, fatherless, and full of optimism. I still thought Dan Dare was a vision of the future. I didn't know he was a dream of the past. I felt prepared for the full weight of adult experience. I was ready, in every way, to change the world.

I didn't know that the world was already changing.

2

Learning to dream

*Deb's delight. The essence of form. First love. The Royal College of Art –
a back door. My personal pantheon: Buckminster Fuller and Brunel.
Shops, playgrounds, airport lounges. The real modern Brunel.*

From the moment I rolled up at the front gates of the Byam Shaw Art
School in Kensington for my first interview, in June 1966, and saw
the longing, expectant eyes of the pearl-wearing, horsy young girls
that were loitering around the halls, I should have known it was not
really the place for me.

It had been, in a former life, an art school for debutantes, and there
were still, even then, a number of young ladies who were undoubtedly
debby. To the thrusting young yokel who had burned down the
winding A roads from Norfolk in his mother's white Mini Countryman, the wood all covered in moss, and the boot and back seat
bursting with huge brown paintings, in the hope of mixing it with a
hip crowd of urgent young visionaries, it was a mite disappointing.
One might even have questioned – with the benefit of hindsight – the
usefulness to me of the course, since it was limited to the instruction of
drawing, painting, and printmaking. But two things were to make
that year – for I was accepted immediately after the interview – very
important for me.

The first was the principal, Maurice de Sausmarez, who was not only a great teacher, but had all the right friends, like Peter Sedgeley and Bridget Riley, two of the most famous 'op' artists of their time, whom he had persuaded to teach at the school. From them I learnt how to see and understand form, and ultimately how to draw it. Not just to sketch the outlines, but to represent the essence, the function of the thing, in the lines I made on the page. In life classes, for example, we were not allowed to draw the outlines of the models, which would have made us think only in two dimensions, and we had to do the same thing with piles of easels – starting from the middle, rather than the silhouette of the pile.

Other strange tasks included making matchstick models of helical shells, and drawing two models as they walked in a figure of eight, or going to Queen's ice rink to draw people as they skated. They would have us at it for nine or ten hours at a time, and for the first time I found myself involved in something for an entire day, so immersed that I didn't even notice time passing.

It was this appreciation of form, as much as anything else in those years, that would direct me towards design and ultimately engineering. As the years went on, I suppose, I tried to get deeper and deeper into the thing itself, from that first vantage point that is mere observation and representation.

As if one momentous impact on my life were not enough for the place, the school was also generous enough to introduce me to my wife.

In classes of up to thirty-five students it is inevitable that you polarise into groups for lunch, and going to the pub, and begin to develop cliques. It so happened that in my group was a girl called Deirdre Hindmarsh, who was very unlike all the other girls. The rest of them were middle-class young ladies formed in the image of their mothers, but Deirdre was a classless, Twiggy-like woman, or like the Vanessa Redgrave character in *Blow Up*.

I thought at first that she was Australian, because I had never heard a cockney accent before. She was warm and open and without pretension, there was no ghost of tradition in her, and she joined in and laughed, and stood out from the horsy, ra-ra posturing of the others. She had long, beautiful, auburn hair and a freckly, Diane Keaton-ish face. She had a slim, neat body and wore tapered ski-pants with foot-straps, a complete sixties chick. Unlike the rest of us, she had not come straight from school but had worked as a secretary for two years in an architectural firm, and de Sausmarez had given her a scholarship on condition that she did a bit of secretarial work for him each day.

We were both travelling into the college every day from East London, me from Herne Hill and she from between Forest Hill and Catford, and we started meeting up on the Circle Line every morning. I remember we started holding hands on a drawing trip to London Zoo, although when I asked her the other day she claimed that she didn't fancy me at all at the time.

We had our first date soon afterwards, at a place called The Ark in Kensington Church Street, one of the trendy new bistros that were beginning to appear where people like us could afford to go because you had to take your own alcohol. I picked her up in my Mini Countryman, which had a dodgy starter motor and always had to be left on a hill, and I paid the bill, which was half my grant gone at a swoop.

From then on I was besotted, and used to go and stay with her at my mother's home in Cley-next-Sea in Norfolk. It was a small cottage on the coast, and we used to walk along the beach picking samphyr and taking it home to cook. Now that it has become trendy among foodies, I often see it on the menu in restaurants, and whenever I do, I order huge platefuls of it.

Perhaps samphyr has mysterious aphrodisiac qualities, for I had proposed before the year was out.

From an unpromising first impression, in other words, the Byam Shaw Art School gave me pretty much everything I have now. I had met the woman who would not only share my life, but make possible all the professional things that I did, and provide the strength to see me through the desperate years of struggle.

It was towards the end of the year that Maurice de Sausmarez turned my attention in a direction it had not really faced before, the future. I had been having a fantastic time, what with the girls, the location, the artistic awakening and the sixties. But what, he wanted to know, was I going to do next? Was I going to stay on and do more painting, or were there other fields I wanted to explore?

Other fields?

I had always thought you had to be a painter. Suddenly this man, who was thin and brown and balding but had the enthusiasm of a child, was uttering dimly heard syllables through the fog of my realisation: 'sculptor ... graphic designer ... photographer ... film maker ... furniture designer ...', and I thought to myself, the way you do at that age, that furniture design sounded interesting. I knew about chairs. I'd sat in a lot, after all. But I'd broken them too, and then glued them together again, and I thought, 'OK then. Let's do a bit of 3-D.'

Now the Royal College of Art, my Alma Mater and the very bedrock of my entire career, was exclusively a graduate school. I had no art degree under my belt, just a year of paint-sploshing and girl-watching. But it so happened that they were running an experiment in educational anti-elitism at the very time when I was looking about for my new direction: they were accepting three students in each intake without first degrees.

The exam, fortunately, did not require one to know very much at all about furniture, but focused instead on intuitive ideas about the use of materials – What should concrete be used for? Is glass or plastic better in a particular situation? – and other theoretical questions related to hypothetical design projects. Even as I sat there sweating out the hours of the exam, my mind was being squeezed in the direction of design.

And, before I knew it, I was squeezing myself into my fashionably restrictive hipsters and driving down to the RCA in my Morris Minor for my first day, along with the two other backdoor new bugs: Richard Wentworth-Stanley, an Etonian who changed later to sculpture, and after changing his name as well, to plain old Richard Wentworth, became one of the great, revolutionary sculptors of our time, and

Charles Dillon, later Lord Dillon, who stayed in furniture, then got into lighting, and invented the very first kite light.

I can't pretend that I didn't feel a little daunted at the beginning. Everyone else was a graduate, with at least three years' experience behind them, while the three of us were expected to catch up in just a year. But it was also very exciting. We were following in the footsteps of David Hockney, Gerald Scarfe, Ossie Clarke, even Len Deighton – it seemed that every big name in the sixties had been there, giving the place an extremely hip and happening reputation.

The design disciplines – interior, furniture, and product design, as well as ceramics – had all been put in a new building next to the Albert Hall and there were a lot of very famous people teaching there. The place did not feel anything like a stuffy old university. And yet everyone was walking around with this feeling that, 'This is where I will make it. This is where I will become great.' The fact that Hockney had become famous while he was actually there gave us all a great will to succeed, and a great many did. It was a very productive period: when the RCA held a centenary exhibition a while back, featuring current work by graduates, about 75 per cent of everything on show was by my contemporaries.

The first year was a preparatory one, in which the rather dilettante foundation provided by the Byam Shaw school was fleshed out to bring me into line with my more conventionally accomplished fellow students. I was buffeted around the various departments of the RCA, spending weeks at a time scratching the surface of film-making, sculpture, industrial design, and encountering all sorts of famous designers who would come in to talk to us, or just to have lunch and be around the RCA.

Putative furniture maker though I was, the course that really caught my imagination was interior design. At least, they called it interior design, but that smacked, even then, of the flighty but fashionable business of interior decoration, the David Hicks-type nonsense that everyone was so excited about in the sixties. In reality, it was a course in architecture of the interior.

Compared to the furniture course, which was all about doing arty-crafty things with wood, this was the nitty-gritty. It was run by Sir Hugh Casson and dealt with the interiors of cars, boats, aeroplanes and restaurants, focusing my enthusiasm for designing things on the real, rapidly changing world outside.

Most important of all, though, was the structural engineering taught by Anthony Hunt, the designer of Waterloo station and the most influential, experimental and ambitious structural engineer of the last thirty years. He talked about the building of bridges and about cantilevered beams, and the theory of structure. Hunt was a structural engineer who was interested in design, and could talk with equal enthusiasm both about how structures worked and about the aesthetics of structure. And I was riveted.

So I jumped ship again. Even in the relatively modern interior design school I had run up against irritating traditionalism: desperate to work in plastic and stainless steel, I had been taken aside and lectured on the importance of wood. I was convinced that it was the role of a young designer to work in modern materials, and rather than continue to bang my head against a wood wall, as it were, I slid into engineering. Every new day, every shift of department, was taking me further from 'art' as my schoolteachers had perceived it, and allowing me to unmake the decisions that had been forced on me at school by the random and ruinous practice of separating the artist from the scientist almost at birth.

Then came Buckminster Fuller. Anthony Hunt often mentioned this American engineer whom I was sure I had never encountered, but whose name seemed almost to sing with the resonances of a pioneering spirit. Rather than display my ignorance by asking Hunt about this man, I found myself a copy of *The Dymaxion World of Buckminster Fuller* by Robert Marles and shut myself away for a rare spell of book-learning.

Buckminster Fuller has been described as one of the century's greatest dreamers – an epithet which I at first took to be critical. A dreamer suggested to me someone unwordly, idealistic, lazy, romantic and, above all, the opposite of a doer – hardly attributes one would seek out in a builder of cars and homes.

But I could not have been more wrong. Fuller dreamt because his vision was of a world that did not yet exist, his thinking was so advanced that his ideas could be related to very little that was already in place. And the value of dreaming – in that sense – was the first thing I learned from him.

The first in his family for more than a century to fail to graduate from Harvard, Fuller had no technical training at all, but absorbed his mechanical education by osmosis during his wartime service in the navy and years as an underling in the construction industry. His first revolutionary effort was a very prescient tear-drop shaped car (he was an ardent admirer of Henry Ford) known as the Dymaxion: a portmanteau of DYnamic + MAXimum + IONs. If this did not catch on, its principles, when applied to the Dymaxion house, made of steel, Duralumin, and plastic, caught the imagination of a generation and throughout the thirties stood as a symbol of the future of mass production.

While these were triumphs of theory, it was not until the fifties that Fuller found commercial success with the geodesic dome, patented in 1954 and reproduced more than 300,000 times since, in such things as sports arenas, subtropical housing and the permanent American base at the South Pole. The best example of Fuller's idea is probably Centreparks, which although it is only a holiday pleasure dome, offers a reminder of Fuller's great dream, to eliminate housing and have families living in secondary pavilions in their gardens.

The geodesic system consisted in dividing a dome into equal triangles so that the surface structure of a dome was followed most accurately. The resultant benefit, besides ease of construction due to the similarity of the triangles, was that a dome shape is extremely strong, and efficient in the distribution of its strength. Consider eggshell, a very weak material that displays remarkable strength when arranged in the shape of an egg. And then compare it with a matchbox, which is made of much thicker material but, because it is a cube, distorts and bends much more easily.

Fuller used this spherical principle, with its inherently high strength-to-weight ratio, to build clear unsupported roofs of enormous span, originally projected to be positioned by Zeppelin, but ultimately, on many occasions, set down by helicopter. And they were not small: the Baton Rouge dome spanned 116 metres, the St Louis project nearer a thousand.

Mocked in the early stages of his career, Buckminster Fuller knew well that the only way to make a genuine breakthrough was to pursue a vision with single-minded determination in the face of criticism. If you try to change things then you upset the establishment, which is why invention and vilification have always gone hand in hand.

I saw then that to do what Buckminster Fuller did, to make real progress in the way we live, or think we live, it was not enough to be just a designer. You had to be an engineer as well. For the first time I saw how creative engineering could produce buildings and products that were not only technologically revolutionary, but whose visual effect, by its fidelity to, and generation out of, its engineering would be exciting, elegant, and lasting. Fuller exorcised from my mind for ever the notion of being a whimsical stylist arriving to paint the stable door a lovely shade of purple long after its inherent inadequacies as a door had offered egress to the bolting nag.

While Buckminster Fuller inspired my first idealistic design dreams, he takes, ultimately, second place in the pantheon of my personal gods.

I have spent my inventing life in the shadow of the great tunnel at Box, with its huge classical portico towering over the track that once brought Daniel Gooch's mighty locomotives, Lord of the Isles and Typhoon, sweeping into the sunlight on their way to Bath. It is a monument to the vision of the man for whom the tunnel could not be a mere hole in the ground, but had to be the triumphal arch to a Roman city. But an arch so brilliantly planned, that when the two teams working at it from either side met in the middle, their respective tunnels were only three inches off a perfect match, and so ambitiously designed that on Brunel's birthday the sun rises at dead centre, and shines all the way through.

Isambard Kingdom Brunel was unable to think small, and nothing was a barrier to him. The mere fact that something had never been done before presented, to Brunel, no suggestion that the doing of it was impossible – he was fired by an inner strength and self-belief almost impossible to imagine in this feckless age. While I could never lay claim to the genius of a man like that – I do not even have a middle name, let alone one which describes the political status of the country I live in (how nice it would be to have been born James Democracy Dyson) – I have tried to be as confident in my vision as he was. And at times in my life when I have encountered difficulty and self-doubt I have looked to his example to fire me on.

When I was deeply in debt, and the Dual Cyclone looked as if it might remain a drawing-board dream, I thought of his father Marc Brunel, who spent time in a debtors' prison when his Thames tunnel seemed destined for failure. When I have considered relinquishing total control, and taking a back-seat consultant's role (and there have been fantastic buyout offers), I have remembered how Brunel never accepted such a position in his life, and the words that he wrote on the subject.

> The term consulting engineer is a very vague one and in practice has been too much used to mean a man who for a consideration sells his name but nothing more. Now I never connect myself with an engineering work except as the Directing Engineer, who, under the Directors, has the sole responsibility and control of the engineering, and is therefore The Engineer ... In a railway the only works to be constructed are engineering works, and there can really be only one engineer.

I have tried, in my own way, to draw on Brunel's dream of applying emerging technology in ways as yet unimagined. He was never afraid to be different or shocking. He never shirked the battles with the money men, and he had to overcome the most incredible resistance to his ideas: when he applied the system of the screw propeller to a transatlantic steam ship he actually filled a boat with people and sent them across the sea. I have asked people only to push my inventions around, not to get inside them and try to float!

And so I have sought out originality for its own sake, and modified it into a philosophy which demands difference from what exists even if only to redefine a stale market. And I have told myself, when people tried to make me modify my ideas, that the Great Western Railway could not have worked as anything but the vision of a single man, pursued with dogged determination that was nothing less than obsession.

Throughout my story I will try to return to Brunel, and to other designers and engineers, to show how identifying with them, and seeing parallels with every stage of my own life, enabled me to see my career as a whole and to know that it would all turn out the way it has. The many people I have upset and offended have considered me arrogant, rude, stubborn and solipsistic. Now, with a hindsight that proves I was right, those faults of mine seem less criminal. And perhaps that is the nature of 'vision': when all has come right, the kind of man who persisted despite constant ridicule from the controlling forces will be said to have possessed vision.

But the dreamers who threw in the towel in the face of adversity have never had the benefit of their ideas being tested, and their dreams – like those of Whitcomb L. Judson, who relinquished his patent for the zipper because he believed that his future lay in the construction of a railway in Minnesota powered by compressed air – appear as ludicrous today as they did to their knockers at the time. By which I am led to the belief that, in the case of inventors, for 'vision' one might equally well read 'stubbornness'. At any stage in my story where I talk of vision, and arrogance seems to have got the better of me, remember that I am celebrating only my stubbornness. I am claiming nothing but the virtues of a mule.

There was, in Brunel's determination, a level of conditioning. His father had been an engineer of almost equally gargantuan vision, building the first tunnel under the Thames and planning one under the Channel, too. For Isambard there was that double-edged Oedipal desire both to impress and to outdo his father. It is what the literary critic Harold Bloom calls the Anxiety of Influence, and the need for a figure to be 'slain' was paramount in the creation of originality – and genius.

My father was dead, and his achievement, anyway, was as a classicist. External figures had to count for a father. It is why a man called Jeremy Fry became so important to me, and Sir Hugh Casson, and Anthony Hunt. But they had to be overcome before I could move forward. If I was to push further there had to be new fathers. There had to be Buckminster Fuller, and Brunel.

My dream was to be an Isambard Kingdom Brunel for my time. It would have been silly, of course, to hope of attaining that sort of status, but there was no reason for him not to be an inspiration. For it is in our engineers that we should place our greatest faith for the present, in that they determine the way our future will be. While novelists, painters and poets are making craven images to the present, ossifying it, offering to the future only ways of remembering, the engineers and inventors are determining how the future will work. A Brunel bridge, or a geodesic dome by Buckminster Fuller, was as much a map of the future as *Vanity Fair* or *The Great Gatsby* were maps of the past. In this way, I think, it is fair to call the engineer an artist – if only you are prepared to see the beauty in mechanics. It is not a claim I can yet make for myself, being still an artist who is trying to call himself an engineer.

A Brunel suspension bridge is a work of art not because it is easy on the eye, but because it mirrors a curve fundamental to the mathematics of nature. It is not beautiful – like the Sistine Chapel – because it is the best way it could have been done, but because it is the only way it could have been done. It is a beauty which, like mathematics and unlike art, is always reducible to zero.

That, perhaps, is what drove me from the artistic road I was travelling, towards a clearer, purer place where my drawings would always be right or wrong. In art you place yourself at the mercy of human judgement and its odious courtiers, human error and human weakness. In engineering and design you are at the mercy only of natural law (physics) and the market (both development capital and income generated by response to the product). They are cruel task masters, but at least they are visible ones. The artist is equally enslaved to the market – the industrialist is just more honest about it.

The other reason for my change of direction, of course, must have been money. For after all those years as a student I discovered that bank balances, unlike mathematics, are reducible not only to zero, but to undefined reaches below.

So my dream was to be a Brunel. But this was never an age of invention. It has been an age when the great monopolies (companies) have been able to dictate that progress has ended. And they did this when they were satisfied not with their product, but with their control of its market. The public has been easily convinced by advertising, and receptiveness to revolution has dwindled. Furthermore, such 'invention' as is now allowed is the prerogative of multinationals, not people. Where are our Wright brothers? Where have the Edisons gone? And the Henry Fords? They are not there. We have broken new frontiers, but where are the names? Who invented the space shuttle? The nuclear submarine? The wind farm? When you go for backing for your crazy scheme it is not enough to be a man, you have to be a group of men. And where is the fun in that?

Cash is king. You can put years of your life into an idea, its development, and realisation, and every paltry penny you had along the way ... but your prospective backer, the banks or corporations, will ask you only how much you are putting up. They will back your money, but not your innovation. And in a world of spreadsheets and account-ants, advertising and shiny-suited businessmen (beings I have ban-ished from my own business), we are growing timid, afraid of our own potential for creation.

So I had to master not only engineering, but product design, finance, marketing, management, and be sure that when the time came, I would be able to take my vision – whatever it may be – to completion entirely on my own. I would have to be a new kind of Isambard Kingdom Brunel. Rougher, tougher, sharper than before. But I had the technology. I could rebuild him...

But before I get carried away, this dream of being compared with Brunel had its concrete side; there was more to it than mere mouth-wash. For it was at about the time that I found these two figures that

I began to turn my hand to some semiprofessional stuff – to test the waters of the outside world, and see how well I floated.

My only business venture until now had been selling cheap wine that a friend of mine was importing from Tarragona in southern Spain. Wine was beginning to catch on in Britain in the late sixties and this unlabelled plonk had a certain cachet among the arty *demi-monde*. I was making reasonable pocket money flogging it by the case to the student union and staff. And I suppose it was here that I learnt the crucial business principle that would guide my later attempts at making money from invention: the only way to make real money is to offer the public something entirely new, that has style value as well as substance, and which they cannot get anywhere else.

It was thus a happy coincidence that one of my first 'work placements', as it would be called now, found me in the Peter Dominic off-licence in London's Victoria Street. It was the summer holidays of 1968, and I was spending twelve weeks under the tutelage of Rodney Fitch of the Conran Design Group, which was quite new at the time, and still the only design consultancy in the country. Everyone on my course had a placement of one kind or another, but to have landed one with Conran, Britain's first real 'design' character, and with twelve quid a week at that, was a great stroke of luck.

We, the wannabe designers, were only supposed to be helping with some ideas for a refurbishment, but it so happened that we had spent the early afternoon in the pub, and I rolled up at the shop roaring drunk, which is very unusual for me, and was so even then. I lurched in through the door and into a pyramidal display of beer cans, which collapsed under my weight and left me arse up on the floor surrounded by cans popping and fizzing all over the place. But I was by no means fazed.

'Let us be out of the ordinary,' I declared, adopting the urgency of a revolutionary. 'Let us tear out the ground floor,' waving my arms here in a ludicrously enthusiastic display of floor tearing, 'and create a room, twice the height, whose floor is at basement level, and reached by stairs at the front of the shop. Then let us line these huge walls all the way to the ceiling with wine racks and fill them with bottles so that the whole place looks like a gigantic library of wine.' A library crammed, I half imagined, with the bottles of cheap wine I was having imported from Tarragona. Who knows, if they had liked my design, I could have been the Booze King of Britain in my early twenties and never even noticed there was anything wrong with my vacuum cleaner.

But they didn't. For the next moment I fell over and was violently sick in the cellar. The rest of my plans remained undivulged, and the world was forced to forego my wine revolution. Although it got something not unlike it, in the end, with places like Majestic and Bibendum in the eighties.

I had a bit more luck with the next project I helped Fitch on: Heathrow Terminal One. Here I designed a foam kiddies' chair for the crèche, which could either be ridden like a horse or a motorbike, or interlocked with others and used as a climbing frame. I also worked on the now-ubiquitous banquette seating, and designed a headrest which they may well have adopted, though I never saw it finished. It was, all in all, a useful early insight into the workings of a design consultancy, but I knew from very early on that it would never be my cup of tea. I didn't want to put the icing on other people's creations. I wanted to make things.

A year or so previously, I had come much closer to something that inspired me, in a project that returned me to my old schooldays' interest in the theatre.

Joan Littlewood, the theatre and film impresario who gave us *Oh, What a Lovely War!* was given to organising lively, bohemian meetings over Clerkenwell pubs, where a motley collection of arty folk would gather to toss ideas about. I had met her through a friend and started attending these meetings where Littlewood, a ball of fire and energy, would talk in anarchic terms about art, and the new 'alternative' culture. She was not concerned about people's pasts, had no respect for tradition, and no time for entrenched values. It didn't matter to her that I was only a student, she saw no obstacles to any kind of achievement, and I felt a real closeness to her exciting world.

She also did a lot of work for the poor in London's East End, and at one of these meetings, in February 1967, she explained that she was organising a City of London Festival as a way of helping poor East London kids, to get them involved in the community and to give them a bit of fun. I chipped in that I knew a lot about Pirelli webbing – a pretty heart-stopping conversational gambit, you will agree – and rubber foam. I said I would make a springy wall, a sort of proto-bouncy castle, out of this giant elastic-band stuff, and then stick on it a giant barmaid, a hippo, and a huge Harold Wilson so the kids could thump them. The models were all full of fart cushions and equally hideous contraptions, and there were squeakers in the barmaid's tits. Ah, how from such little acorns...

The wall was strung up between two pillars at Tower Precinct with the help of some local children, and was a great success – Tim Matthews from the *Today* programme even came down to interview me about it.

Thus, full of the joys of creation and throbbing with confidence in my ability to fashion beauty and function out of the meanest materials, I was up for anything. So when Joan said, 'I want to build a new theatre at Stratford East,' I lurched into, 'Please miss, me miss, over here miss, I'll do it, I'll do it, I'll do it,' mode.

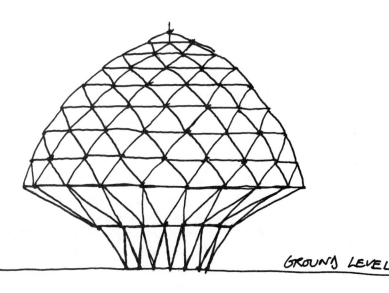

GROUND LEVEL

'Well, then. Go and design it, if you want,' she said. And so I did. Still revelling in the influence of Buckminster Fuller, my design was for a mushroom-shaped auditorium, built of aluminium rods that slotted into nodal connectors in what is known as a triodesic system.

Joan Littlewood loved it, planning permission was granted, and only the question of finance remained. I turned first to Vickers, the owners of British Aluminium. Since my entire structure would depend on aluminium, it seemed a natural place to look. I phoned, I made my appointment, I prepared for my first major head-to-head with British industry. I arrived at Millbank where Vickers had its vast and very overpowering offices. I rode the escalator to the top floor and, whaddya know? They laughed. And even worse, they wouldn't give me any money. What they did do was bring out a cine projector and show me some footage of a factory in Bath, whose flatspan roof had been constructed using the very system I was seeking to fund for my triodesic theatre. In the images on the flickering wall a tall thin man with black curly hair and rolled up shirt-sleeves was pulling on a rope and hoisting the entire roof – which had been assembled on the ground – up into the air by means of a system of pulleys. 'That,' said one of my tight-pocketed interlocutors, 'is Jeremy Fry, the managing director of Rotork. I think you should go and have a word with him.'

In those days millionaire businessmen simply did not wear jeans and pull up their own roofs with ropes. It just wasn't done. And so I was prepared to be impressed. At his palladian Georgian house in Bath I saw, in the leather floors and copper-plated walls, in the whiteness, and the modern furniture, a modern Brunel, who was carrying his professional convictions through into the design of his very own home.

He asked me why I had come. I told him that I wanted to see his factory, and to show him my model of the theatre, and to talk about aluminium, and about maybe getting some help with funding the project. And so we talked about my plans, about Buckminster Fuller, and about my ideas and ambitions in general. As the evening wore on I relaxed more and more and as I leant back in a comfy chair, nursing my whisky, I realised that this was what I wanted to do: to talk about ideas and designs and ways of building wonderful things. And I felt so lucky to be doing it. After all, I had simply dialled directory enquiries after my meeting at Vickers and asked for Jeremy Fry's phone number. And he had invited me to his home for supper. Another seminal journey, another rickety journey in the Mini Countryman, and my first view of Bath, the city where I was to live for the next thirty years.

Another predictive element of the trip was the ultimate refusal of funds. I had shown Fry my model of the proposed theatre, and I think he rather liked it, if not enough to cover me with gold. What he *did* offer me, however, was to prove far more useful in the long run: work, and the first of many collaborations.

What Fry had in mind was, in fact, another theatre job. His friend, the film-maker Tony Richardson, was putting on a production of *Hamlet*, starring Nicol Williamson, at the Roundhouse in north London. Having for the past 100 years been a locomotive turning house, the building was going to need a major rethink – to my lot fell the task of designing the auditorium and seating.

Still smarting from the failure of the mushroom theatre, which was never to get the funding it needed to come to life, I saw in the existing structure of the Roundhouse, the opportunity to make a completely circular auditorium. Beneath the circular stage was an inspection pit, used in the days of steam to work on the underside of the trains, in the same way as the pit in any car garage today. My plan was to make this the entrance for both actors and audience so that an auditorium could be constructed with no breaks at all.

I raced back to London with my plans and got there only a couple of days after the site foreman, a fat fool, by the way, had filled in the pit with rubble and concrete. To excavate again was not possible with the money we had, so that plan, which might have revolutionised the theatre, fell by the wayside.

Though my original dream had been stymied at conception, I continued to work on the design for the auditorium, using all my evenings and weekends and college vacations, and the auditorium was constructed in time for the first night. It stands to this day, though money ran out before I could design the seating, and something rather less ambitious, and considerably cheaper, was used instead.

I was impressed by the irony, even then, of my first paid commission being the redesign of that locomotive turning shed. My greatest inspiration, Brunel, had devoted his working life, his whole life, to the building of a railway system on this island. And yet I had come along at a time when designers and engineers were having to think of new ways to use the buildings that had been left vacant in the twilight of the trains. One hundred years ago I would have been doing things with steam trains, and yet the first professional use of my skills was in brushing over the tracks they had left behind.

So began my association with Jeremy Fry, a mentor as important to me as any of the engineering heroes of the past, with the great advantage of being alive, and keen to nurture such talents as I possessed.

I was really very much in need of a teacher outside the college by 1968. I had taken a look at the industrial design course, which was what I should have been doing, instead of interior design, but the classes did not have the sulphurous whiff of revolution about them. The first time I looked in they were all sitting around fiddling with slightly stylised Ascot heaters. That was their task for the term – to remodel the standard Ascot heater – and they were all being encouraged to produce something essentially the same, but with the odd little variation. There was no change in function, operation, technology, or core thinking.

The next term I peeked in again, and they were all doing exactly the same thing with washing machine fascias. It was like some terrible Kafkaesque design nightmare – but showed me a bleak vision, early on in my career, of what it would be like to design things for other people. It seemed to me that to clock on at work in the morning and be told, 'We've got this kettle, we want you to redesign it for us,' was the very antithesis of Buckminster Fuller and Brunel.

Brunel would wake up and say to himself, 'I want to design the first ocean-going vessel with a screw propeller, it'll look great, be hugely efficient, and change the world.' He didn't wake up and think, 'I think I'll try mixing a few more oats in with the horse's feed and see if it makes the cart go faster.'

Nor did Jeremy Fry. He took me to France and had me designing first a pedalo, and then a pair of 'Jesus floats' which could enable his daughter to walk on water. As a novice designer, as a novice anything I suppose, you are like a sponge looking to soak up mentors and models, and in Fry I had an ocean of experience to absorb. Like Brunel, he operated empirically. He had no regard for experts from other fields (always teaching himself whatever he needed to know as he went along) and he was an engineer interested in building things that derived not only excellence from their design, but elegance as well.

Which is rather important when it comes to building the fastest piece of plywood in the world.

The fastest piece of plywood in the world

Swinging through the Sixties. A better way to water-ski. 'To hell with experts, just get out and do it.' Lessons in sales and sailing. A world tour: Egypt, Israel, Sudan, Malaysia, Libya – baksheesh and a better boat. Scratching the itch.

As I entered my last year at the RCA nothing could have been further from my mind than the job market.

The late sixties was a good time to be at art school – probably a good time to be anywhere in Britain when you look at the acres of media space taken up by baby boomer bores reminiscing about their youth – and with the present so alive and colourful there was no question of the future being any different. When a kid leaves college nowadays, the worries about work begin immediately. Indeed, they begin before. They are beginning earlier and earlier: now it is not only the final-year milk round that shatters the illusions of youth, but whole course modules devoted to job skills throughout student life. And, worse still, every decision that is made from the point of college entry, from A Levels, even from O Levels, must be made with an eye on a specific job somewhere down the line. One wrong move anytime after puberty and pouff! Up goes your future in smoke.

It wasn't like that in 1969. There was no insecurity attached to the notion of employment, no worries that unless you followed a regimented career structure you would be jobless for life. We were the first students to have cars, contraception, our own culture – mobility in every sense – and, as a result, felt ourselves to be a new breed of person altogether. Nonconformity was positively celebrated. It mattered not a jot that I had changed courses continually, from painting to furniture, to interior design, to engineering. I, like everyone else, was just looking for the most exciting thing to do with each moment. The King's Road was the most exciting street in the world, Hockney had just left the RCA, there was wine, restaurants, cheap travel abroad – and you could shock your elders just by the shirt you wore, the length of your hair, or the records you bought. The result was a generation bursting with confidence and determined to run before it could walk.

Conversely, and excitingly for me at least, product design – with the notable exception of Terence Conran and Habitat, which was about interiors really, rather than products – was in the doldrums.

The fifties had seen an unprecedented flourishing in product design. The Festival of Britain had been the great catalyst in Britain, and the Morris Minor, the Morphy Richards toaster, the Hoover Junior and Senior were more beautiful than anything before or since. The kind of absolute vision of men like Sir William Lyons at Jaguar, who dreamt up the XK120 and the E-type, and Ken Wood at Kenwood who envisaged the first food mixer, was what had made the objects on the shop shelves so fantastic.

Then things started to go wrong, for a number of reasons. One was a disastrous design theory that took inexplicable hold on the imaginations of so many, namely that simplicity was the key to perfect design. This was the period of Scandinavian design, of renewed interest in the Bauhaus, and of men like Dieter Rands at Braun who decreed that all must be matt black and boxy. Designers were just picking up on a style, and then slavishly reproducing it. It was tantamount to designocide.

Then, of course, came the rise of consumerism, of which we have heard so much. It may be the capitalist fashion to celebrate the consumer boom of the sixties, but there is much to regret. The rise of the salesman, the Terry Thomas type, was a disaster. When things begin to sell simply because they are in the shops, because people believe they want a new one, and because 'choice' is celebrated for its own sake, then the salesman and the accountant become king, not the engineer. And companies travel the route that *they* prescribe. And so risk goes out of the window, and with it experiment, trial and error (the core of Edisonian progress), difference, and beauty.

Nor, by any means, should blame for the bleak period of the later sixties, seventies and eighties be laid at the feet of plastic. (Does plastic have feet? I suppose it does. By its very nature it can have whatever it likes.) It is a familiar reactionary pose to demonise plastic as the root of all modern ills. But plastic itself was not the problem; the problem was that the wrong people got hold of it.

The plastic pioneers made their greatest mistake only because of the way they had been brought up, for they tried to make it look like the material it was replacing: sheet steel. And so they copied the methods of working steel, justifying the new material by its lightness and cheapness. The result was cheap and nasty objects: plastic corrugated sheet, melamine covered cupboards, plastic loo seats.

But plastic is no use at all in large flat surfaces – only make it curve, and it becomes phenomenally strong. Therein lies its unique potential, and therein always lay its beauty, the perfect beauty that comes with fidelity to function. 'People get shot by people,' says the gun lobby, 'not by guns.' By the same token, do not blame plastic for the heinous crimes committed in its name by designers.

All this led to the happy coincidence of two things: a period which led one to believe that one could do anything, and a period which appeared to need my skills, particularly. Where the things I wanted to do were not yet being done. It was just such a feeling as this that Brunel must have had in the early days of the Industrial Revolution. Imperial expansion created a feeling of national confidence similar to that which we felt, albeit more briefly, in the sixties, and new technology was opening brand new ways of dealing with the world. Brunel felt that as a thinking engineer he could design bridges, ships, trains, tunnels, anything he turned his mind to, and I thought that I could latch onto something a bit tighter than the general sense of freedom. I was sure there was something to be done. This, at least, was the dream. Jeremy Fry was the man who started making it real. Fry must have been encouraged by the work I did for him on the Roundhouse, for it was not long before he came to me with another project.

Jeremy's business was in motorised valve actuators for pipelines, which he had invented himself and from which he had made his fortune. To me as a designer, however, they were not an interesting product, and professional collaboration on a large scale had not seemed likely. But in January 1968, while I was staying at his house in Bath, we happened to be talking about the pedalo and Jesus floats I had made for him, which would never have made commercial products, when he happened to mention that he was thinking about doing a boat. I was amazed. It was a completely new direction for him; he had never done anything even vaguely like it before, and yet there he was, sitting on the sofa and declaring in a very offhand way that he fancied doing a boat.

'Well, it's more of a plywood and foam sandwich at the moment,' he said. And I was hooked.

The idea had come about when he was out water-skiing with his son, and noticed that, when his son kicked off one blade for a spot of mono-skiing he slowed down considerably. Now, this should not have happened – with less frictional area to be impeded by water resistance his son ought to have moved faster.

Intrigued, Jeremy returned to shore, picked up the large plywood motor cover, and persuaded his daughter to climb onto it and be towed by the boat. Sure enough, she scudded across the water even faster than her brother on his skis. Why, he wondered, should a huge flat board plane so well across the water compared to a water ski? The answer, he realised, was that for any given weight, the greater the area supporting it, the less pressure there would be on the water, so the faster it would go.

Pressing on with his theory, he went down to the local timber yard and bought a piece of 8' by 4' plywood, put his daughter on it, and watch it skid still faster behind the boat. This appeared contrary to all the laws of friction and hydrodynamics, and while we later discovered from books that this was, indeed, the most efficient planing hull, Fry was proceeding at this stage purely empirically, adjusting his ideas of the potential vehicle to accord with the evidence of his own eyes.

It was at this point that I came in. 'The trouble is,' he said, 'that we cannot sell a work boat, for that is what this will be, in wood. It will have to be in fibreglass. And I want you to design it for me.'

Now, fibreglass is an eggshell material, fantastically strong in a curved structure, easily punctured when presenting a flat surface. This made it ideal for building conventional hulls, but disastrous for a thing like the launch craft he had in mind.

While it was essentially Jeremy's baby, and I was more of a glorified apprentice, I was expected to take on a lot of responsibility – he was the leader, but I did most of the work. I read a lot about fibreglass and hydrodynamics, and then put my reading into practice as best I could,

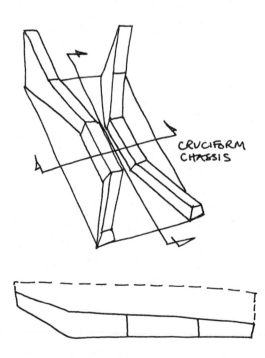

CRUCIFORM
CHASSIS

working on it solidly for most of that year, until I had come up with a cruciform structure that gave us the best of both worlds.

Up until this point, the Brunel business had been no more than a pipe dream, the heady imaginings of an art student inspired by tales of ancient engineering history. And then, suddenly, there was this man who was actually doing it. Having realised at college that I wanted to change the world by building extraordinary things, and shaking people up, I suddenly saw that it was genuinely possible.

At first, certainly, I took Fry for no more than a millionaire industrialist, and interesting enough to me for that alone. But his self-confidence and cavalier approach gradually began to win me over. Here was a man who was not interested in experts. He meets me, he thinks to himself, 'Here is a bright kid, let's employ him.' And he does. He risks little with the possibility of gaining much. It is exactly what I now do at Dyson Appliances – take on unformed graduates to throw youthful ideas around until they have given all they can and are ready to move on to new things. And I was not the only one – the sales director of Rotork, Andy Garnett, was just an arty chap, though highly cultured and articulate, who was bumming around London encapsulating things in Formica and selling them as coffee tables. Jeremy gave him the responsibility for exports. He was brilliant at it, and when he left Rotork, about the same time I did, he set up a company which he recently sold for £35 million.

This attitude to employment extended to Fry's thinking in everything, including engineering. Like Brunel, he did not, when an idea came to him, sit down and process it through pages of calculations; he didn't argue it through with anyone; he just went out and built it. So it was that when I came to him, in the midst of my efforts with the Sea Truck that summer, to say, 'I've had an idea,' he would offer no more advice than to say, 'You know where the workshop is, go and do it.' 'But we'll need to weld this thing,' I would protest. 'Well then, get a welder and weld it.' When I asked if we shouldn't talk to someone about, say, hydrodynamics, he would say, 'The lake is down there, the Land Rover is over there, take a plank of wood down to the lake, tow it behind a boat and look at what happens.'

Now, this was not a *modus operandi* that I had encountered before. College had taught me to revere experts and expertise. Fry ridiculed all that; as far as he was concerned, with enthusiasm and intelligence anything was possible. It was mind-blowing. No research, no 'workings', no preliminary sketches. If it didn't work one way he would just try it another way, until it did. And as we proceeded I could see that we were getting on extremely quickly. The more I observed his method, the more it fascinated me. It was to be exactly the way I went about developing the Ballbarrow.

The root principle was to do things *your* way. It didn't matter how other people did it. It didn't matter if it could be done better. The Ballbarrow was not the only way to make a wheelbarrow that didn't get stuck in mud – but it was *a* way. The trick is not to keep looking over your shoulder at others, or to worry, even as you begin a project, that it is not going to be the best possible example of its kind. As long as it works, and it is exciting, people will follow you.

This is how Fry, in the manner of Brunel, made his progress. If he was convinced that his way was better, then he did it. That was good enough for him.

There were times when he was wrong. In business you will be wrong, by and large, 50 per cent of the time. The trick is to recognise when you have gone wrong and correct the damage – not to worry, at the moment of making the decision, whether it is the right one. The Sea Truck, God knows, is not the best way to travel across water. In bad conditions it is uncomfortable, it smacks the surface of the water, and knocks people's toupees off. But the advantages of it outweigh the disadvantages, and the magic of the thing sees it through.

Magic – the unique way a product does what it does – is never to be underestimated. With the Dual Cyclone's see-through bin, everyone said it would never sell. People did not want to look at the crap they had sucked out of the carpet. John Lewis begged us to make smoked bins; the Japanese are still begging us. And it *is* a potential negative. Our competitors say it looks disgusting. Salesmen think it suffers by looking so filthy in a row of gleaming machines. But the very disadvantage is what gives it its magic. People look at it and say, 'My God, it works!'

If Fry was such a genius, you may well wonder, what did he need me for? The truth is that if he lacked anything, it was the ability to make things beautiful. Not trained as an artist, he did not have the sculptor's instinct that can make a design sexy, but he always said I had a way of making things look good, and that was why he latched on to me. The Sea Truck was not an easy thing to beautify and by taking the architectural, even the interior designer's, approach to an industrial product, I think I managed it pretty well in the end.

You can teach yourself science, in other words, but you can't necessarily make yourself an artist. Leonardo da Vinci could choose to make a helicopter. A helicopter maker could not choose, in the general run of things, to paint a *Mona Lisa*. That's an analogy, by the way, not an invitation of comparisons.

Given my possession of this small skill, then, I realised that I should probably be thinking about designing consumer products – where looks matter – rather than industrial ones. This feeling bubbled away in me for some years, before I first gave it vent in the Ballbarrow.

It took about eight months, in 1969, to get a prototype of the Sea Truck built, which was done in a boatyard near the Severn Bridge, where I would go as often as I could get away from the RCA to supervise. But this was by no means the artful truancy it sounds. Hugh Casson was never anything less than encouraging about my dalliance with the Sea Truck, and treated me just as he would have any student conducting research under a supervisor. That, after all, is how higher education works.

By late 1969 we were in a position to patent it. Rotork paid me £300 for my design and prepared to set up a subsidiary company to make and sell the Sea Truck. For this they waited until I finished college, nine months later.

And so in June 1970, having been at the RCA since 1966, spending one year in furniture and three in interior design, I graduated on the strength of a 40-knot, high-speed, air-lubricated hull conceived as a military assault craft. That they gave me a degree at all was, in the circumstances, quite generous. And yet at the time I was distinctly miffed at receiving only a 2:1, given the obvious market potential of my graduation piece. Here was a boat designed and built by a student which was up and running as an industrial product. But then, the course *was* called 'interior design', and less broad-minded men than Hugh Casson might have thrown me out long before.

Finally, I was finished with education. I couldn't wait to get out into the world. Rodney Fitch, who had by this time left Conran and set up a design consultancy of his own, offered me a job, and so did the yacht designer John Bannenburg. But I had started the Sea Truck and I planned to finish it.

I may have given the impression up to this point, with all my tales of individuality, frustration with the status quo and all that, that I was a self-indulgent, renegade student. Nothing could be further from the truth. I had been very boring, indeed, by no means your typical sixties wild child. I didn't smoke or do drugs, I drank only very little, was pretty well organised and disciplined, and I worked late at night in the holidays on all the projects that I was involved in. I wore the odd flowery shirt, and had quite long hair, but only because I thought they looked nice.

I regret that now, in a way. I saw my own son having a whale of a time at college, going out clubbing, drinking, never seeing daylight and doing all his work at the last minute. It is perhaps the only thing that I actually regret not having conformed with. It is ironic, too, that there was so much more opportunity for me to have fun in the sixties than there was for him in the nineties, a youth culture so much more exciting that was there to be part of.

But then, of course, he had the security of a complete family, a safety net that was there if he should fall. And he had our house in London to live in, whereas Deirdre and I had had to share a single grant of £370 a year, one grant already having gone on our year's rent. I'm not trying to pull the old I-had-to-walk-ten-miles-to-get-the-milk-when-I-were-a-lad-and-I-counted-meself-lucky number, it is just that for a Norfolk country bumpkin, London was a totally new experience, and I was too busy making, or remaking, my own life to go out on the razz every night. Not to mention the fact that I was married.

I never expressed disapproval of my son when he did things differently from the way I had. I suppose that through his 'misspent youth' I was able to live a vicarious one of my own. Maybe it was my own unusual home life, the boarding school, or the lack of money, that made me behave so deadly seriously during my own education. I know that I always felt very insecure at college, because of the way my school had regarded me as a failure.

Maybe it was just a desire to be rich and successful that motivated me – for I was motivated in an almost devilish way compared to the other students – but I think it had more to do with that running business, the wanting to get to the front and get away, and not have to look over my shoulder. At any rate, no amount of ambition for Jacob's professional happiness (the standard parental 'you'll thank us in the end' excuse) could have made me wish on him, or on any of my children, the fear of failure that drove me on then, and still does.

Relevance of all that: to give you a couple of pages to skip so that you feel you are making progress, and to explain just why I was quite as keen as I was to get out into the real world.

With the degree show over, I took a running start and leapt headlong into the fray. I began working for Rotork immediately, starting up and managing the new marine division that had been set up to deal with the Sea Truck, with the immediate prize of £1,500 a year and a company car.

With the job sorted out I bought a three-bedroom terraced house in Fulham for £5,500, with £1,000 left to me by my grandfather, £1,000 borrowed from my brother-in-law, and a hefty mortgage. Here I installed my new wife and child (we had married in December 1968, and Emily was born in February 1971, when I was still only twenty-three) and set about knocking down thirteen inside walls to get a bit of space, revelling in the smash-it-up-and-redo-it-your-way mentality of the time. The silly thing was that we never moved in, but went to Bath almost immediately, leaving the rubble behind.

My approach to my job was fairly typical of the time, too. I was responsible now for selling the vehicle I had designed, and I plunged straight in. I had a cabinless demonstration model at Putney for trials on the Thames, and a notion that the main markets would be oil or marine construction companies, and Scottish lairds perhaps. We thought there might also be a military market.

My initial attempts at salesmanship were not stupendously successful. The vehicle, which then cost £5,000, had as yet no cabin, and I was arriving at meetings with my shaggy hair and floral shirts from Take Six and Just Men. It just wasn't what businessmen looked like then (to be fair, it is not what they look like now, either).

'Couldn't you use Sea Trucks for going on exercises?' I asked one 'tache-twiddling colonel at a military engineering establishment in Chatham, trying to pry open a route into the national defence budget. 'We're not doing exercises, young man,' he bellowed. 'We're waging war!'

After a prolonged period of failure, during which I tried unsuccessfully to sell Sea Trucks to foreign armies and oil companies – and listened to them after each sales pitch tell me, 'Sod off, that thing looks like a Welsh dresser on water' – I returned to the Rotork board with a plea. The thing could not be sold without a cabin. I was trying to convince people that this was a truck of the sea and yet it looked like a detached hull, an unfinished project. We needed a little further investment to get this thing, which I was certain would be a success, off the ground.

'You can't have a cabin until you have sold ten boats,' said the finance director. 'We want to be sure that the Sea Truck can sell.'

But that could have taken for ever, in its present condition.

'If you can sell two a month, we will invest in a cabin,' was the only compromise.

But I could sell far more than two a month if I had a cabin.

'Listen, Mr Dyson, we are going to shut down the Sea Truck in two months anyway, if you don't manage to sell two a month.'

And so I battled on. I sold my first Sea Truck, nine months after the sales project began, to the Cleveland Bridge and Engineering Company, who were engaged in building the Bosphorus Bridge, and gradually began shifting a few to assorted Scottish lairds. I managed my two a month for a while, and went back to the board to talk about getting a cabin.

'Sorry, Mr Dyson. We want to see four sales a month.'

When I managed that, they upped the ante again, demanding sales of six a month. I was butting my head bloodily against a wall of commercial myopia. By hanging this sword of Damocles over me, the directors hoped to drive me into desperate efforts to sell, presumably unimpressed by my assertions that further investment was required. I was young, inexperienced, and oddly dressed, so I suppose they cannot really be blamed. But I learnt then one of the most crucial business lessons of my life: to stint on investment in the early stages, to try to sell a half-finished product, is to doom from the start any project you embark on.

I got my cabin in the end, and sales took off. Scottish lairds were going crazy for it. The Sea Truck's ability to land on beaches meant that they could ferry sheep, coal, provisions, whatever they wanted, from island to island without the need for a jetty. It was, to them, no more than an unsinkable private ferry.

Business was booming. The problem, however, and it was a fairly enormous one, was that there are only so many Scottish lairds in the world. I needed to widen the market, and you know what? The cabin wasn't enough.

My big mistake had been presenting the same craft to each customer and telling them, 'This can be adapted to suit your needs.' If someone wanted a diving boat I would explain that it could be fitted with compressors, heaters and a very slow diesel engine. If an oil company wanted a crew bus, I would tell them that suitable seating and a faster engine could be fitted. To the military I said I would bullet-proof the sides and engine. To constructors in search of a bridging tug I said, 'Special buffers? High power engine? No problem.'

I convinced not a single one of them. People do not want all-purpose; they want high-tech specificity. So, out with the universal modular craft. In with, 'I have just the boat for you, my dear sir: a purpose-built diving boat/bridging tug/assault craft/etc. . . . '

For each function Deirdre designed a brochure, and they began to sell. And it all seemed so obvious: you simply cannot mix your messages when selling something new. A consumer can barely handle one great new idea, let alone two, or even several. Why tell them this thing was universally adaptable when universality mattered to the individual consumer not a whit? It was for the same reason that when I put the Dual Cyclone on the market I kept more or less stumm about its potential as a dry-cleaning tool. How could I expect the public to believe that this was not only the best vacuum cleaner ever made, but also something completely different?

And so, with a quite respectable product to present, I set off around the world to start selling it properly. It was time spent away from designing, but it was to teach me, above all else, that only by trying to sell the thing you have made yourself, by dealing with consumers' problems and the product's failings as they arise, can you really come to understand what you have done, to bond with your invention and to improve it. Conversely, of course, only the man who has brought the thing into the world can presume to foist it on others, and demand a heavy price, with all his heart.

By early 1973, at the age of twenty-five, I was a director of a public company – and desperately keen to make the Sea Truck a success. Despite being a long-haired, seldom suited apparent student, I had to push for a global market. I had to learn fast about selling, not because I was particularly interested in salesmanship *per se*, but because I wanted to make a triumph of this thing I had designed. The world was not a stable place at that time, and my enthusiasm led me into many a troubled water.

During the Arab-Israeli war a market for our product emerged that led to some critical problems. Ford had recently been blacklisted for supplying the Israelis with vehicles and could not shift a car anywhere in the Arab world, a position I could not afford to get into myself, with so much at stake.

I began by selling to the Israeli naval attaché in London, who was a charming man and totally understanding of the predicament that I was in – I was already supplying a number of Arab countries, whose business was far more lucrative than it could have been with one small country. So I was never expected to travel to Israel – which would have prevented me travelling in the Arab world – and dealt with them in London alone, providing them with four diving boats at a total cost of £30,000.

Now, the Egyptians had got wind of the fact that the British navy was interested in the Sea Truck (not quite interested enough to buy any just yet, sadly) and as a result were fascinated. They had bought one to test, were delighted with it, and wanted to fly me over to discuss some modifications. This, by the way, was when nobody thought they stood a chance against Israel, having been hammered in 1972.

I arrived in Cairo on a stifling day in January 1973, which was not so very unusual because every day is stifling in Cairo. So, I wondered, what modification was it they wanted. Armour-plating, perhaps?

The answer to this was, in itself, an education: 'Oh no, that is the last thing we want. We sent one of our men out in a Sea Truck, and tried to shoot him. We shot at him for hours, and couldn't make a mark. The boat rides so low in the water that it cannot be hit.'

This was delightful, and a salient reminder of the blinkered way the British think. Our own navy had spent two years trying to make the Sea Truck suit their needs. By the time they had spent an absolute fortune on armour-plating and special diesel engines to power it, they had turned my lovely launch craft into an iron behemoth that couldn't manage more than about 10 m.p.h. The trial-and-error approach of the Egyptians, on the other hand, had been pure Edison. Furthermore, they had found that outboard motors, which could only power the boat if it had the lightness of the unarmoured model, were much more effective in a combat situation, because if they failed, or got hit by a bullet, they could be tossed overboard and replaced immediately.

When I went back to the navy with these findings some months later, thinking I was doing my country a service by relating to them the very useful results of secret tests by a foreign power, the captain said, simply, 'The Egyptians, eh? And when did they last win a war?'

Not long after that, as it happened. For the modifications they were after involved a set of wheels which were to be clamped to the side of the Sea Truck, allowing it to be pulled across the desert at high speed. It could then be pulled into the boat as it hit the water. I spent a week on the Nile with colonel Ali Naser of the Egyptian Special Boat Squadron, engaged in highly specific speed trials that involved a three-quarter ton weight and a kind of gun that I had never seen before.

I kept asking them what they were doing, in my naïveté, only to be told, quite reasonably, that it was top secret. And when we had managed to get the boat's water speed up to about 58 m.p.h. the Egyptians said, 'Great, this is exactly what we want.' And they sent us home on the next plane. (It didn't seem to bother Colonel Naser, by the way, that I had been doing business with the Israelis. He couldn't help knowing about it because we had mentioned it in all our publicity, but he just said, 'It'll be fine as long as you don't shout about it. If you do I won't be allowed to buy it from you.')

Two weeks later, the Egyptians stormed across the red Sea at Sinai with five of our boats, firing *ciment-prompt*, a quick-drying French cement that hardens in less than a minute, at the napalm outlets the Israelis had placed along the Sinai coast, disabling them and allowing their army to land.

And the greatest irony? The napalm emplacements of the Israeli coastal defences were built on valves that depended on Rotork actuators. The Egyptians were using boats sold to them by Rotork, to destroy Israeli defences sold to them by Rotork.

This presumably sounds an extremely shady business, but the fact is that I really had no idea what the armies I was selling to were planning. Picture again the 25-year-old art student. It was really terribly exciting. The Egyptians merely posed the problem, and I had to solve this apparently impossible task as quickly as possible. I wasn't stopping to think.

They were aware that the Israelis would be watching their activities from the other side of the water, and as a result needed a way to get in and out of the water, and across it, so quickly that the Israelis didn't know what was going on. I wasn't to know that. Since our boats were not actually fitted with guns – though they often carried soldiers who carried guns – I never saw them as, strictly speaking, offensive weapons. And I never thought of what I was doing as particularly harmful. I simply enjoyed selling to the military because their uses were exciting and highly specific, and they were never interested in cost, only what the thing did, and how well it did it. A fantastic situation for a young engineer or designer to be in.

This is not to say that I was without morals, and as I gained in experience and found myself involved in dealings that I was better able to grasp on the spot, I took care to uphold my own values, while working with cultures that might differ from our own in their methods of doing business. I never, for example, took a bribe, though this led me into many a scrape. I remember very well walking into the office of a Nigerian government minister in Lagos and being asked, before I had even sat down, or told him what I was selling, 'So, what's in it for me?'

'Nothing.' I answered.

'Well,' relied the minister. 'Go home, then!' And I did.

I lost a lot of business like that. Not only in Africa, but in Malaysia, too, where bribery is a fact of life – or, rather, of business. It was simply a question of honesty, and of simplicity, for I could not have coped with the complications of bribery. It was also my innocent infatuation with my design: I wanted people to buy it because it was a good boat, not because we bribed them.

I was so hooked into selling the benefits of the thing, the technology, the design, the features – I was on what the parlance of the period would have described as a 'trip' – that it never occurred to me that people might have to be bribed to see the light. I was quite content, in fact, to lose business that way. I would go back and tell the Rotork directors, quite happily, that I had lost a huge deal because I wasn't prepared to bribe. What I was not prepared to do was to go back and tell them that I had lost business because I could not convince our potential customer that it was the best boat.

Both my principles and my desire to keep things simple were given their stiffest test in Libya.

One morning in September 1973, I got a call from the Libyan embassy in London, saying that they were interested in buying a Sea Truck. When I got there, the naval attaché, Commander Orfi, a raffish, mustachioed, Omar Sharify sort of a man, was sitting there in his plush, velvety office with some sort of dancing girl with her breasts hanging out all over the place.

'We want ten of your boats,' he drawled languidly. 'But I can only introduce you, you will have to go out to Libya yourself to do the deal.' And so off I went.

When I arrived at the hotel where I had made a telex booking, I was told that they had never heard of me, and that the place was full. I tried to argue, and they threw me out. Having recently experienced this very problem in Nigeria, I was fazed only slightly. On arrival at the British embassy I was told that all the hotel rooms were bugged anyway, that the only safe place to talk or do business was in the street, and that I should spend my first night there in the embassy, until they could find me a hotel.

Even after I got my hotel room, things did not begin to look up. I had gone out only on the suggestion that there might be a contract in it, but with nothing in the way of a promise. As the days went by I was approached by five different people, all claiming to be agents, all claiming that if I didn't go through them, personally, I would not get the contract.

Nobody had told me about this. I had already visited the Ministry of Purchasing, listened to what they wanted and worked out a contract with the minister. As we negotiated I realised that the deal had nothing to do with money. Whatever we talked about, nothing actually happened. I could quote whatever price I liked – to the extent that I was quoting £3,900 for a spare battery you could buy in Kwik-Fit for £29 – and the minister would accept it, but no contract was being made. These five men – presumably only one of them, in fact – were clearly crucial in some way, but I could not work out how. In desperation, I decided to take the honest approach, and go to the admiral of the navy, my ultimate consumer, and tell him about the five men.

'I've been approached by these five chaps,' I began, 'who say that if I don't go through them . . .' The admiral cut me off mid-sentence.

'Shhh . . . We are not allowed to talk about such things,' he whispered. And that was that.

I went back to the purchasing minister. 'Listen,' I said. 'I don't know what to do. I've got five quotations here, each from a different agent. I'm sure you want these boats – you keep saying you do – and I know that I want to supply them to you. But I don't know who is telling the truth. I simply have no idea who I am supposed to sell them through, or what I am supposed to do.'

All the time he was just smiling and feeding me cups of that revolting Arab tea, which they boil for weeks at a time and serve with buckets of sugar. I kept refusing it and asking for water, which never came.

'Mr Dyson,' the minister finally said. 'If you drink a cup of my tea I will tell you which of the five men is the right dealer.'

It was like some bizarre biblical riddle, or some fairground conjuring trick with a dried pea and three egg-cups. I kept asking myself if there was something I had missed. Could it be worked out? Was I supposed to say, 'The answer is seventy-three', or, 'The man with no trousers learns to carry his wallet in his bum crack'?

But he produced more tea, and I drank it, and he told me which was the right man. And we signed a multimillion-pound contract. And that was that.

If ever proof were needed that to have proceeded with caution in Libya in those days was the right move, it came at the airport on the day, just before Christmas, when I was due to fly out. Some tussle had flared up between Libya and Egypt that day, and my flight was meant to be leaving at the same time as an Egyptian one. They closed the airport, and everyone began queuing to get out. After a few minutes the man in front of me in the queue was dragged off into a room, and I shuffled forwards in the queue, into the spot where he had been standing. Five minutes later the door of the room was opened, and the man's beaten-up body was slung out onto the floor.

I eventually boarded my British Caledonian plane some three hours later. It was full of oil company executives flying home for Christmas, and even surrounded by fat businessmen encountering their first alcohol in months, and hence passing out all over the aisles, my consumption of four bottles of wine and a half-bottle of vodka raised the odd eyebrow.

Selling back then was really pretty easy because I believed in what I was trying to push. As with selling anything, it was about seeing how the boat would fit into the life of the customer, not about mouthing off about how great it was. It was as true of the Sea Truck as ever it was of the Dual Cyclone. You find out what your man wants, and when he comes to you he is buying it as soon as he starts talking, before you even start to sell. It is not about the right adjectives, or shouting you mouth off. It is about discovering a need and satisfying it. Not creating a need, by the way, as many of your cynical marketing men would have it. I have seen many of our own salesmen (I should say ex-salesmen) trying to sell things in meetings, showing the buyer things he couldn't possibly be interested in, making him feel like a sucker, and cocking everything up. I learnt my lesson the hard way. To see what I mean by how easy it is, when you have discovered a need, to let a man buy without selling to him, listen to this conversation between me and a man in a leather jacket, whom I assumed to be a gangster, who showed up for a demonstration on the Thames.

'How fast is it then?' And he whammed the throttle down.

'What sort of load will it carry?' And he drove his car onto it and whammed the throttle down again.

'Great. Can you ram it on the beach?'

'Give it a try.'

He did, and then walked off the front onto the shore.

'Great. I'll have two with engines as big as you can do.'

'I'm glad you like it. What do you plan to use it for?'

'It's a secret.'

'Where are you from?'

'Switzerland.'

'How are you going to pay for it?'

'Cash.'

And he did. All £50,000 of it.

I certainly got a buzz out of selling and all that, and I learnt an awful lot about the Sea Truck, about myself, and about the relationship between selling and designing, but there came a time, of course, when I could hardly sell each and every Sea Truck we made with my own hands (or whatever it is you sell with), and the question of agents had to be addressed.

Without exception, the best agents were the ones who, quite irrespective of their business or financial sense, saw the boat for what it was, and loved it for it. While the temptation (and board pressure) was to hire established boat distributors, who knew the market and would order vast numbers, I was determined to choose people who were mad keen on it. They were the only ones who would be able to overcome all the obstacles and difficulties of selling an entirely new concept, and make a real business out of it.

Best of all, I decided not to sign up any agent unless he would undertake to buy one boat every year. Having twigged that we were wasting a lot of time signing up distributors who never ordered a thing, I realised that not only would it be infinitely easier for our agents to sell if they had a model to demonstrate, rather than just a brochure and a standard patter, but that if they had bought it already, then they would be doubly determined to sell it.

Of course, I sold the concept to the agents as being entirely about demonstratability, but in fact it was far more to do with motivation. That, and the fact that with all the publicity we were getting and the hundreds of enquiries from potential distributors all over the world, I realised that we could make good business just from opening up new markets.

Very often, in a bad month, with no military sales coming through, we would get a decent turnover from sales to agents. Anytime we were short of sales, in fact, we would simply set about looking for new markets.

Well, this was all very well and good. From a soggy plank of plywood we had developed a highly sophisticated, air-lubricated polyurethane landing craft, and sold 250 of them at a turnover of many millions. But I had been away from the drawing board too long. There was an itch there that just had to be scratched. Four years out of college, four years selling with Rotork, four years waiting for something that could be mine, all mine. Something of which they would one day say, 'It was the cleverest thing since the wheel.' Or perhaps, even cleverer than that.

4

Improving on the wheel

Strike a pose. The best thing since the wheel? Leaving the past behind.
Remembering the balls. A bad tool for building a home. A better one. I sever
the umbilical cord, and wheel myself into the great unknown. Putting the
Ballbarrow on the road. Miss Great Britain gets behind me. I invent the
Waterolla, and regret it, while the Ballbarrow becomes big business, sort of.
Looking for a way out of debt, as usual.

Who knows what pose it would be best to strike here? I fancy, on
occasion, the supremely arrogant genius. I imagine myself sitting
around in the company of mortal men, perhaps wearing a velvet cape
over my dinner jacket, when one of them, talking of some fashionable
new product or other, describes it, with that most familiar and tawdry
of clichés, as 'the greatest invention since the wheel'.

I sneer, showing one gleaming fang in the moonlight. 'The wheel?'
I enquire. 'And just what is so great about the wheel?' I smash my
hand on the table at this point, causing huge claret glasses to dance
on the table like drunken sailors, and cry, 'The wheel is flawed, do
you hear me? Flawed! Flawed! Flawed! For I, James Dyson, have
improved upon the wheel. Gentlemen, I give you ... the Ballbarrow!'

At this point my assistant, a hunchback by the name of Squelch,
wheels the Ballbarrow into the room. There is a flash of lightning, the
clock strikes twelve, and I deliver a howling Vincent Price laugh as a
shaft of light from the full moon falls across my face.

Most of the time, though, I admit it was all just a nice coincidence.
Well, better than nice; but a coincidence all the same.

In fact, it was three coincidences. There was this situation in which I was getting fed up with the life of a salesman, and looking for something to make for myself. Then there was a nice little turn of events involving final improvements to the Sea Truck, which gave me the materials and technical advantage that I would need. And there was the fact that in 1972, with a view ultimately to leaving London forever, Deirdre and I had bought an old farmhouse with one and a half acres in the Cotswolds. The confluence of these three apparently disparate conditions was what gave me my 'Eureka!'

The first you know about, and so I take the second two in sequence, hoping in that way to show how, with a little help from Dame Fortune, great technical leaps can be generated out of the smallest things in domestic life.

Now, the sad truth is that people were abusing the Sea Truck. Having, as it did, a very low draught – it drew, in fact, only six inches of water – people tended to develop an inflated idea of its indestructibility, to feel that it could never touch the bottom, no matter what the conditions. As a result, they tended to ram it into rocks rather more often than was strictly good or wholesome.

Fibreglass, as I have said before, is an eggshell material. People wax lyrical about its strength, and with good reason. But they are talking about tensile. Poke it with a walking stick, and you have a hole.

As designers, we knew that we could enhance the product by making it unpuncturable. And the best way to do that was to take our lead from those big plastic water pipes which will not break even when you hit them with a hammer. Using an extremely tough material, like washing-up bowl plastic (otherwise known as low-density polyethylene), which would obviously be too bendy to use in sheets, but was ideal for making pipes, we determined to make what was effectively a Kontiki raft of polythene pipes. The pipes would be bunged with what looked like plastic footballs, there would be a steel frame, and the raft would bend up slightly at the front to give it a wave entry form. We did not know, of course, what the hydrodynamic performance would be like. Would the most effective hull shape look, in cross section, like this:

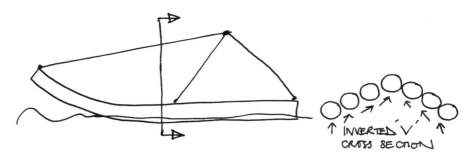

Or like this:

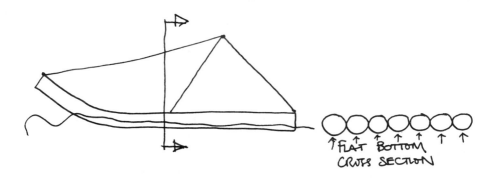

Should we use three massive pipes, or ten small ones? Dozens of similar questions needed answering, and so, towards the end of 1973, I set off with an engineering assistant and my entire family – which now comprised myself, Deirdre, Emily and Jacob – to a small village in Haut-Provence owned by Jeremy Fry. I was delighted to leave off running the business for a while, and spent eight glorious months out there testing the boat exhaustively on a reservoir.

We built a succession of eight-foot models which we tested in what I still consider an ingenious way. Unable to afford the type of long tanks used in NRDC labs, in which a frame along the top uses a tramline principle to drag your boat through the water, and not permitted to pull it behind a boat, for the reservoir was a drinking one, and motors were not allowed on it, we instead attached a rope to the boat which was coiled at the other end around a large drum powered by a petrol engine.

We rowed **the boat** out into the middle of the lake – which was, incidentally quite fantastically beautiful, bounded on one side by sheer cliff face, and on the other by a beach, where we secured the motor – and then let it go. The motor would coil in the rope onto the drum and the boat would shoot back towards the beach. We simply measured the resistance in the wire to determine the efficiency of the hull. Cunning, eh? We determined, among other things, what the optimum number of tubes was and that a

MAXIMUM LIFT

shape was more efficient than a

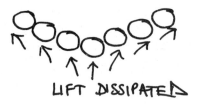

LIFT DISSIPATED

shape. We perfected the steel superstructure to keep it strong (it was essentially a glorified lilo, after all) and returned to Britain to complete a full-size prototype. And you know what?

It never went into production.

In the period when the prototype was being built, I was turning my attentions to the Ballbarrow, which should not, in itself, have presented any real problem. But when difficulties arose they just shelved the whole thing – something that always seems to happen when the original designer does not stay on his project. The self-belief is not there to press on through the hard times.

I would like to think that if I had stayed on it, the Tube Boat would have worked. In none of the projects on which I have worked has success ever been certain until I was a fair way down the line, and if it is not your own baby then there is just not the conviction to make it work. To hand over a thing like that and see it founder and disappear almost makes you want to go back and prove the new developers wrong, to make it work. But you do not, because you are on to new things. Rotork still make the flat-bottomed one, and it is doing fine. But the Tube Boat would have bounced off rocks, invulnerable, inde-bloodystructible. To coin a bit of tmesis.

I cannot do anything about it now. You can't repeat the past. How fitting are the final lines of *The Great Gatsby*, proving as they do the impossibility of changing what is gone, and yet of always wanting to, and using such a beautifully Sea Trucky metaphor to do it: 'So we beat on, boats against the current, borne back ceaselessly into the past.'

Now, I do hope you have kept those balls in the back of your mind, the plastic football-shaped bungs that we plugged into the ends of the pipes to make the raft watertight. For while the Tube Boat never came to anything, I had, at least, learnt how to mould plastic into a sphere – to make a perfect pneumatic ball of polyethylene. And it was while engaged in doing this one day that I said to myself, 'Hello, this could be the answer to my problems.' The problems in question arose as follows.

When we moved out of the Fulham house in 1971, never staying to reap the benefits of all our torn-down walls, we had bought a large farmhouse on the Badminton estate in the Cotswolds. Nay, a dream farmhouse, the sort of place every city-dweller hopes one day to escape to. For all the excitement and glamour of the metropolis, it had begun to pall for me, and I guess I was always a country boy at heart.

This farmhouse was well over 300 years old, and having been inhabited for the duration of that time by tenant farmers, it had never been improved or modernised in any way. Having underestimated how much we would need to borrow to buy the place, we found ourselves unable to employ anyone to get it in shape. And so we set about rebuilding it ourselves.

With drystone walls to be built, ditches to be dug, and cement to be mixed, I found myself, naturally enough, spending a lot of time in the company of a wheelbarrow. And in socialising with that piece of equipment on a regular diurnal basis, I discovered what a crummy piece of equipment it really was. And this was no common or garden, or even garden-centre, wheelbarrow. This was a navvy barrow, the model used in the building trade and considered by the gentlemen of that profession to be, in their own parlance, 'the dog's bollocks' where wheelbarrows are concerned.

Well, it was riddled with faults:

i) It had a wheel that was
    (a) prone to punctures
    (b) unstable when carrying heavy loads
    (c) inclined to sink in soft ground, such as the mud usually found in environments where it is used
    (d) likely to dig ruts in your lawn.

ii) It had thin, tubular legs that again sank in soft ground, ruined lawns, and caused the thing to fall over.

iii) It had a folded steel body with four faults of its own:
    (a) hard, sharp edges that bashed your legs and smashed wooden door jambs when you went through doors
    (b) when you filled it with cement it dribbled out through the cracks
    (c) cement left in it stuck to the steel sides
    (d) an open shape so that when you filled it with cement it slopped out over the sides as you wheeled.

It seemed to me, in short, a remarkably primitive derivation from the days when wheelbarrows were no more than shafts of wood with a wheel on one end, on which Stone Age man balanced things and wheeled them about. In all those thousands of years since its first conception, nobody had ever stopped and said, 'I could design this thing better.'

The reason for this is simple: a builder does not care if he smashes door jambs – after all, they are not his door jambs. He doesn't care if cement spills out of it, that only makes his load lighter. He doesn't care if cement sticks to it, because it isn't his wheelbarrow. And he certainly doesn't care if it digs furrows in other people's lawns.

So, to keep myself amused while I was performing these repetitive navvy-type tasks, pushing cement and stones around all day, I set my mind to possible improvements.

I saw that it needed fatter feet so that it didn't sink (goats, after all, do not live in deserts, nor camels in mountains). It need fatter wheels for the same reason. It needed a soft container so that it didn't smash knees or doors. And it needed to be more of a dumper truck shape, more bucket-like, so that it didn't spill things so easily. Ideally, too, it would be made of a non-stick, indestructible material so that cement wouldn't stick to it.

So I ruminated on these things in the year or so after we bought the place in Badminton, letting them turn over in my mind, and wondering how I might achieve them, not, at this stage, with any view to patenting a product, just to making my life a bit easier.

Then it was off to France to test the Tube Boat – catching up on our-selves, now – where we needed to bung the polythene pipes, and where I learnt to mould unpuncturable low-density polyethylene into a sphere. And even as I turned my first plastic sphere, I knew what was happening and I said to myself, 'This is it, matey. This is the answer to all my problems.' For not only had I learnt how to mould the sphere that would give me my revolutionary wheel, but I had learnt how to use an indestructible material that resisted the sticking of barnacles (the natural, marine equivalent of cement slops), which would serve me well in the design of the body. This, I reckoned, could go all the way.

The wheelbarrow market was a very attractive one to me at that time. It seemed a relatively unambitious market, where I would not be competing against any multinational giants as you do in, say, electricals. A kinder, gentler market altogether, or so I thought.

Furthermore, the fact that no one had contributed anything faintly new to it in 10,000 years (rather as the vacuum cleaner went unchanged for over 100), meant that anything new, with major design improvements and innovations, would have enormous impact.

So, while I was still in France working on the Tube Boat, I spoke to an old friend from the construction industry, who was as enthusiastic about the Ballbarrow as I was, and as keen to get out and work on something new and exciting. We decided to set up a company together. I then set about creating a very rough prototype, the emphasis very much on 'proto'. I built a crude fibreglass body with no handles, and then bought a football and moulded fibreglass around it. This wasn't going to tell me much about the ball itself, but it would give me a feel for the thing and prove whether or not a ball, in principle, would be more effective in soft ground than a wheel.

On my return from France in August 1974 I went to see Jeremy Fry and told him I was leaving. I felt a complete heel, and a complete mug, the two competing for prominence in my petrified mind.

I had never handed in my notice before, and here I was kissing goodbye to the best job in the world, a £10,000-a-year salary and a company car, driven only by the desire to do something on my own. Having worked, effectively alone, for five years at Rotork I had seen most of my efforts go to rewarding the shareholders, and I just thought it was time I started doing it for myself. It was, in retrospect, a stupid decision, not least because my mortgage was large and my two children, Emily and Jacob, were small. I still marvel at Deirdre's encouragement of me at that time. It could have meant losing everything. But she was always philosophical, and insisted that if everything failed she could paint pictures for money and I could make furniture – there's a vocational training for you!

The heel part of it was to do with leaving Jeremy, the man who had given me my first chance at such a young age, and been such a good friend to me ever since. I felt very grateful to him for all he had taught me and felt deep down as if I might be betraying him. But I had been working under a great man for a long time now and it was time to be my own man at last.

Jeremy was shocked at first, quite understandably, and then, to his undying credit, offered to back me financially. I thanked him, but declined. Again, because I wanted to be free, and because I already had a backer.

Or so I thought. Sadly, however, not long after my return to Britain, my construction friend called me up to say that his business had taken a bad turn and he could no longer come in with me. And so, for the first time since leaving college, I was quite alone once again. But I was not really all that worried. Deirdre was very supportive of me at home and knew very well from previous experience how unstable and unpredictable business can be. We were both curiously mellow, even with two children to feed, a big overdraft and a bigger mortgage, and we kept faith. I was also pretty certain that Fry would have repeated his offer of backing. Still, though, I wanted to prove I was ready to fly the nest.

Down to ICI at Welwyn Garden City, then, I drove with my fibreglass prototype in October 1974, initially to discuss the feasibility of moulding the pieces I needed, how best to do it, and what materials to use, but also with half an eye on the notion that they might be interested in funding the operation. It was from them, after all, that I would be buying the plastics.

'Can't be done,' they said. 'The Ball is not feasible. You cannot mould plastic into a complete sphere. And even if you could it certainly wouldn't work as a pneumatic wheely ball thing, or whatever it is.'

This, typically enough, only strengthened my resolve and made me determined to prove them wrong. With a view to setting up my own company, I went to see a lawyer friend of my brother-in-law called Andrew Phillips, who was not only a damn good lawyer, but a chap canny enough to have got himself an advice slot on the *Jimmy Young* show on Radio 2. Phillips not only helped with the formation of the company but fell in love with the Ballbarrow and persuaded said brother-in-law (Stuart Kirkwood, husband of my sister Shanie) to invest in it.

This was extremely good news. Stuart was the son of one Lord

Kirkwood, the former Chairman of the mining company RTZ who had overseen its great rise in the fifties and sixties. He and his brother, the current Lord Kirkwood had, as a result, inherited some family money. Which is always nice.

We both stood as guarantors on an overdraft of £12,000 each – which on my part involved putting up the Badminton house as security – and engaged in a 50–50 partnership in a new company to be called Kirk-Dyson. (I had tried to register Dyson as the name, but the Registry of Names wouldn't let me for some reason, although they have let me have it now. This one was obviously an amalgam of my name with Stuart Kirkwood's, but I quite liked the sound of it: it smacked of Kirk Douglas, which seemed rather appropriate for our tough, no-nonsense, square-jawed little barrow.)

By March 1979 we had a decent prototype. With it we approached a Mr Duffin of Flextank, the undisputed king of rotational moulding, who displayed great belief in the barrow and agreed to build the tooling at his factory in Pontycymr. So I completed the designs and Flextank produced the bucket and the grass-box extension using the very low-density polyethylene I had envisaged all along – and it proved, indeed, to be virtually unbreakable.

The ball itself, about which ICI could not have been more wrong, was made from a similar plastic with a vinyl additive: ethylene vinyl acetate, the same sort of material as goes into a Spacehopper, but a bit more rigid! It was moulded as a complete, sealed sphere and then punctured and fitted with a valve, making it the first plastic pneumatic wheel ever made.

The steel tube frame was made in Birmingham, the bearings inside the ball came from an injection moulder in Caerphilly, and the thing was ultimately put together by a couple of Irish blokes in the pigsties (estate agents call them loose boxes) at my house in Badminton.

Our original idea had been that the barrow would tip like a dumper truck, operated by a twist handle, but when the prototype was ready for demonstration we realised that while it was fun, the dumper facility was giving the customer too much – and risking the possibility of confusing him. The spirit of the thing, you see, was in the ball and the dumper shape – anything else would be gilding the lily. This principle is a crucial one. Just as the spirit of the Sea Truck was in the flat hull, and the spirit of the Dual Cyclone is in the cyclone, so there was a simplicity about the Ballbarrow that displayed its newness and superiority and shouted its usefulness. To attempt other gimmicks might lead to a customer believing it was just the same old thing with something added. So, off came the dump facility and the twisty handle, a swift redesign, and we were ready to launch.

But you can take nothing for granted in this game, not even kings. Six months into production the moulding monarch mentioned above decreed that his machines could no longer produce enough mouldings. *And* he tried to jack up the price.

And so I found another moulding magnate. It was a terribly expensive business, paying off Flextank, and moving all the tooling down from Wales. And, keen not to get into such a pickle again, we made it clear to our new moulders that the price had to be fixed for a year, that certain volumes had to be achieved – and to all of this they agreed with the obsequious nodding of heads and rubbing together of hands.

A month later, it was the same story: low output and an attempt to raise the price. These people seemed to be lining up to prove that I couldn't make a go of business alone and should head back to Rotork with my tail between my legs. But sick though I was of this treatment, I was by no means ready to give up. Borrowing yet another £45,000 at a time when interest rates were up to 25 per cent, I bought a rotational moulding machine from America, a new kind of machinery that had never been seen here before. We had to assemble it ourselves and then learn how to operate it. Since nobody else was up to it, we would build the bloody parts ourselves.

In May we launched 'the Ballbarrow from Kirk-Dyson Designs'. Well, perhaps 'launched' is a bit strong. But we did, at least, begin making them, assembling ten or twenty a day in the pigsties.

The reason I balked at the word 'launched' was because I really didn't have any idea what I was doing at all. Rotork had taught me to sell capital goods, not consumer products, so that apart from the designing and engineering bit of the operation, where I felt reasonably comfortable, this was a real seat-of-the-pants, kamikaze approach to getting a product off the ground. I had not drawn up any business plans or anything. I had merely partitioned off an office in the loose boxes with a piece of chipboard, persuaded Deirdre to help me with the business when she could, and painted 'Ballbarrow Is Here' on the side of a van. But how to start shifting the things, I had no idea.

The first attempt was almost laughable. Almost? No, it was bona fide, side-splittingly hilarious – at least in the context of traditional hardware sales strategies. I had a friend called Gill Taylor whom I had met in Badminton and who just so happened to have been Miss Great Britain 1964. She was blonde, attractive, curvaceous and a typical 'travel around the world and help people' beauty queen. She was also at a loose end and quite prepared to tour the garden centres of the West Country touting Ballbarrows.

Next thing I knew, a friend of hers showed up at my 'office' wanting to do the same. And then another, and another, until I had a great sales force of attractive, middle-class thirty-something ladies, descending on the garden centres of Britain.

Descending, unfortunately, with absolutely no success whatever.

It was not the fault of my 'bevy of beauties' that they had no success. It was just that the garden centres wouldn't buy this ridiculous-looking thing. When the ladies showed up with their demonstration Ballbarrow, people assumed it was a joke. And so, sadly, they gave up.

Quite why they thought it was a joke remains unclear. But there are a couple of possible reasons, more clearly visible in retrospect, why the Ballbarrow might have failed to catch on at first. It might, for example, have been the colour scheme. The barrow was green while the ball was orange. The thinking behind this was that: (a) a bright orange ball would make it more visible on a building site, thus reducing the likelihood of its being run over by a JCB; (b) it was very important that the ball be noticed in shops as it was the main selling point to the consumer; and (c), well (c) is rather a silly one.

When I had first applied to the design council for their triangular sticker of approval the ball had been red and, as a result, they had refused to approve it because they felt it did not tone in adequately with a garden and should, in fact, be green. I was appalled. These people were not designers, just a bunch of civil servants who happened to be evaluating designs. I determined at that moment to make the ball as luridly and fluorescently orange as possible, simply to annoy them. Mature, huh?

It was not only the colour, though, that was putting retailers off. In the building trade, for whom a slightly bigger barrow was produced (the ball having a 350mm diameter as opposed to 250mm) the resentment was almost masonic. They pushed wheelbarrows around all day long, and had done for years, they would explain. And who was I to come along and tell them that the tool they'd been using all these years was no good? What did I know about it?

What, indeed? It was an interesting lesson in psychology, teaching me that the entrenched professional is always going to resist far longer than the private consumer. Many of the advantages, you see, were simply not perceived by the builder as advantages at all, for the reasons I mentioned earlier, and all the things that would make it so popular with gardeners were utterly irrelevant to him.

And so we forgot the building trade – which was a shame for I feel that if we had pressed on, something could have been made of it – and gave up on the middle-class ladies. In desperation, I turned to the newspapers. I did a nice little drawing of the Ballbarrow and slapped down some direct response ads, among the baldness cures and incontinence pants, for 'The Ballbarrow From Kirk-Dyson Designs – £19.95'.

BALLBARROW is here...
Tough, rust-proof non-stick barrow riding on a unique E.V.A. ball. Rides easily over ruts and broken ground. Leaves no marks on lawns — even fully laden. Massive grassbox extension available.
WATEROLLA- rust-proof garden roller. You decide the weight (from 10 to 210 lbs) Maintenance free.
Send for brochure & prices: Dept. 4
Kirk-Dyson Designs Ltd.,
Badminton, Avon tel 045-421 425

And what do you know? The cheques started rolling in.

I was astonished. This was the same object that had been rejected completely by builders and retailers, who had been able to see it in the flesh, and it was being bought up by members of the public, who were sending off cheques for twenty quid to a company no one had heard of, all on the strength of a weedy little drawing in a tiny newspaper advertisement.

It was fantastic. We were getting a good class of customer, from ads in the *Sunday Times* and the *Sunday Telegraph*, and the business began gradually to show a profit, producing up to thirty a day, and shipping them off by post. From here on, things snowballed. Or rather Ballbarrowed.

The gardening correspondent of the *Sunday Times*, one Graham Rose, had seen one of our ads and called me up asking if he could see one. I drove up to his home at Uffington, which was not all that far away, and took a Ballbarrow with me. He loved it.

Soon afterwards, an article appeared on the 'Prufrock' page on the back of the business section, headed 'Perfectly Spherical Winner'. There was a photograph of me with my long hair and flares standing on a pile of rubbish behind my house, along with some fairly hagiographic copy.

It always seems to be journalists that are first to see the potential of a new invention, which is odd when you consider that they are not, in their nature, particularly commercially minded people. It is also the very best way of convincing the public. One decent editorial counts for a thousand advertisements. People are far more likely to believe someone who has tested something for themselves – and it is assumed that a journalist has done that. From that point on, and throughout my struggles to launch the Dual Cyclone, I made editorial comment the basis of all my thinking about publicity.

A stall at the Chelsea Flower Show continued the build-up of interest in the Ballbarrow, and helped to get us written about in magazines like *Homes & Gardens*, which contributed to the general glamorisation of the product. And then along came a man called Scott.

Bob Scott, to be precise, of Scotcade, the man who introduced nonstick pans and cordless irons and kettles to the world while working for Tower Pots and Pans. He was an American who had come to Europe in the 1960s, at the height of the Vietnam War, and had set up a direct-selling operation that involved buying whole pages in the broadsheets and presenting products not so much as if he were advertising them, but was simply writing a story about them, complete with juicy photographs.

He, too, loved the Ballbarrow and agreed to take it on not because he expected to do well commercially, by his standards (and he did not by *his* standards), but because he wanted, in his own words, 'to attract a better class of customer, the middle-class gardening people whom I have found it difficult to reach with my carriage clocks'.

Scott's other trick was a list of names and addresses to whom he sent catalogues, thereby vastly increasing the profitability of each sale, because it did not involve paying for space. His sales were huge, by our standards, and the orders began to roll in. He would make the sale and then send us labels addressed to the people he had sold to. All we had to do was slap the label on a barrow and pack it off to the customer, then send an invoice to Scott. He wasn't having to hold stock, and neither were we, we were practically building to order, with all the savings on overheads that that entails.

By March we had taken a 50 per cent share of the market and were selling 45,000 Ballbarrows a year, turning over about £600,000 annually. We had even gone so far as to introduce another product to the public and were enjoying a 50 per cent market share with that as well. Its own story is worth a small digression, I think.

The tale of the Waterolla, designed and patented at the same time as the Ballbarrow (its baby brother, if you like), is interesting largely because of its grotesque illustration of a single commercial principle. In the annals of designing history the Waterolla will go down, if it goes down at all, as the perfect example of making a product too good.

The Waterolla was a garden roller that, instead of being a large metal drum full of concrete, was a large plastic drum full of nothing. In this state it could be chucked in the back of a Volvo and taken home, where you filled it with water to give it weight when you wanted to roll the lawn. This system meant that when you wanted to take it somewhere else, you had only to empty the water and refill when you got to wherever else you wanted to roll. The old-fashioned rollers were, by their very nature, condemned to spend their entire lives rolling the same patch of grass.

It was marvellous. It was even reckoned at one time that we had 90 per cent of the market (albeit of the world's tiniest market, I do not think you need me to tell you that not many people buy garden rollers). And then sales dried up altogether. Just like that. Over. No more sales. Finished.

Why? Well, though the market was small, at least, in the old days everyone who wanted to have one had to buy their own – you couldn't very well nip round to your parents' place and borrow their half-ton lump of iron and concrete. The Waterolla, unfortunately, was ideal for borrowing. People were so mean that if someone in the neighbourhood had a Waterolla everyone would borrow it, and no one else would buy one.

The great, indeed only, selling point of the thing was the quality which ultimately made it unsellable. We had, in short, moved into the garden roller market, closed it down, and moved on.

Now, at last, with the growing exposure of the Ballbarrow, people were starting to ask for it in shops. The time came to move towards a new kind of selling, and with the involvement of wholesalers, retailers and the rest, the board felt we should take on a sales manager.

That sales manager's name was John Brannan. His experience of our kind of business was limited, coming as he did from a background in haberdashery, and worst of all, he turned out to be a complete bastard.

I do not use that term lightly. The worst of Brannan is yet to come, but in following his advice to abandon direct selling and supply shops via wholesalers, we began to lose that contact with the consumer that was the basis of our success. As with the Dual Cyclone, so with the Ballbarrow: the establishment of a client base by word of mouth is what gives a product longevity and integrity, a sort of wise man building his house on the rock principle. And quite apart from the loss of that intangible heart, in bald economic terms we were only making half as much money on each sale because he had had to incorporate a margin for wholesalers. The business became cash negative, and we started to find ourselves sinking into debt.

What was the response of the board? To expand. 'Oh, we're doing terribly well,' they thought. 'Let's get a proper factory. Let's injection-mould the barrow.' Now, in principle I would have been all for injection-moulding the barrow. It was cheaper than rotational moulding, produced a better-quality product and allowed greater output. But it would cost £55,000 to convert.

What can you say? The cost of the new equipment and the liability of the new factory we had to rent in Corsham was extremely onerous, but it was born of ambition and confidence on the part of the board, I thought, and it was all terribly exciting.

The problem was that we were doing it all on borrowed money. Under Heath and then under Wilson, interest rates spiralled and we were running an overdraft by this time of £150,000. We needed a new investor; we would have to dilute our share power.

George Jackson was a property developer from Cirencester to whom we sold one third of the company for about £100,000. I was now a minor shareholder, holding, like Jackson and my brother-in-law, only a third of Kirk-Dyson. Furthermore, I was the only industrialist on the board, becoming a more and more isolated voice, despite being the inventor of our product and the only one who had a real relationship with it.

I brought in an old friend of my father's, Robert Beldam, to have a bit of moral support on the board. He was chairman of the CBI small companies section, and though his presence created a little, never expressed, resentment on the board, having him there made me feel somewhat better.

Through 1976 and into 1977 we were a hot seller in shops and garden centres, and while there were no figures for wheelbarrows, we had soon taken something like 70 per cent of the entire market. At £25, we were three times the price of the old tin barrow, so that wasn't bad at all, but exports were negligible because the freight costs on such a bulky, low-cost object are pretty much prohibitive – the price against the indigenous wheelbarrow in France or Australia was more than tenfold.

The problem was this: while the company was a reasonably healthy one with thirty-odd employees, it wasn't good enough to continue with this kind of debt around its neck. With interest rates at 25 per cent and borrowings of £150,000–200,000 we're talking £50,000 a year in back interest even before you think about paying off the capital. Kirk-Dyson just couldn't support that kind of debt repayment.

What we needed was a big cash-injection, and fast. Exporting was not going to be the answer, so there was only one thing for it. We would have to try and sell a licence abroad. The biggest and easiest market was obvious. America.

5

Betrayal over a ball

America – land of the free. Ripped off rotten by a real rat. Dealing with the traitor. I am ousted outrageously and learn about creative jealousy. The company sells out, and I am well out of it.

Ah, yes. America where the buffalo roam, where seldom is heard a discouraging word, and the skies are not cloudy all day.

The discouraging word thing is true enough, but not necessarily a good thing; in fact at times the problem can be words that are too encouraging. So it proved to be in the case of the Ballbarrow, and so too with the Dual Cyclone, both times in very different ways.

One of the strains of this book is about control. If you have the intimate knowledge of a product that comes with dreaming it up and then designing it, I have been trying to say, then you will be the better able to sell it and then, reciprocally, to go back to it and improve it. From there you are in the best possible position to convince others of its greatness and to inspire others to give their very best efforts to developing it, and to remain true to it, and to see it through all the way to its optimum point. To total fruition, if you like.

This did not happen at Kirk-Dyson. The story so far, if I have told it right, has been about my dream of doing something on my own, how I gradually had to let others in, how they occasionally let me down, how ultimately it came down to boards of directors, and how gradually my own voice and influence became watered down. This process was to continue to the very end, sadly, and to the ultimate detriment of the project.

When the time came, in October 1977, to try to sell a licence in the United States, a seminal moment in the life of any consumer product (as seminal, indeed, as 'making it' in the States is for any pop group, novelist, actor or film-maker), I was simply too busy running the business to attend to the licensing myself.

I tried, at first, to involve myself in organising things – simply on the principle of bringing my baby up all the way. Having seen it through birth, vaccinations, kindergarten and school, there was no reason to let someone else take it off to university. I spoke to 3M, Plascor, the Glassco Plastics Company, and The Faultless Starch Bon Ami Co., among others, all of whom proclaimed themselves very interested in the Ballbarrow, and eventually drew up a list of five companies that would be worth a visit.

But the actual visiting had to be done by our sales manager, John Brannan. He was sent off to vet the five companies in November and returned a few days later, having visited only two of them. 'Glassco is the one for us,' he said. 'It's absolutely perfect. And you'll never guess what – they've offered me a job.'

'What about the other three companies?' I couldn't help asking.

'Well, here was this fabulous offer, so I didn't think I needed to carry on.'

This came as a bit of a blow to the board, who were shocked at Brannan's disloyalty. I wasn't, by the way, for I suspected he was a rat all along. The only thing that surprised me about this genuinely shocking act of betrayal was that he didn't go to the other companies on the list – they might have made him an even better offer.

So, in the end, I did have to go out there for myself. I looked at all the companies, found that Glassco, a Chicago plastics manufacturer, was not suitable at all, and plumped for Plascor of New York, with whom I began negotiating a licence.

Brannan, meanwhile, left us for what was ostensibly a job in Britain. In fact, what he did was to buy some Ballbarrows, take them out to

Chicago with him, and begin copying them with his new employers. We had a patent and a trademark; it simply wouldn't have occurred to us that this could happen. Even if, that is, we had known about it.

The first I heard of it, however, was when, in the midst of our negotiations with Plascor, we learnt that Sears was already selling the Ballbarrow.

You what?

Glassco had stolen our slogan 'The Ballbarrow Is Here'; they had used an identical green bin and red ball; they had stolen our logo; they had even used a Kirk-Dyson Ballbarrow in their publicity because they were in such a rush to beat Plascor onto the market they had not even had time to build their own yet. For the Lord's sake, their brochures looked the same as ours, with the single difference being that the woman pushing the thing was not my wife, Deirdre, as it was in our own campaign. Even Brannan had balked there!

I was fortunate in only one thing at this time, and that was the personality of the President of Plascor, Stanley Roth. You might have expected him to renegotiate the terms of our licence agreement when he heard about Brannan's rip-off, but, to his eternal credit, he did not. To encounter, in the midst of so much back-stabbing, a truly honourable man, gave me a great deal of heart to persevere.

I was very low at this point, but business traumas were put in perspective towards the end of my negotiations with Plascor by the sad, though not unexpected, death of my mother. For the previous six months she had been suffering from incurable cancer of the liver, a disease whose discovery in her own body had seemed a bitter twist of fate after the death of my father from it twenty years before. To be deprived, in only her mid-fifties, of seeing her children and grand-children mature, was very cruel. During her sickness, Deirdre had been pregnant with Sam, who was born just before she died, and I will always remember her cuddling him.

The death of my last parent was a terrible blow, and outweighed all my own personal disasters. Touchingly, Plascor's external legal counsel was well aware of this and made a donation to a New York cancer charity in memory of my mother.

But business did have to go on and the board of Kirk-Dyson was, naturally enough, very keen to commence legal action against Glassco. I was not so keen, myself, for reasons I will come to shortly, but I consented initially to their wishes. I got myself a hardcore New York lawyer called Carl Goldstein, with an office on the forty-eighth floor of a Wall Street skyscraper and an egg-timer which he flipped over whenever the phone rang so that he could charge the caller accordingly. That experience alone, the hiring of a Wall Street lawyer, was a lot of fun. And he willingly took the case.

Now, I had advised the board very strongly against taking legal action. The last thing we needed, I explained, was a fight in America. We were in debt as it was and the battle would be expensive, time-consuming and probably futile, since patent cases are very rarely won outright. The thing to do, I told them, was to file a complaint through our American lawyer, to let them see we meant business, and then return to our business in England, strengthen it, and then set about production in the States at a lower price, and take Glassco's market. My conviction that this tactic would work was born, once again, of my belief that only the person with the closest relationship with the product could make a success of it.

I warmed to my theme. The money we saved on law suits, I informed the board, could go towards subsidising the US production of the barrow. And, best of all, we should not set about competing with Brannan until he was well and truly up and running. But by biding our time we could allow him to open up a market, which we could then exploit, and with a bit of luck punish him for his treachery that way.

But the board was not impressed. 'No, no, no,' they cried. 'We must go over there and teach him a lesson. We must show him that we cannot be trampled on.'

They were wrong. I tried to warn them. We would waste cash we didn't have (we had only entered the US to try to rescue ourselves from debt in the first place); we would take our eye off the ball, so to speak, and we would suffer the occupational hazard of all men who bang their heads against brick walls.

They didn't listen. To the courts we jolly well went. I spent the next year flying backwards and forwards between Britain and the US, wasting time on legal minutiae. And it did us no good at all.

We even lost the case about Glassco's theft of the Ballbarrow name, which was the one we might most reasonably have expected to win. But the presiding judge ruled that our trademark wasn't valid because the word 'ballbarrow' was purely descriptive; it only described, he said, a wheelbarrow with a ball instead of a wheel. I was struck dumb. What a bizarre thing to say, I thought, when there was no such thing as a wheelbarrow with a ball until I invented it and gave it a name.

'If you go up to the man in the street,' he said, 'and ask him what a ballbarrow is, he will say that it is a wheelbarrow with a ball.' This was particularly poignant for me, since I had spent years telling people I had invented a ballbarrow, only to hear them ask, 'What on earth is that?'

By the end of 1978 we had got nowhere. If we made a mistake in our choice of lawyer, it was only that we employed a New York attorney to fight a case in Chicago, thereby opening ourselves up to suffer by the enmity between the two cities. The importance of using a 'local' was brought home to me, and when I came to fight the biggest lawsuit of my life some ten years later, again in America, I didn't make the same mistake.

To keep costs down at home we were now making the ballbarrow frames ourselves, doing all the bending, cutting, and painting with powder epoxy. The business had bedded down, and while not earth shattering, was perfectly OK.

We had also launched another new product. The Trolleyball was a boat-launching trolley that used pneumatic balls instead of wheels to make moving heavy boats across beaches much easier than it had ever been before. With the addition of a frame bearing a sling of seat-belt webbing you could also use it to haul any boat you liked, whereas in the past a system of wooden chocks and carpet meant that you needed a different trolley for every boat.

Because these balls floated you could just float the boat onto the webbing and wheel it out of the water, whereas with the old kind, the trolley would disappear into the mud and you'd get the positioning wrong and end up with a chock through the hull.

I used to go out to the Datchett Reservoir by the M4 at nights, where there are hundreds of dinghies, and walk along the grass pulling each type of boat out of the water with my trolley, to make sure that I could claim its suitability for any type of hull. It was good to spend a little time on making and testing again, to distract me from the financial troubles of the business, and the thing proved enormously popular, helping to keep some cash flowing into the company.

But we were still not doing well enough to sustain our debt, and having failed to sort things out by selling an American licence, we still needed to get ourselves out of the red. Debt, you see, is a terrible thing for a small company. It fosters a bizarre reverse psychology that comes from the darkest depths of the human psyche and makes you even more inclined to overspend. The reason for this, is that when you have no money and are in debt you start thinking about all the things you could do if you had money, and that sets you to dreaming up all sorts of schemes and projects, which lead you into further debt as you try to realise them.

When you have money, on the other hand, you tend to be more careful, largely because the occasion does not arise where you sit around desperately trying to think of ways of making money. You just get on with your life without thinking up hair-brained schemes you couldn't possibly carry out. Thus, without an overdraft you are not only freed of the interest burden, but your mind is freed to think more clearly and you can negotiate more effectively with both suppliers and customers, because they can see that you are not stretched financially and desperate to make a deal.

The only way that I could see to get the company out of this debt was for the three of us who owned Kirk-Dyson to capitalise our loans. The other two were not willing to do this, and we grew to be more and more at loggerheads with each other.

There were other things, too, that were creating unease on the board. The others resented very much the fact that I had brought in Robert Beldam. His was a voice on the board that always echoed mine, particularly in such matters as the capitalising of our loans, and it made them feel uneasy.

This pressure continued to build until, ultimately, one cold morning in January 1979, I was invited up to Jackson's place in Cirencester for a board meeting. I pulled up at his house and climbed out of my Citroën. From the other cars in the drive I could see that Kirkwood was already there, probably sitting in a back room with Jackson. As I was walking towards the house, Andrew Phillips came out to meet me.

'You're out, mate,' he said. And I was.

Despite everything, this came as quite a surprise. But an observation in the past helped me to understand a little of why it happened. At Rotork, Jeremy Fry was the inventor, owner, principal shareholder and chairman. Some of the other senior executives seemed to resent that his ownership was absolute, and they were, to all intents and purposes, hired executives. At the time I was baffled by this antipathy towards such a charismatic and brilliant man – I did not feel it myself, because I always knew that I would one day create things of my own. And I never imagined that anything like it would ever happen to me.

It did. In name we were three equal shareholders, each with 33 per cent. But whenever the Ballbarrow was featured in the press, or at design fairs or within industry shindigs of any kind, it was always me that people wanted to talk to. I was the one immediately identified with the product; I was the one with the understanding of it. It was part of me. And yet the others felt, quite reasonably I suppose, as much right to the product as I. This generated the kind of jealousy that led to George Davis being forced out of Next, where one man's personal identification with the business irritates all the others. It could even be said to have been part of what led to the ousting of Margaret Thatcher from government.

In my case, though, it could also have been born of creative jealousy. Accountants, executives, money men are often jealous of their creative counterparts, because they themselves have never created anything. They are always very quick to do the creative ones down, to be negative and destructive in everything, and to insist that the creatives know nothing of business as a way of defending their own importance in the scheme of things. I guess it is a pretty frightening thing to be uncreative.

What transpired after I left was even more interesting. Almost immediately, they sold the Ballbarrow to another company and, presumably, recovered their debts at the expense of rights to the product. They held on to the factory and to all the machinery, planning to subcontract, and make mouldings for other companies, as well as making new products of their own. Soon afterwards, they sold that too.

It appeared that they had got rid of me because they knew I would never agree to sell off the rights to the Ballbarrow, and had become, in their eyes, nothing but an irritating obstacle to the business. It had cost them almost nothing to usurp me, because the business was not worth anything. Furthermore, and I weep to recall it, I had, in my naked naïveté, assigned the patent for the thing to the company, rather than to myself. I had no rights at all to the invention I had created and laboured over for so long. It was not a mistake I was ever to make again.

It wasn't a money thing, by the way. It had nothing to do with me and my family being suddenly deprived of my £10,000-a-year salary. Nor the fact that I felt I had been pickpocketed by my friends and family. It was a bigger loss than that. To lose my invention (not the company, which was never the point) was like losing a limb. No, it was worse than that. It was like giving birth, and then losing the child. And I was completely shattered by it.

My friends rallied round at the time, and our very close friends Penny and Stephen Ross looked after me and Deirdre in our despondency. I felt no rage towards the other directors; I knew there would be other inventions in the future. I even stopped Andrew Phillips from crawling to me with apologies, telling him, as we stood there in Jackson's drive, 'Look, if you want me to go, I'll go.'

The effect on my relationship with my sister was sad. She and her husband claimed they couldn't talk to me for legal reasons. But I didn't even try to put up a fight. I hated legal actions back then, and once they had thrown me out of the business I had built, I wanted only to turn my back on them, and get on with my life. I didn't speak to my sister or brother-in-law for ten years, and I suppose it only goes to prove the old cliché that you shouldn't go into business with relatives.

From a business point of view, I suppose, I was well out of it. I had gone into the project to prove that I could make something on my own, to be free of the boring side of business that had bogged me down eventually at Rotork, and to enjoy a little autonomy. Those things I had done, and my invention had been a huge sales success, if not a commercial one.

And so I was back where I had been when I left Rotork. Alone, and a little wiser. But, just as had been the case when I stopped work on the Sea Truck to concentrate on the Ballbarrow, so, in leaving Kirk-Dyson, I was taking with me a little something for the future.

6

'It really was no miracle, what happened was just this…'

A journey through time. Hubert C. Booth and a Victorian paradigm. A cleaner fit for a king. A bag on a broomstick: the American dream. Hoover and Electrolux rest on their laurels. Nothing happens for a long, long time. The inadequacies of the 'modern' vacuum cleaner. A night-time vision at the sawmill. How I solved a suction problem at the Ballbarrow factory, and had a revelation. Cereal packets, sellotape, and the world's first bagless vacuum cleaner.

Before we arrive at the main event, for it is now not very far off, I want to take you on a journey through time.

It is the last year of the reign of Queen Victoria, and we are in the London office of an engineer called Hubert Cecil Booth, famed for his success in designing the Big Wheels that are proving so popular at the fashionable fairgrounds and great exhibitions in London, Paris and Vienna.

In the corner of the room, Mr Booth, a small man with large whiskers, is kneeling on the carpet. He has placed his pocket handkerchief on the floor and, with his lips pressed firmly to it, he appears to be sucking with all his might, as if hoping to lift the carpet up off the floor by his mouth alone.

After some time he straightens up and, picking the handkerchief up off the floor, holds it up to the light, apparently for examination. A smile spreads across his bonhominous face. 'Aha,' he whispers, 'I thought as much.'

If you approach Mr Booth (he will not notice us, we are like Scrooge and the Christmas ghosts, seeing but unseen), you will notice that the handkerchief is impregnated with dust, sucked up by him from the carpet into its fabric. Now, why should he be so pleased about that?

Some days earlier he had been, at the instigation of a friend, to witness a demonstration of a new American device for extracting the dust from the upholstery in railway carriages, at the Empire Music Hall in Leicester Square – though other sources say that it was at the St Pancras Hotel, or even at St Pancras station itself. At any rate, the cleaning method on show involved blowing the dust away by means of compressed air, so that it dispersed into a great cloud and then, eventually, settled again on the furniture.

Hubert C. Booth had not been impressed.

'Would it not be more effective to use suction?' he had enquired of the machine's proud inventor.

'No, it would not. And besides it would be impossible,' said the infuriated man, or words to that effect, and promptly stalked away.

But Booth was not convinced, hence the little demonstration we have just witnessed. For the record, it should be pointed out that many historians describe the handkerchief test as having first been tried out on the seating in a restaurant close to his Victoria Street office, but as we have just seen what happened on the carpet, we know which story to believe, don't we?

Satisfied with the result of his test, Booth invested in an electric motor and a vertical-reciprocating pump, and sent out to the Army & Navy stores up the road for some cloth. By February 1902 he had formed the British Vacuum Cleaner Company (later called Goblin), and had men all over the country providing a cleaning service by means of a horse-drawn 5hp engine that turned over in the street while long hoses were fed into people's homes to suck out the dust.

The machine was an instant success, with parties being thrown by pukka ladies so that all their friends could watch the carpets being cleaned, and Booth even fitted transparent hoses so that they could see the dust being sucked up into the bowels of the machine.

At this stage Booth planned only to offer a cleaning service, not to sell cleaners. But the annals of vacuum cleaning legend had a little surprise in store for him. During preparations for the coronation of King Edward VII at Westminster Abbey, it was noticed only very late in the day that the blue carpet on which the royal thrones were to stand was extremely dirty. It was too late to have them sent away for the laborious cleaning process that was the norm at the dawn of the century, and nobody knew what to do. (It does all sound rather implausible, doesn't it? But that's legend for you.)

Booth got wind of this pretty pickle at the Abbey – God knows how – and stepped in with an offer of assistance. The carpets were vacuumed, everything looked lovely, and the new king was crowned.

When the king got wind of what had happened (again, it sounds unlikely – can you imagine some royal courtier, trained in the days of Victoria, approaching the king to ask if he might like to hear how the cleaners got the carpet looking so lovely?) he demanded, indeed commanded, a royal performance. A machine was brought to Buckingham Palace and he and Queen Alexandra watched with approval. So impressed were they, in fact, that after the demonstration they ordered two vacuum cleaners for themselves, one for Buck House and one for Windsor Castle, making them the first people ever to buy a vacuum cleaner.

In 1904 Booth's company began production of a more mobile machine for domestic sale. It had the motor, pump and collecting canister mounted on a trolley, and was plugged into a light socket to be operated by servants, though it still weighed in at a hefty 88lbs. A man after my own heart, Booth worked tirelessly to protect his patents, both for the cloth-collecting bag and the assertion that his was indeed the first vacuum cleaner.

But if the thing was really going to make it big, it was going to have to happen in America. And so it was that in 1908 a leather and saddle company called Hoover, looking to diversify the business as cars began to replace horses, bought the rights to an electrical carpet sweeper invented by one James Murray Spangler, the true prototype of the machine we know today. (Or knew until 1993, anyway.)

Spangler was an asthmatic janitor working in a department store in what was then New Berlin, Ohio, in the early part of this century, who found that the dust thrown up by his broom was damaging his health. In response to this he fashioned a machine out of wood and tin that incorporated a vertical-shaft electric motor mounted on a pair of wheels, with an electric fan which sucked up the dust and blew it into a pillow case – slung from a broomstick which stuck into the back of the trolley – cadged from his wife for a dust-bag. He may well have been smarter than the average janitor, but he was not up to marketing himself and had no option but to sell the rights.

With the patent made over to himself, W.H. 'Boss' Hoover set out to conquer the world. And conquer it he did, for his model 'O' suction sweeper, which came out in December 1908 at a cost of $70, was, after the electric fan, only the second device in history to use an electric motor. At the time electricity enthusiasts were coming out second best to the coal gas lobby, who insisted that lighting, heating and cooking could all be better done by gas. It was this impasse that led to the boom in electrical appliances, as a way of spreading the word, which itself brought about the power revolution after the First World War.

But as far as the vacuum cleaner was concerned, revolution was over. Sure, Electrolux came up with a cylinder and hose cleaner in 1913, and the 1936 Hoover Junior introduced rotating brushes that helped to dislodge dust from the carpet, but the world had been given its electric fan and pillow case on a stick, and that was that. At least as far as Hoover, Electrolux and their cronies were concerned.

And that's about enough history. Back to the future we go, to 1978, arriving somewhere near the end of the last chapter, so that I am still at Kirk-Dyson, but tiring of the line of garden-oriented products which represents our trade.

Life in our new home in Bathford, a very Jane Austeny Georgian sandstone building called Sycamore House, where we had moved to be nearer the Ballbarrow factory, and the joys of the city of Bath, was as busy as ever. We had three children by now, Sam having been born that year, and I had not only got my maths wrong in purchasing the house, so that I had to borrow £12,000 more than I planned, but had opted for a building that required replumbing and wiring, which, as a result of my mathematical mishap, I could not afford to have done professionally, so was doing myself in what spare time I had. Nor did these butch and manly chores mean that I shirked my responsibilities as far as the housework was concerned. A little light vacuuming was the least I could do.

The model we had at home was an old reconditioned Hoover Junior. Old because I couldn't afford a new one. Reconditioned because I had not been able to afford a new one even the first time around. A Hoover because they were the only reconditioned models available at that time. And a Junior, or at least an upright, because that was the kind my mother had (more of which genetic prejudice later).

It had been annoying me for years, this poxy machine. But I had not really had any time to think about why. I don't think it ever had much suck, even in its callow youth. It just seemed to push the dirt and dust around the house, and I came to think of it as more of an expensive broom than a cheap vacuum cleaner. It took a little further investment in contemporary vacuum technology to get my head working.

The new place in Bathford had a lot of wooden floor space and not much carpet, which meant that I needed something with much more suck. And so we bought ourselves a great big cylinder cleaner that was advertised as the most powerful on the market.

For a room or two, when we first bought it, the new machine was fine. But after a while it, too, lost interest in sucking, and as it was a cylinder cleaner with a hose, I was able to put my hand over the end very easily to see how hard it was sucking. It was that, in fact, that led me to start thinking about 'suck' in general.

I noticed that it was often I, who used it mainly at weekends, who found it most useless, rather than Deirdre. This was because by the time I picked it up, after a week of use, the bag was often filling up. On one such weekend, with the machine wheezing around the house, nosing at the dust like an old labrador sniffing diffidently at cold turds on a pavement, I went to the hoover bag cupboard, and found that the cupboard was bare. Ingenious chap that I am, I decided the logical thing to do was to cut open the bag, a sausage-shaped thing that wrapped around the motor and filled like a colon, empty it, and stitch it up again.

The first thing that surprised me was that the bag was really not that full at all, and yet it was clearly preventing the machine from working. I eviscerated it anyway, and taped it back together with masking tape. To my blank astonishment, the thing could muster no more suck than before my impromptu surgery.

On the following Monday I bought some new bags, and the cleaner worked again. I tried my emptied bag once again – no change. Sensitised to the problem now, I did a fair amount of vacuuming with one of the new bags, and noted a rapid decline in performance, while the bag, which I checked constantly, had only a thin coating of dust on the inside.

What was going on here? It was a rainy afternoon and I sat with my vacuum cleaner for some time, asking myself why it should be that it failed to work with a partially full, or completely emptied, bag, but worked fine with a brand new one. What was the difference between these bags?

I opened up the three bags – the reused one, the new but partially full one, and a brand new one – and the only difference was a fine coating of dust on the inside of the first two.

It had to be that the pores of the bag, which were meant to let out only air, were in fact clogging with dust and cutting off the suck. This, of course, was why I had noticed an enfeebled suck when putting my hand over the hose nozzle after only a few minutes' cleaning with a new bag. It also explained why the old Hoover Junior, which had a reusable rather than disposable bag, had never actually worked properly at all. It had been permanently clogged.

I was furious. I felt the same anger towards the vacuum cleaner as I had towards the wheelbarrow. We were all victims of a gigantic con by the manufacturers. They fit these bags and the bloody things clog up immediately, and had done for 100 years. I had spent all this money on the most powerful vacuum cleaner ever produced, and it was essentially just as useless as the old one I had always had, which was permanently and irrecoverably clogged.

All suggestions of new technology were mere marketing hype. The way they responded to the fact that their product was crap was to bring out a more expensive one, and simply ignore the fact that it was still crap. By the time the public realised, they would have brought out yet another one which the public might believe wasn't crap – until they tried it. It could go on for ever.

And it would have done, but for one stroke of fortune: it so happened that I was having suction nightmares elsewhere.

At the new Ballbarrow factory, which was now up and running (the one we had bought, you remember, because of our problems with contractors), we had just installed a powder-coating plant. To toughen the frames of the barrow each one was sprayed with an epoxy powder that melted when baked and formed a coat of paint. The powder was sprayed out of a thing like a child's water machine-gun which electrically charged the powder as it came out of the gun so that it would cling to the metal frame.

As the frame arrived in front of the gun, on the conveyor belt, huge amounts of the spray would miss, and had to be collected for disposal by means of what was, in essence, a huge vacuum cleaner. This consisted of an 8ft × 8ft cloth screen, behind which was some ducting and a gigantic fan with a three-phase motor – it sounded like Concorde when you started it up – which provided enormous suction power and drew the waste powder into the screen.

The problem was that production had to stop every hour so that the screen could be brushed down and the powder gathered up to be reused. In practice, the screen was behaving exactly like a vacuum cleaner bag. It became clogged after an hour's work and prevented the suction from getting to the powder storm, so that instead of being collected, it went all over the factory. The hourly delay was also extremely expensive, and it was clear to one and all that this was all terribly inefficient. So we went back to the people who had provided us with the spray equipment, who told us that the really big industrial users of their stuff used a cyclone.

'A cyclone?' I said. 'What the hell is a cyclone?'

It turned out to be a 30-foot high cone that spun the dust out of the air by centrifugal force – the kind of thing, if you ever looked, that you would see on top of a saw mill. I had, in fact, noticed them before, but had never had any idea what they were for. At any rate, this seemed like a decent idea, so I got a quote to have one built at the factory.

£75,000. I just laughed.

But there was a sawmill nearby, so I thought I would try and make one myself. It was what Jeremy Fry would have done.

The next night I drove up to the sawmill, parked a little way away and approached under the cover of dark. I climbed over the fence and surveyed at close hand the gigantic symbol of my future, the image that was to dominate my life for the next fifteen years. I made some sketches by moonlight and climbed all over it to determine exactly how it worked, what the proportions were, and what it was made of.

The only thing I couldn't see was the entrance of the chimney. It clearly went down into the cyclone, but how far, and at exactly what point, I could not tell (this was to become a point of major concern in the Dual Cyclone and the subject of many months' research). I made some sketches of the possibilities and scooted off to the car before the security guards discovered me.

Back at the factory the next day, Sunday (I do not believe in fiddling about in the face of imminent revolution), we welded up a 30-foot cyclone from sheets of steel, blew a hole in the roof, and stuck this Vulcan's ice-cream cone defiantly out into the sky. I gleefully tore the cloth veil from the opening of the duct and started the conveyor belt. The spray came at the barrow frame and whatever passed on went straight into the gaping hole, up the ducting and around the walls at the top of the cyclone, spiralling down through the inverted cone to be collected by a bag at the bottom, while the air escaped into the sky. Production just went on and on, no stoppages until the end of the day. To reuse the unused powder we just removed the sack at the bottom of the cyclone and stuck on another one. The machinery was transformed and the way was paved for the unparalleled success of the Ballbarrow. Not to mention the unparalleled skulduggery of my fellow partners, who were even then plotting to toss me out of the company like a clogged vacuum cleaner bag.

But things were very soon about to turn me away from the Ballbarrow anyway, and from that part of my struggling career, for ever.

As I was kneeling there on the factory floor that Sunday, welding up the sheet metal for the cyclone, and wondering what Michael Brown was doing now, and thinking of how his dad used to weld the tiny footplates to his scaled-down steam engines, I was also fantasising about the cyclone.

To begin with, I didn't understand it. I racked my brains trying to work out this peculiar phenomenon that allowed you to separate dust without a filter. As far as I could think, there was nothing else that could spin matter out of a fluid or gas in this way – except perhaps a spin drier or salad spinner, which seemed an altogether different principle.

I could imagine something like this happening in a rather crude way, but the fact that it operated to this degree of sophistication made it fascinating to me. A filter that collected dust without any barrier or membrane.

Barriers ... membranes ... I suddenly twigged. Vacuum cleaner bags! The dirty, stinking little pouches of domestic faeces that had been exasperating me at home for months.

By the time we had the cyclone erected in the factory, I was in a fever. As I ripped off the cloth filter it occurred to me how similar this was to throwing out a bag – and never replacing it!

It was not, perhaps, the 'Eureka!' that it should have been, considering how important its ultimate application was to be, because I already had the fundamental idea up and running. But it occurred to me at that moment that there was really no reason why it shouldn't work in miniature – using a cyclone about the size of, say, a Perrier bottle.

That same night, a cold, bleak one in October 1978, I leapt into my car and dashed home through the storm, thinking of nothing but bagless vacuum cleaners. In my kitchen I set about the old Hoover Junior with the zeal of a revolutionary. I tore off the bag and tried a little vacuuming, just to establish that the mechanics were all in order. Sure enough, the dust that the fan sucked up was blown out into the room in a horrible spray.

My next move was to lay my hands on a quantity of cardboard and model up a miniature version of the 30-foot thing I had been building at the factory: a foot-long cone shape, covered over at the large end and with a hole in the top to serve as a chimney for the escaping clean air – using kitchen scissors and then lots of gaffer tape which I wound round and round the structure to make it as airtight as possible. Then I attached a short length of hose pipe to the outlet hole of the machine – where the bag had once been – and connected that to the top of the cyclone, which I had fixed onto the shaft of the cleaner. I plugged the vacuum cleaner in and flicked the switch, expecting the worst. But there were no explosions, no blasts of dusty air into the kitchen, I just pushed it around the house, and it seemed to be perfectly happy. After a few minutes I disconnected my cardboard construction and peered in to find a deposit of dust in the bottom of the cone.

I vacuumed the whole house, from top to bottom, and then once more for luck, occasionally disconnecting the cyclone to empty it and check that it was not all a dream.

I was the only man in the world with a bagless vacuum cleaner.

Inside the cyclone

Where the dust goes. Faster than a speeding particle. Mathematics is bunk. Patience, patience, patience.

'Look, James, can you tell me, just one more time: where exactly does the dust go?'

If I had a vacuum cleaner bag for every time I have heard that sentence, I could probably manage for the rest of my life with a Hoover Junior, chucking the bag away every time I had finished a room. Not that I would want to, of course.

I shall try to explain, as best I can, the principle behind cyclonic filtration.

A vacuum cleaner develops its suction by means of a fan which, as it spins, discharges a powerful stream of air in the opposite direction from that in which you intend to clean, exhaling it through the back of the casing, or in the case of the Dual Cyclone and most other vacuum cleaners these days, through the front, above the suction head. This sets up an equally powerful inflowing current of air which picks up and carries with it any dust particles or small debris brushed up from the floor or carpet by the rotating brushes of an upright cleaner, or sucked up directly by the nozzle of a cylinder cleaner.

This fan is driven by a small, high-speed universal motor and has a

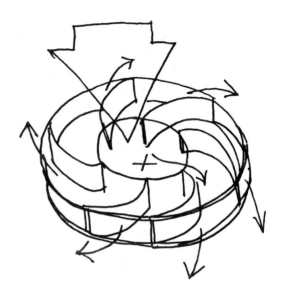

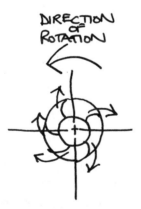

DIRECTION
OF
ROTATION

number of blades set an angle, whose rotation sets up this flow of air in the axial direction. Now this incoming air has to be filtered in some way so that the air leaves and the dust remains behind. Without filtration you would have either all the dust going back into the room, or all the air being trapped and the vacuum cleaner blowing up.

In the case of a bag vacuum cleaner, this filtering job is done by the bag, the air passing through the pores and out into the room, leaving the dust behind in the bag. People have long known that suction power diminishes because of the increasing air flow resistance as dust enters the bag. They assumed that the problem was to do with the bag filling up. It was not. For what they did not know was that the pores in the bag do not do their job properly; they clog almost immediately so that filtration is prevented and there is very little flow of air at all in the axial direction, no matter how fast the propeller blades spin.

What we were doing in the Ballbarrow factory, and what I was doing with my little prototype, was drawing the air up the pipe and blowing it into the top of a cylinder, which tapered down into a cone shape – one that, in the cardboard version, was perhaps a foot deep and six inches in diameter. The dusty air enters the cylinder at a tangent, coming straight into contact with the curve of the cylinder wall. This is where the first physical phenomenon occurs.

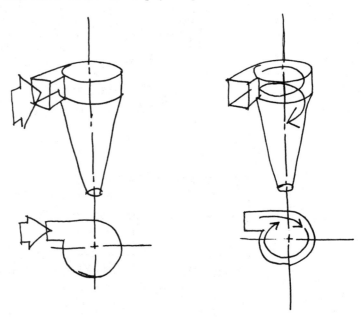

It is a law of physics – don't ask me why, I don't make these laws – that when a particle with mass makes its first turn around a curved wall its speed is multiplied three times. You can see it happening when the ball is spun onto a roulette wheel, or better still when you shoot a ball in a pinball machine and it accelerates round the corner.

Now, the reason that the cyclone is cone shaped is that when you reduce the diameter around which your object is travelling it will accelerate again, by about 50 per cent. In this way the cyclone in the vacuum cleaner, for example, accelerates the dust particles from 20 m.p.h. to 600 m.p.h. and then to 924 m.p.h., or about 324,000 r.p.m.

In saying that you have 324,000 r.p.m. at the bottom of the cyclone, it is worth remembering that washing machine manufacturers make great play of any machine that offers more than 1000 r.p.m. for the spinning of water out of a bundle of clothes. We are increasing that efficiency by 32,000 per cent.

Or I could put it another way, just to be silly. There is a ride at Alton Towers called The Cyclotron. It consists of a huge wheel that spins on a central pivot. Holidaymakers out for a cheap thrill stand in this thing with their backs pressed up against the wall. As it starts to spin it turns up to a vertical position and the people are pressed against the wall so hard by centrifugal force that they just stay there, pinned, even when they are upside down. The force is so strong that you can't move your face, your tongue, or anything at all. At its top speed it is probably spinning no faster than 20 m.p.h. In the cyclone we are talking 924 m.p.h. – faster than the speed of sound. So there.

Under this force the dust is spun out of the air and against the walls of the cyclone by centrifugal force. Particles of whatever size, even the particles that comprise cigarette smoke, have a mass that is vulnerable to gravity. By applying this 324,000 r.p.m. you are applying a g-force that increases that mass several thousand times. So a tiny particle that appears to be quite happy floating around in the air, and would continue to do so for ever without the slightest encouragement, suddenly assumes a huge weight and is forced by the imparted momentum of the cyclone into the bottom of the cone where it is collected (in the huge Ballbarrow factory example by a big bag, or in the vacuum cleaner by the plastic drum).

Now, there is clearly a huge amount of air entering with the dust, about thirty Perrier bottles (or 30,000 cubic centimetres) of air per second. In a bag cleaner it is supposed to escape through the bag; in the cyclone it does something very different.

You need to think of the whole caboodle, dust and air, as being like a long sausage. As it enters at the top of the cyclone it is being pushed round and round the walls until it comes to the bottom. The dust and rubbish, which has this great weight, is not enjoying the journey, just as when you drive your car hard at a bend it wants to keep on going straight and you have to exert pressure on the steering wheel to keep the car on the road. The air, which has no mass, doesn't have this problem, and rather than straining at the walls, which would ultimately blow the whole thing up, it can get to the centre of the cyclone, and take the easiest possible exit.

So, at the top of the cyclone, in the middle, is a chimney. The air happily escapes out of the hole; the particles cannot. Thus, the only thing that can get out is pure air, so no expelled dust, and no smells.

As I began to develop the cyclone, I thought it would be worth having a look at what had been written on the subject, for if there were simple mathematical models for the principle, it would be easy to work out how best to design the thing. This was not a fruitful exercise. I have one book which has at least six different formulae for explaining the movement of particles in a cyclone; they all seem to contradict each other; and they are all useless (three of these incomprehensible algebraic confections are shown below, just for fun).

(a) Shepherd and Lapple, Equation (7.21).

$$Z_E = 16ab/D^2_2 = 16 \times 0.2 \times 0.5/0.5^2$$
$$= 6.4$$

(b) Stairmand, Equation (7.23).

To find ϕ, we have $r_E/r_2 = 1.6$, $c_f = 0.01$, $C_f A_f/2A_E = 0.62$, and so from Table 7.2, $\phi = 0.9$. Hence

$$Z_E = 1 + 2\phi^2(2r_E/r_2 - 1) + 2(A_E/A_o)^2$$
$$= 1 + 3.56 + 0.52 = 5.1.$$

To find τ_L we use the relationship $\tau_L = Q/2\pi\mu^2_m(L - h)$, where μ_m is the tangential velocity at $r = r_2/2$ (p. 255). We have

$$\mu_E = \phi v_E = 13.5 \text{ m/s}; \ \mu_m = \mu_E(2r_E r_2)^{1/2}$$
$$= 13.5 \times 3.2^{1/2} = 24.1 \text{ m/s}.$$

Hence

$$\tau_L = 1.5/(2\pi \times 24.1^2 \times 3.5) = 1.17 \times 10^{-4} \text{ s},$$

corresponding to a diameter of 6 μm for unit density spheres in air at 20°C.

(c) Barth, pp. 261–3.

We have $r_E/r_1 = 0.8$ and so $a = 0.73$; also $C_f = 0.018$ and $K = 4.4$.

You could, theoretically, write a formula which would tell you whether or not a particular cyclone would separate a particular micron size, but that would depend on only one kind of particle, with a single micron size, entering it. In reality, what you get are thousands of different sizes of particle entering. The smaller ones get caught up in the slipstream of the larger ones – indeed, the slipstream of one group of particles will pull along with it whole colonies of much tinier ones – so that much smaller particles than you would expect a particular cyclone to collect will follow the larger ones into it. Like many industrialists, the particle has an insurmountable sheep mentality.

So if, say, one mathematical model told you that particles with a diameter of half a micron would escape your cyclone, but that particles with a diameter of one micron would not, that model would work as long as you loaded into it particles of either one micron or half a micron. And loaded them one by one.

From a practical point of view, this equation is what is known as 'a fat lot of use'. If the cyclone was going to work as an effective filter for a vacuum cleaner, it was going to have to be able to deal with millions of bits of detritus of millions of different sizes. Because it is such a simple principle, it is also a ludicrously complicated one: so many factors affect its efficiency.

When I came to develop the cyclone there would be hundreds of questions that needed answering:

Is a circular shaped entry the best way to get the air in?

What size should it be?

Should it poke in slightly, or not?

Should it come in at a pure tangent, or a half tangent?

Should it contract as it enters?

Should it be angled down to follow the natural spiral down the cyclone?

How many entries should there be?

And those are just questions about the entry point. In the absence of formulae, you have to take the Edisonian approach: test, and test, and test until it works best.

I made hundreds of cyclones in the early years, and then thousands of them. Testing all the different styles, I found that the important thing was the entry point, that it should enter peripherally, and at a pure tangent. I tried it with one entry and with two entries, I even made one with 140 entries, just in case it was better, but you only ever got one flow of air. (In the cylinder model, much later, we did actually use two entries, because it is such a squat little thing that you could not get the required cross-sectional area with only one).

Then there were questions about the positioning and size and shape of the exit point, and every other part of the thing, and all of them had to be answered by testing.

Slow, slow, slow. These things cannot be hurried. When you develop a prototype you have to change only one thing at a time. If you are really going to improve things, and that is what inventing is all about, then you are going to have to be patient. Very patient.

I was being so bloody patient that I still had only one cyclone in there. The best was yet to come.

8

In the land of the blind...

Thank you, no – we're quite happy in the gardening market. They don't even get excited about a stripper. So I set up in business with some help from Jeremy Fry and a vegetable garden.

After this amazing weekend I could hardly wait to get back to the office in Corsham, horrible though it was. It was an unusual feeling for me, for I had for some time been growing tired of life at Kirk-Dyson, for all the reasons I gave earlier, and was, though I didn't know it of course, approaching the termination of my relationship with the company. But on this particular morning, I was returning to work having just made the first steps in developing what I felt sure was to be one of the inventions of the decade, and which could solve all of Kirk-Dyson's problems at a blow.

As I drove in, I turned over in my mind, as you do, the conversation that would follow my revelation. The board would be bound to object that the vacuum cleaner was not a gardening product, and that we had better stick to the market we knew. Boards of directors are predictable like that.

We *had* come to realise, some months before, that we needed to diversify. The selling operation, management structure, factory and enormous bank overdraft that we needed to finance the company could no longer be supported by the sales volume and profit margin of the Ballbarrow. But we were still thinking purely of the gardening market.

By way of diversification, we had been developing a hydroponic drip-watering system that involved a network of thin plastic pipes running under the garden, delivering water directly to the roots of the plants, so that nothing was lost by evaporation and you watered only the plants you wanted to without encouraging weeds or slugs and snails. Sadly, for it was a fine product, we had made a major marketing error.

What we were attempting to offer was a panacea to all your gardening troubles. But, rather as had happened with the Sea Truck, consumers were simply not able to grasp so many improvements in one fell swoop. And the thing was too universal, too all-purpose. Had we begun it as, say, a greenhouse watering system, with a single timesaving benefit, thus appealing to a specific need, it would have bedded down nicely into the real market. We could then have gradually introduced the other ideas and made a real success of it.

But we didn't do that, and Roots – so named because the Alex Haley book of that name and the television drama series based on it were hugely popular at the time – never made us much money. Other hydroponic systems came along later, and the principle became ubiquitous. But ours was the very first – small consolation when you fail to capitalise.

But the principle of product diversification was the right one. When salesmen visit showrooms, shops, or in this case garden centres, the way to maximise the effectiveness of one's time and expense is to make multiple sales. If the salesman has to go all that way just to say, 'I see you are down from five Ballbarrows to three, you'll be needing another two,' then you are wasting time. If, however, he can say, 'You need two barrows, three Waterollas, and ten packets of Roots,' then you have quite a worthwhile order.

Worthwhile, but still by no means dazzling. I was getting heartily sick of the seasonality of the gardening market. People bought Ballbarrows from April to June, and we made occasional sales after that until mid-October, after which we sold none at all until the spring. And if there was a wet summer or a late start to the spring then sales were hit very badly; cash reserves went through periods of terrible drought, and there was very little predictability, so planning was difficult.

I felt that the gardening market was simply too small for the sorts of things I believed I was capable of producing. I thought we should be making a higher value product, retailing for £100, £200, even £300, that sold in enormous quantities throughout the year, not just in summer, and to every kind of household, not just the ones with gardens. Something like, oh, I don't know, like a vacuum cleaner, for example.

And so it was that when I sat down with the board I was ready to defend myself against their objections that the vacuum cleaner was not a gardening tool. But even as I was doing this, I was more than somewhat miffed that they showed so little excitement about my invention. As directors of a manufacturing company, they should have been hopping about in delirious glee at the discovery that one of their colleagues had invented something that could instantly dominate an enormous market, save the company, and make them extremely rich. Instead, they sat there with faces as long as hoover bags, grumbling about staying in the garden market and focusing all our efforts on Roots, until, in the height of my harangue – and the moment is as fresh in my mind as if it was happening even as I write – I was stopped by one of them with the words I was to hear over and over and over again for the next ten years.

'But James,' he said smugly, simperingly, like a father patronising an over-enthusiastic but educationally retarded child (I do not remember exactly which director it was), 'your idea can't be any good. If there were a better kind of vacuum cleaner, Hoover or Electrolux would have invented it.'

The British industrial mentality in a nutshell. British mentality full stop, come to think of it. You can't imagine a Russian saying to Lenin in 1917, 'Ooh, Vladimir, we can't have a revolution. If there were a better way the Romanovs would have thought of it.' Or an American saying, 'But Mr Ford, if cars were better than horses then the breeders would put wheels on them and feed them petrol.'

I explained that it was nonetheless a good product for us to look at. I had gone so far as to draw up a business plan, which is unusual for me; I had examined the market, and everything about it was good, in the way that the market for the Ballbarrow wasn't.

The refusals of the board then turned to outright hostility. 'Look, James, you are not to develop this any further, it's a stupid idea.'

Hardly surprising, really, that Kirk-Dyson and I parted company not long afterwards.

But it rankled terribly at the time. It is often very difficult to justify a new product in the very early stages of its development and this leads to a cripplingly vicious circle, for the cost of development is huge, and it is just at this very time that one most needs an injection of outside cash. When you come up with entirely original technology, particularly for something as entrenched in the public imagination as a vacuum cleaner, it is very difficult to argue lucidly for its ultimate success. You can say, 'I think it will be successful because bags are disgusting things and everyone hates them.' Then they say to you, 'What proof have you got that people don't like bags?' 'Well,' you reply, 'none. It is just my personal view.'

Your 'personal view' is more than enough to give your dream credibility in your own mind, but all anyone will say, when asked to put money up to pursue it, is, 'Well, bugger off, matey. I'm not backing your "own personal view" with my own personal cash.'

What you want to be able to do, because it is the only kind of talk businessmen can understand, is to walk in and say, 'Within three years 65 per cent of the population will not be buying bags, they will be buying something else, and if we have a cyclonic vacuum cleaner then we will get a 40 per cent share of that 65 per cent, thereby guaranteeing us a turnover of £30 million a year.'

I would have loved to do that, but all I had was a cardboard model of a filtering system I could see would not clog, but whose true efficiency I could not yet quantify. I didn't know then, for example, that by the time a bag vacuum cleaner has picked up 500 grammes of dust, it has lost two-thirds of its efficiency, as *Which?* magazine was later to discover. I had, in short, no idea of the degree of technical success I would achieve, that it would be three times as powerful as any other cleaner, and all those other things that might have impressed them. All I knew was that this was *a* way of making an uncloggable bagless vacuum cleaner.

Thus, when doubting Thomases cross-examine you, and fire at you all sorts of negative responses, you are pretty powerless. On the question of why Hoover haven't done it, for example, you can say little more than, 'Well, Hoover are a bit dim,' or, 'I'm cleverer than they are,' or, 'I've come across it and they haven't. So there.'

These, I need hardly tell you, are weedy arguments in the face of unwilling accountants, whose inevitable response will be based on the assumption that Hoover and Electrolux are more likely to invent a better vacuum cleaner than that Ballbarrow idiot, James Dyson.

In desperation, and still in the hope of convincing my own company of the virtues of the cyclone, I translated the idea into their own language.

The late seventies was a time when people were madly keen on stripping. Everything from pine tables to floors and walls were being sanded bare, and I had found myself using my Black & Decker with its sanding attachment an awful lot. The dust this thing threw up was incredible.

It seemed to me foolish that the back of the spinning rubber disk was not ribbed like a fan and housed in a casing with bristles at the bottom so that all the dust was sucked back into a bag. I developed one, with a cyclone, of course, rather than a bag, and returned to the board. This was, after all, a product they might be better able to understand. It was almost a garden implement, after all, if you had wooden outdoor furniture.

They were not interested. The board was implacable, and a parting of the ways was inevitable. My attempts to persuade them to capitalise their loans had made them uneasy; they did not like Beldam; and their jealousy was embittering them to my every move. In short, to bring us back to the end of chapter five, by January 1979 I was gone.

Back home in Bathford, I was despondent. Why could no one see the potential of my cyclonic dream? I was not, however, in any sort of mood to give up the ghost.

There was a big, late-Georgian coach house beside the house, a sort of stone garage that had been used as a garden shed, with a timber store upstairs. It was very draughty, had only stable doors, few windows, and no water, heating, phone, gas or electricity. I put a power point in first, and gave myself a single lightbulb to work by. I had nothing but a work-bench and a few simple tools, but I was determined that here I would make the damn thing myself.

Overdrawn, though, and with no imaginable inflow of cash in the near future, I knew that I had to raise funds, and fast. I had two options: to go to a merchant bank, or to try a few old friends.

As far as old friends were concerned, the obvious man was Jeremy Fry. He had offered to help me before, in the days of the Ballbarrow, and he was someone who knew that things don't always work out immediately, that innovation takes time and persistence. Furthermore, I was fed up with the type of non-executive directors I had been lumbered with at Kirk-Dyson, who knew little of manufacturing business, assuming that you had only to set up a company and rake in the profit.

Fry had waited nine months for me to sell the first Sea Truck, and two years for me to get the thing into profit. He was always likely to be my best hope. And so it proved. With £25,000 from Jeremy, and £25,000 from me, £18,000 of which I raised by selling the vegetable garden at Sycamore House, and the rest borrowed with my home as security, we set up the Air Power Vacuum Cleaner Company. And, at last, I was in the vacuum cleaner business.

9

Double vision

Cyclone after cyclone after cyclone ... The virtues of iterative development. Man cannot live by bread board alone. Two cyclones prove to be better than one. I prepare for battle with fire-belching giants.

So there I am out in the coach house on a blisteringly cold morning in the first days of the 1980s. Maggie is only just beginning to wreak her havoc; yuppies are as yet no more than a marketing department's dream; there are no Filofaxes, or New World Chardonnays; the utilities are publicly owned, and most people didn't even know what a share is. The dark days of boom and bust, and the death of British industry, lurk menacingly round the corner.

My fingers numb with the chill, I huddle like Bob Cratchit over a single candle and prepare to hammer out another prototype cyclone. There is some way to go yet, you will have noticed, if not by the weight of pages in your right hand, then by the fact that I have said somewhere before that before I went into production with the Dual Cyclone, I had built 5,127 prototypes. So far, you know about only one, the cardboard and gaffer tape thing that I tossed together on the kitchen floor.

Well, this little room in the coach house is where I built most of the other 5,126. With the relative solidity of the Air Power Vacuum Cleaner Company at my back – and with little interference from

Jeremy, whom I saw for perhaps half an hour a week – I got down to the business of development. This, the real hands-on stuff, was, after all, one of the things I had wanted to get back to.

Day in, day out, I made cyclones. I would have breakfast with Deirdre at half past seven, take Jacob and Emily to school, and then at 9.00 a.m. walk across the yard to the coach house. I would break for half an hour at lunchtime, walk across to the house to eat and see a bit of Sam, and then go back to work until half past six. If the phone rang, Deirdre would come out and yell, and I would jog in and talk for a while, and then trudge out again to my workshop.

With money by no means flowing easily in through me, Deirdre was holding art classes, teaching life and still-life drawing, as well as painting. She sold her own paintings through art galleries in Bath, Bristol, Henley and London, and had a regular job doing illustrations for the 'Shophound' articles in *Vogue*. To save money, we did everything around the house ourselves, from cleaning and curtain-making to plumbing and structural maintenance.

And all the while I was making cyclones. Acrylic cyclones, rolled-brass cyclones, machined aluminium cyclones (which looked like prosthetic limbs for the Tin Man in *The Wizard of Oz* – whose life was also changed by a cyclone). For three years I did this alone. I could not afford anyone to help me, and what would have been the point, when I could do it all myself?

When you start out, you just don't think it is going to take that long. Time passes by, and it is always *mañana*. Sam grew up and started walking, then talking, and all the while I made cyclones. Deirdre did everything else. Sometimes I would lose control completely when a model went wrong after weeks of planning, and Jacob told me only recently how well he remembers the sound of sheets of acrylic shattering out in the coach house, or down in the cellar, and me exploding in a typhoon of vociferous profanity.

Over the next three years we used up all the money that had been borrowed for the Air Power Vacuum Cleaner Company, and our mortgage grew steadily bigger and bigger.

I was looking at two issues, principally, during this thankless time:

the ability of the cyclone to separate the visible bits of rubbish like mud, hair, finger nails, fag butts, bottle tops, half-munched crisps, dry bogey, Rice Krispies, coins, rings, dog fluff, cat sick, fish food, feathers, pins, pine needles, biro tops, ash, couscous, earwax, biscuit crumbs, toe jam, navel fluff, flies, spiders, roaches and beetles, sugar, and spice and old pilau rice . . . and its ability to separate the very fine dusts you can't see.

For this second category I had to find a way of measuring how much dust was coming out of the machine, in relation to how much I was putting in. How much was being filtered out of the air by the cyclone, in other words, and how much was coming straight back out into the room again.

At first I tried to do this by applying a piece of black cloth to the exhaust of the cyclone, loading in white powder, and comparing the whiteness on the black cloth each time I made an adjustment to the cyclone. In the end I had 200 bits of cloth with white circles on them of varying degrees of greyness, which were impossible to preserve, and told me absolutely nothing at all. Fantastic.

Eventually, I discovered a thing called an absolute filter, which claims to capture 99.997 per cent of all particles fed through it – so that you weighed it, put it in the exhaust, sucked for a bit, and then weighed the increase in mass. The less the difference, the more effective the cyclone. Simple. Then, of course, there were airflow tests – for which I built an airflow measurement box – because I did not want to develop the perfect cyclone only to discover that it restricted my airflow, now did I? And so it went on; for every little property, a new test, a new day.

All this, of course, was being done in the hope of providing that conclusive proof, those all-important figures, that might impress some purblind money man to get behind the cyclone.

I was in something of a hurry. The fastest method of making the things turned out to be the rolled-brass method: I would cut out the shape of each cyclone in sheet brass, roll it on a set of rollers not unlike a mangle and then solder up the edges. I then applied the new cyclone to my bread board, a plywood screen with vacuum cleaner

motors attached to one side, and with a hole so that on the other side
a cyclone could be mounted, saving at least the effort of making an
entirely new machine each time. In this way I was able to make one
test each day. I could test one new entry point, or one new diameter,
or one new angle, and so on.

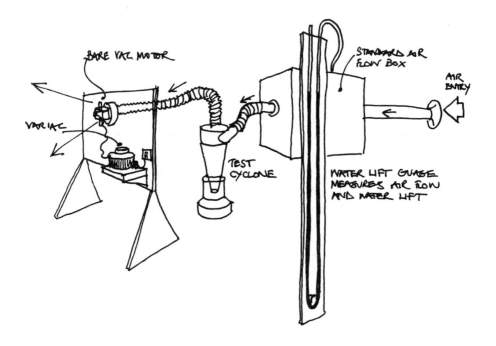

That is what development is all about. Empirical testing demands
that you only ever make one change at a time. It is the Edisonian
principle, and it is bloody slow. It is a thing that takes me ages to
explain to my graduate employees at Dyson Appliances, but it is so
important. They tend to leap in to tests, making dozens of radical
changes and then stepping back to test their new masterpiece. How
do they know which change has improved it, and which hasn't?

Let us say that we are looking at the brush bars. They are inefficient,
and we don't know why. 'What we need,' says some bright spark, 'is
softer, longer bristles.' So they order a brush bar with softer, longer

bristles. And the new brush bar is better. But they still don't know why.

What that bright spark should do is order three new brush bars, one long and stiff, one long and soft, and one short and soft. And test each one against the other, to see wherein the improvement lies.

This is why development is such a slow process. But the British obsession with the quantum leap holds us back. We always want to create something new out of nothing, and without research, and without long hard hours of effort. But there is no such thing as a quantum leap. There is only dogged persistence – and in the end you make it look like a quantum leap. Ask the Japanese.

While it is easy, of course, for me to celebrate my doggedness now and say that it is all you need to succeed, the truth is that it demoralised me terribly. I would crawl into the house every night covered in dust after a long day in the coach house, exhausted and depressed because that day's cyclone had not worked. There were times when I thought it would never work, that I would keep on making cyclone after cyclone, never going forwards, never going backwards, until I died.

But looking at it now, in view of the fact that I was making only one change at a time, and working alone, I think that a decent working prototype in four years was actually quite speedy work. It sounds a bit Hare and the Tortoise, but those old fairytales knew what was going on. It would have been a lot quicker, though, if I had not spent the first few years looking at the whole thing upside down.

I spent all that development time, you see, on what appeared to be the most difficult part of the cyclone's job: the filtering of the fine dust. I worked exclusively on that for month after month – in hindsight it looks ridiculous. And after two years, when I had that licked, I built a vacuum cleaner, a lovely red and blue thing that had the most perfect fine dust filter the world had ever seen. Not that it ever saw it. For although it looked great for a while, as I used it round the house, I noticed that the odd thing would suddenly escape, for no apparent reason: a dog hair, or a long bit of cotton.

With one of these cyclones set up on my bread board I fed into it a long thread, and noticed that it wrapped itself around the wall of the cyclone and then stuck out at the other end, escaping from, rather than being captured by, the cyclone. It was clear, then, that this type was not going to be able to cope with awkward-shaped objects. And it was not going to be a very impressive marketing campaign that advertised a brand new vacuum cleaner that 'cleans better than any vacuum cleaner you have ever seen, as long as you don't have any awkward-shaped bits of dirt in your home'.

There was a real problem here. Was it ever going to work?

Well, of course it was. I just hadn't quite been able to make out the forest for the trees, or rather the cyclone for the dust. Or perhaps I had been trying too hard to run before I could walk. Or perhaps there is no cliché that can quite express what I was doing.

The thing is that awkward things, like fluff and long fibres, like to decelerate quite quickly – not really an option in a cyclone spinning faster than the speed of sound. It needs to get down out of the air stream and not get caught up in the air exiting back up the middle, in which it can easily be caught up and brought out again.

The answer, of course, was that we needed a cyclone that did not taper quite so dramatically, so that it did not keep on speeding up all the way down. We needed one, in fact, whose walls were parallel. In such a cyclone the larger objects, which do not need so much g-force to increase their gravitational weight, would sink happily down.

Given that this would not do at all for the finer elements, we clearly would have to have two cyclones. It did not take long to work out that the smaller, more sharply tapering cyclone would fit happily inside the gentler one – if you look at your own Dyson Dual Cyclone (or at one of the pictures in this book if you have not yet woken up and smelt the coffee) the clear cylindrical bin is the larger cyclone, the yellow cylinder inside it houses the faster one.

The results at first were not bad, except that there was still some unwanted escape of these large fiddly bits of debris, because they were still getting sucked into the central cyclone, rather than decelerating

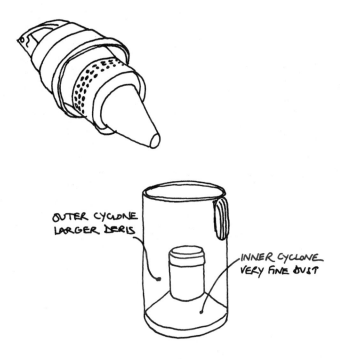

OUTER CYCLONE
LARGER DEBRIS

INNER CYCLONE
VERY FINE DUST

happily against the outer walls and settling safely at the bottom, out
of harm's way.

The solution was what became known as the shroud: a plastic mesh
that wraps around the top of the inner cyclone so that, quite simply,
the larger objects cannot get into it, but carry on their business around
the walls of the outer one, while the finer particles are drawn in
through the holes and filtered out in the unforgiving whirls of the
924 m.p.h. cyclone. When you pull the bin (which comprises the two
cyclones) out of its housing on the front of the vacuum cleaner, and
tip it out, a grey dust of talcum powder-like fineness comes out of the
middle one, whereas your chunkier commodities fall out of the outer
one.

With this set-up completed late in 1982, I had, at last, 100 per cent
efficiency – in my vacuum cleaner, that is, not in my body. After three
years of constant work in the coach house, making at least one model

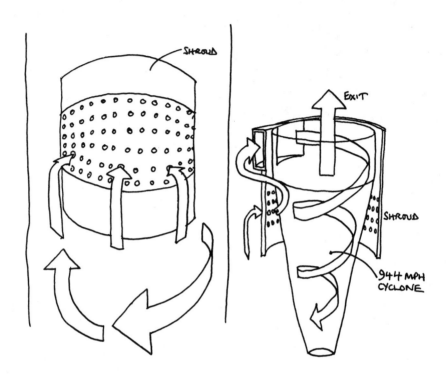

a day for well over a thousand days, I was becoming very tired indeed, and Deirdre was trying harder than ever to make me work less maniacally.

When we set up the company in 1979 it had been with the intention of manufacturing the product ourselves, but by 1982, what with my exhaustion and overdraft, and with the company not having made any money, it seemed unlikely that that was ever going to happen. The money problems were getting more and more serious every day, and I had to make this project work, or we would go under. I was pretty driven, and a combination of fear and hope had kept me at my task. But now I was too keen on getting out of debt – my personal overdraft was £8,000, my business overdraft was £36,000, and my mortgage was a further £35,000 – to start borrowing millions of pounds to go into production.

What is more, I had spent most of my working life involved in manufacturing, and I wanted to eke out a few more years at the drawing board, doing what I really enjoyed, rather than getting involved in management and problems on the production lines, and the welfare of a large staff.

After lengthy discussions, Jeremy Fry and I decided that rather than attempting to produce the thing ourselves, we should try to sell a licence for its production. We felt that we both had pretty good track records in innovation and manufacturing – his considerably longer-established, of course, than mine – and as a result would have some credibility when it came to presenting industrial ideas. Others, in short, should take our proposals seriously enough that we should not have to make the things ourselves any more – if your principal skill, and first love, is design, invention and creation, as it was for both of us, then that is what you want to spend your time doing, rather than manufacturing, marketing and selling.

With the name of our company changed to Prototypes Ltd, to indicate that we developed products rather than manufactured them, I picked up my single-cyclone red-and-blue prototype, which demonstrated the look of the thing and the ancillary features, and a tank vacuum cleaner equipped with a dual cyclone to demonstrate the true efficiency of the technology, and set off, like a travelling vacuum cleaner salesman of old, to tackle the fire-belching giants of British industry.

'Have you got a licence for that?'

Getting the show on the road. Hoover attempt to extract the Mickey, but I burst their bag. Two minutes with Hamilton Beach – but no sucking. A bit of German resistance. Tomorrow and tomorrow and tomorrow. I make a break for the home of the brave. In the land of the free they all want something for nothing. I lock horns with the Grizzly Adams of the electrical wilderness. A product that nobody has, everyone needs, and only I make.

In setting out to find a licensee for the vacuum cleaner, what I was doing, in effect, was offering manufacturing companies the exclusive rights to my patents and my intellectual property, for a period of time, in a particular place, in return for a percentage of their profits from its sale.

Everything in a licence is negotiable, and no two licences are the same, which makes them a very big deal to negotiate and a huge hassle generally. The bigger a company is, the less they want to sign one. Some even expect you, quite bizarrely, just to give them your invention. Just hand it over and bog off.

I was not about to do this, nor was I going to sell out completely, for any amount of cash. You *can* sell your invention off in one go and accept what is known as a 'paid up' royalty. You take a lump sum and that is the last money you ever make; you literally sell it off lock, stock, and cyclone to the manufacturing company. That kind of deal is final and irreversible. All licence agreements, on the other hand, are reversible, and if the licensing company does not satisfy you that it is using its best endeavours to produce and sell the thing, or it is ripping you off in some way, it is possible, though fraught, to terminate it.

I was looking, initially, for a five- to ten-year deal, in Britain or Europe, with a royalty of no less than 5 per cent of the wholesale price, with about £40,000 up front. What I had to offer in return was a hypothetical product combining the dual cyclone technology I was able to demonstrate in a tank cleaner prototype with the look, feel, and other innovations of the upright red-and-blue prototype (to make a fully operational dual cyclone upright would have taken me another five months, time I just didn't have).

Unusually, because I was a designer, I was also offering as part of the licence my own services in the design of the final product. Rather than just selling a piece of raw technology, I was licensing a marketing proposition, one which said, 'Bags are a problem, people don't like them, here is the technology and complete design to offer people a vacuum cleaner without a bag and conquer the market.'

Nor was the red-and-blue machine unimpressive. It was not quite as imposing as the models we now have on the market – and I have occasionally wondered what the response might have been if I had gone on the road with something like the DC-01 – but I don't think it would have made any difference. Manufacturers, investors, retailers are either excited by new technology or not, and anyway that is carts before horses stuff: it is not finished products that need investing in.

But there was plenty in the prototype to get excited about. There were two cyclones, but they were perched next to each other, and both were the same. I can't quite remember why, but they were both fine dust filters. There was a telescopic hose attached, and an instant changeover valve, which allowed you to switch immediately from floor-level to overhead cleaning.

I had put a lot of effort into the styling of the thing even then, because I knew that if I was going to sell a licence I had to show, at least in principle, that it could look good. With its two parallel cyclones, it looked a bit like a rocket-pack powered by twin-jet engines. It already had a two-wheel base, which made it more manoeuvrable than the four-wheeled models that dominated the market, and it conformed pretty well to the design principles that I had brought to the Ballbarrow – it looked purposeful, technologically original, and visually unusual.

And with it I hit the road. Quite literally. A few phone calls to manufacturing companies to set up appointments and then I loaded my prototypes in the back of the car and set off to impress people. I had been a salesman before and hardly expected everyone to be immediately taken with the machine and start covering me with gold, but there had to be someone out there who would want all this. Didn't there?

My first thought, obviously enough, was to approach Hoover. But it never got much further than a first thought. When I phoned them to set up the appointment they told me that I would have to sign an agreement first. This seemed reasonable enough, since we would both want to protect our interests. Many companies are so afraid of being accused of stealing inventors' ideas that they won't even look at them. And others use middlemen to try to distance themselves. When I tried to license Black & Decker, for example, they refused to let me into their main building, instead putting me in a portakabin and sending down an independent patent agent to look at the vacuum cleaner. Highly strange, because she could have stolen it for them as easily as anyone else.

Hoover did not bother with such niceties. A clause in the agreement they wanted me to sign meant that anything that came out of discussions between me and Hoover would belong to Hoover. Considering that we were going to be discussing my new technology, not theirs, this was an exceedingly rotten deal. It was like a burglar writing to you to inform you that he would be burgling your home and assuming that, by warning you, he rendered the theft morally acceptable.

I asked them to remove the offending clause. They would not. That was the last Hoover saw of me, until they sent their VP Europe, Mike Rutter onto the *Money Programme* in 1995 (by which time I had overtaken them) to say that Hoover regretted not buying my invention, because they would have seen to it that it never saw the light of day. What touching respect for the consumer's right to choice.

Everyone else, though, was prepared to sign a confidentiality agreement. And so it was, that over the next two years, until 1983, I approached every manufacturer you could think of.

I think it was Hotpoint, in Peterborough, that I tried first after Hoover. I had a meeting with their marketing manager, explained the benefits of my technology, showed him my machine, and a little brochure I had had made, and then listened to him say, 'This project is dead from the neck up.'

I went on to try Electrolux, Goblin, AEG, Electrostar, Alfatech, Shopvac, Black & Decker, Zanussi, Vorwerk, Vax, Hamilton Beach, and each time the scenario was different in structure but similar in theme. By and large they would give me half an hour and then lunch in which to put my case, but I never knew, each time I arrived at some new company, whether I would be talking to one person or twenty. I would turn up with a model and a brochure and some test results, never forewarned as to whether it would be an informal chat or a formal presentation.

Hamilton Beach, for example, said, 'You've got two minutes to convince us.' What a nightmare. What a pointless exercise. And what a fundamentally flawed piece of thinking. Why was it I who had to convince them? Their immediate approach was, 'This product is rubbish, try to deceive us.' That is the only way I can understand what they were trying to say. For if the product were good, why should they need convincing? I knew they were loonies anyway, because they wouldn't let me use the word 'suck', presumably because it hinted at fellatio, which would have been unseemly, or because if something 'sucks', in American slang, then it is bad. These people were nuts. Utterly hat-stand.

But there was enough interest for most of the major people to see me. Dozens of people would always be called in to have a look. I would sit there with the managing director, and people from the sales department, and the marketing department, and the technical department, and talk about the advantages to the consumer, in terms of not having to use a bag, and pointing out also all the other innovations that I had developed.

The extraordinary thing was that, even when they were satisfied that the technology worked, none of them seemed to be listening to me – I had given plenty of presentations in my time and knew perfectly well when people were listening to me and when they weren't. The reason for their deafness was that they were interested in only one thing: defending their own product, if not directly to me, then amongst each other as I sat there.

Electrolux, for example, told me quite simply that I would never sell a vacuum cleaner without a bag. They added, as an incidental point, that they made a lot of money selling bags. The only positive thing they said was, 'we like the hose, though.' (I didn't realise *quite* how much they liked it until some years later, when, in 1986, one such hose appeared on an Electrolux machine.)

I gradually deduced that I was being turned down not because these people thought the machine didn't work, but because they just didn't want it. In England, I think, companies rejected it just because they were English. In Germany they rejected it because *I* was English – what I called the 'vossn't inwented here' syndrome.

So desperate were they to rubbish it at AEG in Frankfurt that the engineering director tipped a great bin liner full of rubbish onto the floor and then rammed my prototype into it so that it was completely engulfed by this heap. Not a job that upright vacuum cleaners were ever supposed to do.

'See,' he cried. 'It doesn't vurk!'

And then he pulled out the latest AEG cylinder cleaner and started sucking the big lumps of dirt up through the hose. Pure defensiveness, ignoring that my machine was (a) an upright, and (b) a prototype. He just didn't want to know.

The other side of the German mentality was displayed by Herr Schottal of Electrostar. He had the cyclone put through loads of tests, liked it and then rejected it, in my opinion, because he couldn't bear to pay royalties. A few years later they came out with the 'Zyclon'! Other companies just retreated into their shells and defended.

It really was extraordinary, and quite unexpected. Every single one of them seemed to miss the point: that here was an innovation of real benefit to the consumer, a massive leap from a crappy old carpet sucker to a cleaner of total efficiency and undiminishable power. For each manufacturer in turn, it represented an opportunity to bring out a new product with a major technical advantage over their competitors. The most ironic in this respect was Goblin, who had trouble finding time to see me because they had all their staff on a two-day week because sales were so low. As if it were better to save time by not seeing me, rather than buying something better than anything their competitors had, starting to sell again, and going back to work full time.

All anyone could ever think of to say was, 'Ours works perfectly well already,' 'People are used to bags,' and, 'We like selling bags.' And if they weren't repeating these trite little objections, they were sighing, or looking the other way, or smiling conspiratorially to each other, even laughing. Enough of that could drive you mad.

Electrolux went so far as to rebuff me twice. Some years after my first rebuttal, when a couple of my cyclone vacuum cleaners had got into production elsewhere under licence, I went to Sweden to meet the man who ran Electrolux's worldwide domestic appliances division. I provided a model for his engineers to put through its paces, and after two days of testing I was present when he asked them, 'Does it work better than a bag?'

I heard them say, 'Yes,' and him reply, 'Does it filter better?' and them say, 'Yes.' And then he turned to me and said, 'In that case we should go for it, because we can charge more for it than other vacuum cleaners, and make much more money.' And I thought, 'Hallelujah!' for this was the first person to understand that what we had was a product that no one else had, that worked better than any other product on the market, and could make more money than anything before or since.

Two weeks later I rang the chap to ask how it was coming along, only to hear that he had proposed the thing to their centre of vacuum cleaner production in England, who were just at that time bringing out a new model of their own, and were therefore not interested.

In those two years that I plodded around Europe I survived on a sort of *mañana* attitude: tomorrow would always be better. You have to think like that, otherwise you just can't go on. After each knock-back I would find a reason to be optimistic about the next meeting. 'They'll want it because they are into new technology,' I would think. Or, 'They will want it because they are German.' And as you suffer each rejection you learn a little bit about your product, and what people want from it, and why – and you can sometimes justify your profitless ploddings that way, too.

But there is, unfortunately, a 'Can't Do' mentality in Britain that afflicts every sphere of life. I soon realised that attempts to license in Britain were a waste of my time and money, because a combination of apathy and chronic defensiveness about their own products, and poxy little market share, had killed any interest there might have been in developing anything new. All I was doing – and it is inevitable if you are trying to sell a licence for something – was offering everyone advance warning of a potential competitor.

You can see this 'Can't Do' mentality in Britain wherever you cast your eyes. Think of the average British builder. The minute you ask him to do something, anything at all, his first reaction is to say, 'No.' If you ask him to move a pile of bricks from one place to another, he will roll his eyes, take a deep, exaggerated breath, point out all the difficulties, and say, 'It could take a very long time,' or, 'It'll cost you, mate,' usually both.

British Industry is very similar, and so is the DTI when it comes to handing out grants. They go through all the reasons why they shouldn't do something, why it's wrong, why it's a risk. It is a very easy attitude to adopt. It is the path of least resistance, after all, for there are always a 101 reasons why a project could fail, compared to far fewer, but much more compelling, reasons why it might succeed. And it is the very reason why, in Britain, nothing ever gets done.

And that included my used-to-be potential backers, who are now my competitors. Very few of them ever actually said, 'No,' they just never said, 'Yes.' They liked to think of licensing as the easy option,

My father and mother's
war-time marriage, 1940

With my mother, 1 day old, 1947

Playing with fire at my first birthday, 1948

Punting along the
Backs at Cambridge.
My mother and Tom
are passengers, 1962

Racing up dunes
with Samie and Tom
at Blakeney Point,
1951

Winning the cross-
country at Gresham's
school, 1965

Reaching high at rugby at Gresham's school, 1965

Playing Trinculo in *The Tempest* at the open air theatre,
Gresham's school - the bottle was wooden, 1965

With Jeremy Fry in Provence, building a pedalo from a scrap bike, 1968

Speed trials on the Nile with the Egyptian Special Boat Squadron one week before they stormed Sinai. I took the photo, 1973

Deirdre and I with our children, Emily and Jacob, at Holkham (near Blakeney) in clothes, 1977

Deirdre, 1980

Deirdre modelling for a new Ballbarrow brochure at Dodington House, 1976

Jacob and Sam outside the workshop Bathford with the Builders Ballbarrow, 1986

Family outside Sycamore House for *Car Styling* magazine, Japan, 1987

(above) Sawmill-cyclone above Hill Leigh Timber, Bath. Inspiration for solution for bag clogging problem

HILL LEIGH TIMBER IM

With Japanese G-Force (£1200 cost) for *Car Styling* magazine, 1987

4.00am Tokyo negotiating licence deal with Kanaya, Kajiwara and Tomochita, 1985

Iona SF7 - dry powder shampoo/vacuum cleaner designed for
Iona Appliances, 1988

Our first factory line for DC01 -
Chippenham, July 1993

Fantom Technologies - upright vacuum
cleaner (annual sales $200 million), 1988

Jacob, 24, product designer, demonstrating the DC02 de Stijl at the Design Museum, October 1996

Sam, 18, demonstrating the DC01 at the Design Museum opening of 'doing a Dyson', October 1996

Me demonstrating the DC02 to journalists at the Imagination Gallery launch, January 1995

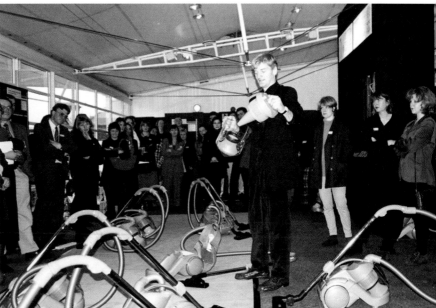

Magazine advertisement for *Interiors*, *Marie Claire* and *Evening Standard*, created by Tony Muranka and photographed by Alan Randall, 1995

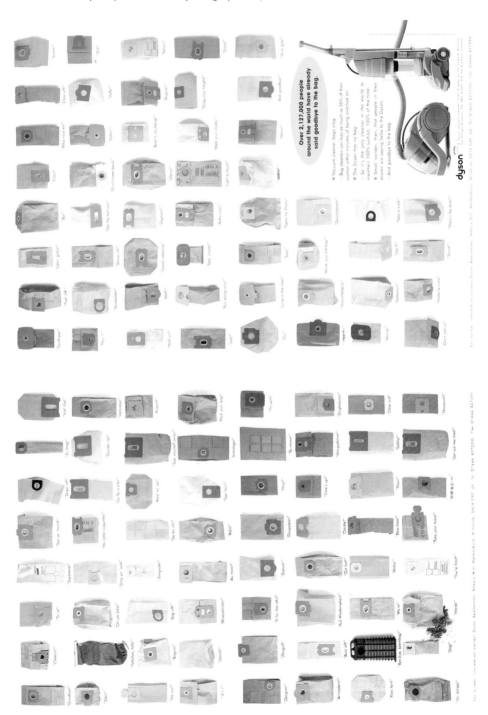

The evidence against vacuum cleaners with bags keeps piling up.

viruses
pollen
dust mite faeces
pet hairs

Because bags clog, bag cleaners lose suction...   **...leaving this behind in your home.**

The Dyson has no bag, so it's the only cleaner to maintain 100% suction, 100% of the time.

Bag vacuum cleaners perform inefficiently because they quickly lose suction as the pores inside the bag clog with dust. This reduction can happen so rapidly that, after just a few minutes, suction can drop to 50% – and keep going down. ● This means that most people, in the course of normal vacuuming, are using cleaners which operate at a fraction of their suction power. ● Dyson vacuum cleaners have eradicated the bag and its problems by using centrifugal force to remove dust, dirt, allergens and minute particles (as small as 0.1 micron). ● Tests were carried out under normal conditions in average family homes. ● Dyson vacuum cleaners are available from all major electrical retailers. ● For further information, call Dyson Sales on 01666 827200 and quote reference number 970416.

dyson *dual cyclone TECHNOLOGY*

Dust pile advertisement for national press by Tony Muranka and Alan Randall, 1996/7

Deirdre and I at Jeffrey Pike's daughter's party at the Hurlingham Club, 1992

My daughter, Emily, 25, fashion designer, at the Design Museum

Invitation to my solo exhibition – 'doing a Dyson' at the Design Museum, 1996/7

Silent salesman put on the top of every Dyson product

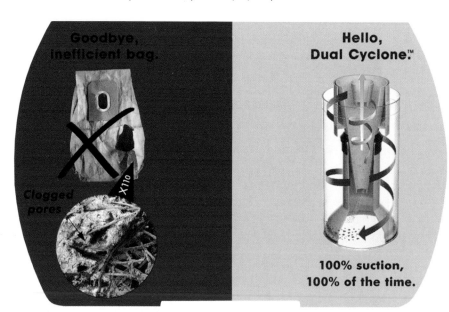

that they could string you along for years, until you realise that nothing is happening, by which time you are either bankrupt or dead.

After a couple of years of this, with bankruptcy or death indeed looking the most likely outcome of my efforts, I turned my gaze westwards once again. The Americans may have shafted us over the Ballbarrow, but you could not say that they were unambitious. I looked to America for the very opposite mindset from the one I had found at home. And sure enough, I found it.

To be fair, for a moment, to British industry, it is not only greater ambition and vision that allows an American manufacturer to make advances where a British one cannot. The US market is a more competitive and aggressive one than our own because there is so much more at stake. With a five-times bigger market, and greater spending power per head, the potential winnings are so much greater.

Thus, for a piece of brand new technology like the Dual Cyclone, it is bound, or ought, to be a more fruitful hunting ground. My vacuum cleaner looked to everyone but me like a niche market product, if it was anything at all. And in a country like Britain of only 60 million people, niches are just too small to be worth risking the expenditure for tooling and setting up a company. In America, with a population five times bigger, each niche is five times bigger, and since each person has about twice the spending power of someone in Britain, that niche is in real terms ten times bigger than it would be here, and the risk is thus reduced tenfold.

The question should not have arisen, however, for my vacuum cleaner was not a niche product at all, it was quite gobsmackingly mainstream; but it was only in America that they could risk finding that out, for if it did not ultimately appeal to the mainstream consumer, it could still survive.

This situation, as well as a natural inclination towards optimism and opportunism, not to say greed, has allowed Americans to take a very positive attitude towards new technology. Let's face it, the car, the telephone, and the television were invented in Europe, but it was in America that their commercial potential was exploited.

So I had a first-hand taste of the 'Can Do' mentality. I would sit down at meetings with directors shouting, 'Hi, James, meet the guys. We're gonna do great business James. We're gonna talk turkey. We're gonna hit the streets with our feet running. We're gonna kick us some serious butt. We're gonna conquer the world.'

The plan to tackle America had come about as the result of some interest generated over there by a small picture in a TWA in-flight magazine of a vacuum cleaner I had made for Jeremy Fry's company, Rotork.

I know I gave the impression that my attempts to license in Europe had proved a complete failure, and that was largely true, for the little licensing deal I made with Rotork never made me any money, and only resulted in a few hundred vacuum cleaners being sold, but it was instrumental in starting me off on my American efforts – and while those efforts ultimately proved fruitless I should mention how the first commercial cyclone came to be made.

It was towards the end of 1982, when I had been flogging round Europe for nearly two years to no avail, that Rotork's chief executive, Tom Essie, said to Jeremy one day, 'Whatever became of James Dyson?' When Jeremy told him my tale of woe, Essie asked him whether Rotork shouldn't perhaps take a look at it. Together we drew up a business plan for the production of an upright dual cyclone vacuum cleaner, and the Rotork board of directors, swayed presumably by Jeremy's dual involvement, approved it. We thrashed out an agreement that paid me £20,000 and gave me a 5 per cent royalty, and I went off to develop the vacuum cleaner.

Within a couple of months I had made a wooden model of how it would look, and produced a bread board that showed how it would work. By August 1983 I had a fully fledged version, incorporating the dual cyclone as planned, and with a see-through bin because, while developing the technology on a tank cleaner, I had used a clear bin so that I could see what was happening in the outer cyclone, and reckoned that the customer would want to be able to do this too. Apart from anything else, it was fun. The telescopic hose was there too, but I had it all coiled up on the outside, Richard Rogers style, which looked rather dramatic and, coupled with the pink colouring, made the thing look almost alive.

Almost immediately something happened that is always disastrous: Tom Essie moved on to another project, a financial director was put in charge of the vacuum cleaner, and I knew that everything was doomed. To start with, it is always terrible when the man who has brought a project into a company moves on: it is only the originator of the project who will identify with it closely enough to see it through. Bring in another man, and all he is doing is midwifing another man's baby. He will not want this, if he has a grain of ambition in him. He will want to impress everyone with his own ideas and projects. And so 'Pouf!', up goes the old project in smoke.

Furthermore, the man they brought in was a money man. Innovation requires builders not bean-counters, and the last person who should be running something is the man who controls its costs. Sure, you need that man in there somewhere to keep a rein on things, but he shouldn't be at the top.

I completed the designs all the same, and hung around to help this manager when they asked me to. But I could only watch in horror as the wrong toolmakers were commissioned and the whole project was put in jeopardy.

As the months went by, I could see quite clearly that this chap was never going to get the job done, and so I got in touch with Zanussi, whom I had recently discovered made a lot of plastic components for other people as well as themselves. By putting Rotork in touch with the Italians I was able to orchestrate a situation where Zanussi made the thing, and Klene-eze sold it, while Rotork acted only as bankers.

And they did manage to get about 500 units onto the market, which was very handy for me. Few though the Cyclon (as it was named) sold, it provided me with invaluable feedback on consumer reactions, various functional issues and, of course, durability. It was real live market research, with the advantage that, because it was being sold direct rather than through shops, and to only a small number of people, not too many people would be annoyed if there were problems.

But there weren't, really. And many of the 500 or so that we sold are still in use today. We hear quite often from their owners, who often ring up hoping to exchange them for Dysons, or because something has gone wrong, in which case we are always happy to help out.

This deal didn't last long, though. Rotork began to lose their bottle when they saw that a few modifications would have to be made, and as it was not a core business they were only too happy to roll over and have their tummies tickled when another company arrived to gobble up their UK licence, and then squash it for ever (more of which anon).

For all its failure to make a mark in Britain, it was a picture of this Cyclon that appeared in the TWA in-flight magazine, and was spotted by a number of manufacturing executives in America. I made myself some appointments by phone, calling all the people who had written to me, and then flew over there, early in 1984, to try my luck. I would arrive at airports, and have to hoik all my luggage, and my Cyclon and my tank cleaner across to the car-hire desk, and then hoik it all out to the car, and then drive for hours and hours to some meeting, until I was as worn down as much by the physical effort as the mental strain that came with sleeping in a different hotel room every night, missing my family, and the general misery of the whole thing.

But the 'Can Do' approach of the Americans was at least a great relief after the grim negativism of Britain. At companies like Grand Met, Black & Decker, Kirby, Conair, Shopvac and Filter Queen, they made a huge fuss of me. They would bring all the corporate vice-presidents, or VPs – their equivalent of directors – together and start flapping their arms about and yelling, 'We've flown people in from all corners of the globe, we're gonna get corporate backing, we're gonna bake dollar pies!' Of course, the bullshit factor is huge. It is the downside of the 'Can Do' approach. My hit rate was really very low.

I would get home to Bath and then receive phone calls saying, 'Yeah, James, we're right behind you, one hundred per cent, we're coming to a decision, we're talking finance, we're talking legals, we're talking due diligence.' (Due diligence, by the way, is an American corporate expression for doing financial investigations and models, auditing, market research, feasibility studies, patent searches, all the background palaver to see if a project is worth getting into. When I first heard the expression I thought, because of the American accent, that it was 'do diligence' – and wondered what on earth it was, assuming that it just meant they were doing things diligently.)

They would give me all this crap, and then it would all fizzle out.

There were a number of disappointments of this kind, and it began to get quite depressing, just travelling around the continent from state to state, thinking I had made a deal, and then having it pulled out from under me every time. What kept me going, though, was the quasi-religious following that my vacuum cleaner attracted. When a particular VP managed to persuade his company to take up the cyclone project, only to see it fall apart further down the line, he would, more often than not, quit the company in disgust. It is not an exaggeration to say that my meanderings around America in the early 1980s left a trail of wrecked careers across the continent. Well, maybe it is an exaggeration. At any rate, the fact that so many others seemed to share my obsession gave me great heart, and convinced me that perseverance would eventually be rewarded.

The trouble is, though, that perseverance is by no means cheap. Once, for example, I was getting close to a deal with a division of Grand Metropolitan called DP Products when, after weeks of negotiations and sitting about in Mississippi, they changed their minds one morning and walked away, leaving me with a chunk of my life wasted and a legal bill of £35,000. And legal fees incurred on a failed deal cannot even be set off against tax. (This situation came about, historically, because dodgy property developers would go around offsetting all kinds of legal fees against their ill-gotten gains – until the Inland Revenue closed the loophole, suspicious that people were deliberately engineering failed deals to have something to offset. This has been particularly unfortunate for me, as my past is littered with failed deals.) The lesson I learnt was to teach myself the basics of contract law, and hammer out the basics of each deal on my own, only calling out my lawyer, at a cost of £3,000 a day or whatever it was, when the deal looked absolutely certain.

And deals just kept falling apart. For one reason or another. The general will to produce the machine was far greater than in Britain, but there were so many other things to go wrong.

Black & Decker, for example, had a long history of making honourable deals with inventors, and of making a success of new inventions, from the Workmate to the cordless power drill and the hot-air wallpaper stripper. Nothing would have been nicer than to have signed a licence agreement with them. The first time I tried them was when they sent out their patent agent to look at my vacuum cleaner in a portakabin, rather than send out an engineer whom I might subsequently accuse of stealing it. At least an engineer might have *understood* it.

The second meeting with Black & Decker, some time later, drew out my agony much longer, and really showed up the rot at the core of the American way.

We got on terribly well this time, and everyone was terribly keen on the product. Negotiations went humming along until I left thinking, 'Wow, this is it!' and returned to England. A few days later the Black & Decker VP responsible for worldwide product development, together with the VP legal, came down to Sycamore House, and we carried on negotiations in the dining room, hammering out the details until such time as I reckoned it was worth pulling in the lawyer. We had agreed everything in principle and all that was left was to determine the amount of front money I would be paid, and to negotiate minimum royalties.

Now, front money is very important indeed. It is a non-refundable down payment which, for someone like me, is crucial to pay legal costs, and to prove to me that the licensing-company is serious about going into production. When you negotiate a licensing deal you are handing over your own technology for them to exploit, and the first year or so of the agreement, at least, is spent designing the product they want. Then it can take up to a year to get all the tooling made and put in place to produce the thing. In short, from the moment of signing on the dotted line you are probably at least two years away from launching the product and further still from your first royalty cheque.

The front money is perhaps the most important part of the initial deal, because until the thing is made I will otherwise get nothing at all. This sum, unlike an author's advance from a publisher for example, is not reimbursable out of royalties – though many have tried to negotiate that with me, and I have always refused – it is a one-off lump sum I expect to be paid to sign my name. It might have been anything, back then, from £30,000 to £200,000, but the bigger the better, not only because it makes you richer, but because it shows greater commitment from the company. Without being bled of a little cash, you see, a big company like Black & Decker might sit on the project for God knows how long, deciding whether or not to make it (as Vax were to do to me some years later). In the meantime you are powerless.

The inclusion in a contract of minimum royalties, and of a trigger date for their payment, is also crucial. This way payments are activated on a certain date when both parties expect the product to be in production, and help persuade a licensing company that might other-wise never go into production at all, and never pay you any royalties, to keep to its part of the agreement.

What most, indeed all, manufacturers want, however, is to pay you no money at all at the beginning, have you working for them all the way through the deal for nothing, and then only start to pay you your measly percentage when they start selling the product, and making money themselves – at which point they will think of all sorts of different ways to renegotiate the royalty rate, and pay you practically nothing at all. That, at least, is the pattern of every licence agreement I have ever signed, and so, as I mentioned my insistence on a front-money payment to Black & Decker in the dining room at Sycamore House, I was not surprised to hear their VP Legal, one Paul

J. Lerner, a smug, pipe-smoking man with a bow-tie, say, 'Oh no, James. Nothing till we start selling.'

Pathetic, isn't it? For a gigantic corporation to quibble with a small inventor over a few dollars, expecting him, rather than themselves, to take financial responsibility should the project fail. In my dire financial straits I was more interested in this lump sum than anything else – I needed the front money to keep myself and my family going.

The product manager, meanwhile, who was desperately keen to make a deal, was tearing his hair out, as his legal man refused to offer either of the basic assurances necessary to a licence agreement.

'If you won't pay,' I asked, 'then how do I know that you are serious?'

'Oh, we're serious,' he said. 'We're Black & Decker.'

'Fine. I'm James Dyson. But I could be ten months into this thing, having given you all my technology and cut out all my other potential licensees, and you could just walk away leaving me with nothing. It's blatantly unfair.'

'You've just got to trust us.' He said.

'Sorry. That won't do. You have to give me £100,000, then I'll trust you, and you can trust me.'

But Lerner stood firm. The product manager was in tears. And they flew home to America.

The deal was lost. Still no one wanted to produce my vacuum cleaner. I would have to continue living in debt. But at least, by keeping my lawyer out of it till the last minute, I had saved on legal fees. And, best of all, I would never have to see Paul J. Lerner again.

Or so I thought.

Six months after that I was back in the US negotiating with a company called Conair, the world's largest manufacturer of hairdryers, with a $500,000,000 turnover, who, on seeing the Dual Cyclone, had decided to move into the vacuum cleaner market. Prescient chaps.

Once again, my hopes were high. I was back in Connecticut, not far from Black & Decker, and just next door to Remington, where Victor Kiam liked his razor so much he bought the company. The guy who owned Conair, Lee Rizutto, was very keen on the product and everything was going very nicely indeed, with only the 'due diligence' to be completed.

I was pretty confident at that time, because I was sure that my product could satisfy any of the demands that the due diligence routine could put it through. But there are always dangers. A large part of 'd.d.', for example, is the patent search – in which the prospective licensee tests the strength of your patent, whether it is valid, and whether it is likely to be enforceable. The last thing he wants is to go into production, only to discover that someone else brings out a copy.

Even when a patent had been filed and granted it doesn't necessarily mean much, just that the patent office was satisfied – but if a plagiarist can find something in it, anything at all, that the patent examiners had missed when they examined your application, such as a piece of 'prior art', then they can contest your patent, and might just win. ('Prior art' is simply a piece of technology claimed in your patent as an innovation, that has in fact been published before your patent application. It doesn't have to be identical, only similar, and it can invalidate the whole patent.)

So there are pitfalls, and if someone really wants to reject your product, there are plenty of ways. But that wasn't the case here: both Rizutto and the VP in charge of the project, an Englishman called David St George, were behind me all the way. It was then, however, that they mentioned the name of the VP responsible for their due diligence: Paul J. Lerner! The very pipe-sucker who had done for me at Black & Decker, and had, in the interim, moved to Conair.

'Oh well then,' I said to Rizutto, 'that's the end of the deal then.'

'Don't be silly,' he said. 'We're dead set on it. There won't be any problems.'

'I know that guy, Lerner,' I told him. 'He's so bloody negative, he'll kill the whole deal.'

And he did.

I got my familiar consolation though, which was that David St George left Conair in disgust. But that, flattering though it was, wasn't going to feed my family.

Yet, something had to. So I doggedly continued in my one-man licensing tour. But trying to find a major licensee as a one-man show is a punishing experience: you have to prove your product's marketability on your own; you have to hammer out the front money alone, and alone you have to run the gauntlet of in-house engineers testing your machine, determined to prove that it doesn't work because it isn't their idea. Only after that do you get down to the licensing nitty-gritty. Negotiations of that kind are normally battled through by two teams, but for me it was still, and always, alone. I would be in a room with the company president, and the VPs legal, sales, financial, and engineering, as well as their own outside lawyers (mine, of course, still waiting to be activated by phone at the last minute, to keep costs down). I cannot overstate the soul-destroying drudgery of sitting in a board room with all these specialists, each with their own little area in which to attack you. The executives of big corporations like to hunt in packs and surround their small prey, frightening it one by one before baring their fangs and all pouncing together. One of them says, 'We'll give you a 5 per cent royalty on the first 100,000 units, and then 2 per cent on the next 100,000.'

And you say, 'But that's unfair because . . .'

And before you have finished another one will interrupt with something else. So while you try to answer that, another one pre-empts your answer, saying, 'I know that, but . . .' and begins his own attack. Each one is trying to impress the president, by getting his own two penn'orth in, and they derive confidence both from the presence of each other, and from your own evident bewilderment.

It is not unlike a school playground situation in which one child is being picked on, and can't turn the situation around because of the sheer weight of numbers laughing at him. Or it is like a debate in which one person's views are ridiculed by every other interlocutor, so that no matter how right you are, you will be defeated by the frustration of so many people shouting you down. As the smallest and youngest at the big house in Norfolk, I had learnt all about that a long time ago.

As I said earlier, there is no such thing as a standard licence agreement. They differ from country to country and from company to company, and everyone has different finances, and different needs. They are huge documents and can take years to negotiate, even if you do have a professional lawyer (doing it myself, I made some terrible mistakes). A licence agreement is really a considerable piece of creative work in its own right, and it is easy to get out-created.

Once again, my point of weakness was my smallness, isolation, and dire need. A licence agreement is not like any other kind of agreement between companies. The people I was dealing with knew perfectly well that there weren't other companies clamouring for my product and, because a deal takes so long to negotiate, and each is unique, I couldn't go round negotiating other agreements in parallel with other companies as a back-up, should the deal fall through. The licensee knows this, too. And takes advantage of this sword of Damocles that hangs over me. He knows I am captive, and the more sure of this he becomes, the tougher he gets, the more he tries to screw me.

I had to learn a good deal of brinkmanship in those years – but a strange kind of brinkmanship, for it is only the big corporation that has an ongoing business and can get up and walk away. I can't, and I am the one who has made the investment, paid the huge patent costs, has the heavy overdraft and the big R&D costs – the longer the negotiations go on the more desperate you become for the money, the more desperate to do the deal . . . and they know it. This situation, the large-team-plays-hardball-with-lone-inventor scenario, was best exemplified when, some time before I got muddled up with Black & Decker and Conair, I became involved in a licence negotiation with Shopvac.

Now, Shopvac really are quite big. Their founder, William Miller, who was still alive and the great overseeing patriarch of the company, had invented the tank vacuum cleaner – a sort of dustbin with a motor on the top – years before and made millions. So called because Americans keep it in a place they call the 'shop' (a sort of den, garage, workshop type of room), it was the rock on which his empire was founded. And now that he felt like expanding that empire, he wanted to license my technology both for their tanks and for a mainstream vacuum cleaner that would allow them to take on that section of the market too. I travelled out to their headquarters in Williamsport, Pennsylvania, where I stayed for a few days while we went through a series of very successful meetings and put the cyclone through lots of tests, the results of which they seemed to be delighted with.

When the time came to bang out a deal they arranged a meeting, rather bizarrely, in a room at the Marriatt Hotel in Saddleback, New Jersey. It was a typical Marriatt hotel room, pastel bed sheets, ghastly floral-patterned sofa, acrylic carpet, the kind you get in the armpit of America. The VPs engineering and legal sat on the bed, the VPs financial and sales sat on the sofa, and another one, the marketing VP if I remember rightly, kept disappearing into the bathroom, for reasons of his own. The great founder, William Miller, was also there, squeezed into an armchair, watching, and saying nothing.

I stood up for most of the time, wearing a wild Johnson suit covered in silver flecks, trying to behave like a lawyer, as we sketched out the agreement. They all tried to grind me into submission, sometimes one by one, and sometimes altogether, and as I felt myself losing ground I began to wonder if perhaps it was the suit that was the problem. Towards the end of the meeting, as we were getting close to a deal, they began insisting on utterly unacceptable terms.

And I said, simply, 'No. That won't do.'

At this point, and we had been there for some hours, the old man heaved himself out of his seat for the first time, this great, barrel-chested Grizzly Adams of the domestic appliance wilderness, and lost his temper in a great flash of thunder.

'Just who do you think you are? You're lucky to have us, here. We know how this is done – you should listen to us and accept just what ever we offer you.'

'Well, that's absolutely fine and dandy,' I said, and started packing up my briefcase. I turned to the door, and said, 'I've got to go and catch a plane to Washington to see Black & Decker. But if you want to modify your opinions, you know where to find me.'

I turned my back on them with my heart beating, but trying to look considerably taller and leaner and meaner than I was, in the hope of leaving a sort of Lone Ranger 'who was that masked man?' effect in my wake.

Once outside, one of the men, a quieter one called Jonathan Miller, ran after and caught up with me.

'Take no notice of my father,' he said. 'He's just in a foul temper today.'

'If he is involved in the negotiations,' I said, 'then I have to take notice of him. There's seven of you buggers in there, and only one of me. The last thing that any of you should be doing is losing your temper and trying to bully me into an agreement. I'm off to Black & Decker.' And I carried on walking.

As I walked out of the hotel's main door, I paused at the top of the steps to smell the evening air, and remind myself that it was only a licensing deal I had lost, not a limb, or a close friend.

As I stood there I heard the doorman say, 'Dig the suit, man.' And my faith in corporate America was all but restored.

What I was trying to do at this time, which was not easy, was to keep as many of the potential licensees in the air as was humanly possible, rather than get tied down to one company too quickly. For most of the period this looked like pathetically wishful thinking, but the idea was that when, and if, I did get made some offers, I could ensure that I chose the best possible ones.

But by 1984, having been touting the cyclone around the world for the best part of three years, I had not yet made a single penny. I had been spending very little time at home so that, unlike in the development stages, Deirdre had had to manage pretty much on her own. Prototypes Ltd was pretty much out of cash, and I feared that even Jeremy's Job-like patience might be wearing thin. It was then that I got a call, very early one morning, from a smooth-talking man I had never heard of before.

'Hi, James,' he said suavely. 'I've seen your publicity. And I think that what you have there is a product that nobody has, that everyone needs, and only you make.'

'Well, nice of you to say so,'

'That's my philosophy, James. We want products that nobody has, and everyone needs, and only we make.'

'How convenient. Who are you?'

'I'm the vice president of global operations for Amway Corporation. I'll fly over and see you right away.'

Short chapter, big deal

The odd quandary but, hey, a deal's a deal. They claim fraudulent conduct, deception, and misrepresentation. Disagreements over a wheelchair. Jeremy says goodbye. I sink deeper and deeper into debt.

Amway's vice president of global operations flew into Heathrow on Tuesday, 13 March at 13.13. Roughly. He hired a Jaguar at the airport, and drove down to Sycamore House, ringing my doorbell at about four o'clock.

He was a rotund man, but not obese, wearing a pinstriped suit, and about as charming a person as you could hope to meet, in an Americanised Australian sort of a way. Over a cup of tea in the coach house he talked about Amway.

Amway was and is, in fact, a very famous company indeed, and there are not many Americans who do not know about it – I notice, as I write, that even the spell-check on my computer, which does not have an enormous reservoir of company names, is familiar with it, whereas Shopvac, Miele, Zanussi, even Kenwood, all get the bewildered red underline that says Microsoft do not know who they are.

The VP was a very nice man indeed, which meant a lot because he was our only point of contact with the company. So nice. So nice. He said to me, after our chat in Bath, 'Come over to our US headquarters, and we'll put you up. And we'll have a limo pick you up at the airport.'

And so, in April 1984, I did.

After a few days, to cut a long story short, they offered me what seemed a huge sum for a licence for the Dual Cyclone. It sounded particularly huge to a man who had not earnt a bean in five years.

Cheques were flying about in the spring air and I thought to myself, 'This is the life, this is what it is all about.' At last, at long, long last, I had found a company that was going to make millions and millions of lovely Dual Cyclones, and sell them to everybody, and make me and my family rich and happy, so that I could get on with inventing lots more wonderful things and making the world a lovelier place.

I rang Jeremy from the hotel (I still owned only 51 per cent of Prototypes Ltd, he had the other 49 per cent) and told him that I had been offered this great deal.

He flew out to join me, we hired a local lawyer, and we had a deal hammered out, with some helicoptering of documents between Amway's many VPs, within four days. It would take a couple more before everything was ready to sign, so we took the opportunity to fly out to California for a couple of days to stay with Tony Richardson, whom I had not seen since the old days at the Roundhouse. I had been travelling around so much, though, that I was suffering from chronic jet-lag by the time we arrived, took a mogadon, and slept for two days, thereby spending my first trip to Hollywood in bed.

Suitably refreshed, we flew back on the red-eye, and walked into Amway's boardroom expecting to just sign the deal. To my blank astonishment, the deal had changed, with Amway proposing new figures for what I would be paid.

Still, not wanting to give up the very real possibility of at last profiting from the cyclone, we decided to sign the new deal anyway. It was still a good deal. We excluded everyone else we had been talking to, signed the deal, and flew home with a cheque.

Back at Sycamore House, a great cloud was lifted. It seemed as though the years of struggle were over at last. I can be quite a monster when I am annoyed, or irritated, or frustrated with something, and there had been a lot of frustration over the last few years. I was a great big teddy bear all over again, and my family were getting their fair whack of my time, at last. Deirdre and the children were so delighted they celebrated by buying an eighteenth-century marble statue of a woman, who was to become part of the family.

That was in May 1984. Between then and the beginning of August I travelled to Amway's headquarters twice more, to hand over drawings and to discuss the project.

Then in September, I received a telex saying that Amway wanted to come over and see me to renegotiate again.

They never came, and a few days later we received a letter from their lawyers accusing us of fraudulent conduct, deception and misrepresentation on the grounds (amongst others) that it was not ready for the market. Strangely enough, though, it did not actually include anything about terminating the agreement.

So we wrote back that we assumed, from the nature of their letter, that they were abandoning the project.

There was, thus, only one thing for it: a company worth about minus £100,000 was going to do battle with a multibillion-dollar giant.

It was then that Jeremy decided not to continue his involvement with Prototypes (although he did not finally resign as a director until October 1985). The vacuum cleaner was not his baby, it was costing everyone money, and things were about to get very hairy indeed, so I couldn't really blame him.

The time for a parting of the ways had seemed to be around the corner for some time. In recent months Prototypes had been developing an indoor wheelchair, at the instigation of Jeremy's great friend, Lord Snowdon. Snowdon's idea was a very good one, because the old multipurpose wheelchair was terribly clumsy round the house, not to mention the fact that it brought into the home all kinds of muck and dogshit – and the kinds of specific functions that an indoor model would need would be superfluous on one that was also used outdoors.

In response, Jeremy and I came up with a good motorised prototype that had angled wheels for better manoeuvrability, and could be folded up easily and put in the back of a car. But while I believed our design had the charisma necessary for a substantially original project, the other people involved kept trying to compromise – to make it more like every other wheelchair on the market, and thus, essentially, multipurpose – and since I was only a lieutenant in this it did not hold my attention the way that the vacuum cleaner could, which was all my own.

Jeremy's interests and my own began to diverge considerably. He was nearing retirement, and taking a principally altruistic interest in the wheelchair. He had imagined that once the deal in America was signed we would be able to sit back and count the royalties, but as the skies began to darken he decided he had had enough. I, on the other hand, was determined to struggle, and did not particularly need the distractions of the wheelchair, much though I would like to have made the design viable, given time and space to concentrate on it.

As far as Amway was concerned, it became clear to me that, so long as the agreement was being contested I could not license the thing to anyone else, and with every passing day the legal costs were plunging me deeper and deeper into debt. I had to reach a settlement fast.

After months of negotiation my US lawyers settled with Amway on terms that meant I had to pay them back all the money, in return for their termination of the licence and the return of my patents. This all 'resolved' itself in the early weeks of 1985. I was broke, hungry, and depressed. But at least I was free. It was then that hope returned, and not a minute too soon, in the form of a promise from the East.

'We ruv G-Force!' –
Japan to the rescue

A nation of shopkeepers. Jeeves shimmers in, and then shimmers out again pretty sharpish. The allure of the East. The Occidental blind spot. I am large, smelly, and unattractive. Why the Japanese liked me. Why they liked the cyclone even more. The fingerprint test. The most expensive vacuum cleaner in the world. The uselessness of brilliance. Britain sinks ever lower.

Back home at Square One, a place I was getting to know pretty well by now, the outlook was dreary. Everywhere I had been with my invention had been a disappointment of one kind or another. First of all I had been turned down by my own company because, 'If there were a better kind of vacuum cleaner Hoover or Electrolux would have invented it.' Then I had been turned down in my requests for backing by bean-counters who assumed that, since I was a designer, I knew nothing about counting beans. Then I had been turned down by several major electrical companies because they did not dare change direction away from bag-dependent machines, or were simply opposed to revolution as a matter of principle. And I had encountered nothing in America but disappointment and a massive law case that had financially crippled me.

I was very close to despair – and the state of the country under Margaret Thatcher was ramming it home to me every day. We had become the nation of shopkeepers that Napoleon had mocked us as so long ago. Eighties values were vaunting the efforts of city bankers who moved money around but created nothing. Advertising was fast becoming the British disease, and Britain was choosing to advertise its way out of recession.

From the inside, the contemporary notion of the eighties as the 'Design Decade' was a mockery. All it meant was that they were revamping the shops a bit, and places like Next, Sock Shop, and Tie-Rack were becoming popular. But the products inside the shops were not changing, not from a design point of view at least.

And so British companies decided that the best way to give themselves an overhaul was to call in a big advertising or PR consultancy, and spend millions on persuading the public that they were better than everyone else, and were in some way new and exciting. It never occurred to them to invest the money in the research and development of something genuinely, and tangibly, new and exciting.

That, I am afraid, is the only way to achieve long-term growth, wealth, and stability. Slow, boring and initially expensive it may be, but the cataclysmic boom and bust of the years that followed were the price we paid for excitement.

My first effort to drag myself from the mire took me to Hampstead to see a man called Sidney Jacob (with whom I had negotiated during the litigation with Amway), a dry-cleaning millionaire who had recently sold his business, Jeeves of Belgravia, to BSM, and was looking for something new to do with his millions. I was worn out and desperate, and perhaps he smelt it in the air: no one I have encountered before or since was quite as tough as Sidney. At first, when we sat down to discuss the possible deal, he was as charming as Cary Grant. But there was a glint of steel in his eye, and when it slid from its scabbard to administer a sharp slash, it was all the more surprising for the charm that preceded it.

Jacob claimed to be afraid that the royalties would be enormous, and that, as a precaution, my percentage should decrease as sales rose.

'But Sidney,' I protested, 'that is the nature of royalties. The more you sell the more I get.'

'No,' he urged. 'It's totally inequitable that you should get £5 million a year for doing nothing at all. It is only right that your money should be concentrated at the beginning and then tail off.'

Nothing at all! That was nice. It seems to be the case that whenever you sit down with a businessman he cannot see past what is being put on the table at that very moment. I had come up with a new piece of technology, I had done all the development and testing and patenting and spent vast amounts of money, but now that I needed another man's money to get off the ground, he felt entitled to say that I had done 'nothing'.

I asked for a 5 per cent royalty. He offered me 3 per cent. As I tried to control myself in the face of his miserable offer, he went on, 'That is three per cent reducing to half a per cent in time.'

I would drive home each evening feeling as if I had been through a mangle, and realise as I drove that I couldn't possibly agree to his offer of that day. I would ring him the next day to tell him so, and he would come over all hurt and offended, and make me feel like a heel.

Sidney Jacob could see the negotiations only from his point of view, and had no inkling that I, like any businessman, needed to be motivated into doing the deal too. That combination of charm and steel is very nasty indeed to encounter. It leaves you feeling utterly shafted and unwilling to do a deal.

So I didn't.

While I was mooching around in Bath, despairing over one thing and another, and while my doggedness and self-belief, in the absence of any real evidence that they were justified, were beginning to look more and more like insanity, a picture of the Cyclon – which had been off the market since the beginning of the Amway affair in November 1984 – was gracing the pages of a glossy American product design annual where it generated one single request for information. From Japan.

It so happened that Apex Inc., the Japanese company who had taken a vague interest, had a representative in Britain, a woman called Rachel Carter, and even her little story (though she was only an opening pawn in the great game plan) was illustrative of the new mindset I was about to encounter.

She lived in Islington, and had been the landlady of a Japanese businessman called Kenji Kajiwara, (a good, unbusinessy businessman whom I came to respect very much) when he came to London to learn English in the late seventies. Having become friendly with this chap she took his advice to go out to Japan herself, and teach English. Soon enough, though, she began to suffer from the culture shock, and all the difficulties in adjusting, that any westerner who spends more than three weeks out there inevitably does (I should know, the first time I returned from an extended business trip in Japan, Deirdre was shocked to find that I had completely changed. I kept bowing my head all the time, she claimed, and behaving meekly. I never shouted anymore and seemed to suppress all my natural instincts. Compared to the bear with a headache that had left England only weeks before this was a disturbing alteration, and it took me quite some time to recover.) As a result of her own experience, Rachel Carter felt compelled to return to England.

Having nothing else to do on her return, and Kajiwara feeling more than a little guilty for his role in her downfall, she began acting as an Apex agent in Britain, and when Apex tipped her the wink, it was she who came to see me.

It was a gentle, trendy-looking woman, about five or ten years younger than me, and with all the designer accoutrements of the time from Filofax to Chanel suit (though she was unpretentious and quietly determined, with enough sensitivity and intelligence to work hard to understand how the Japanese think), who showed up on my doorstep in Bath to tell me what sort of a company Apex was, and what they wanted from me. Although I suspect her role was mainly to find out what sort of a person I was. Years later, when we had become good friends, she told me that the first thing they asked her when she reported back was, 'Does he want to go to Geisha bars?'

At the end of our meeting I knew, broke though I was, that I had to go. The cheapest flight I could find was an Aeroflot one via Moscow, and so I flew out to Japan in a clunking aircraft like a prewar Hoover Junior with wings (in which the passengers travelled in the bag), entirely on spec, with no promise at all of any sort of deal, and utterly unsure what to make of this company that had approached a ridiculous little British company and professed an interest in a vacuum cleaner that appeared almost unpurchaseable in Japan.

Even in the late twentieth century there is still an Occidental blind spot about the Japanese. We profess to have come so far in race relations, to understand each other better than ever. And yet the Japanese continue to fascinate, bewilder and frighten us in equal measure. A television and newspaper culture that tends to sneer first, and laugh later, while going through only the motions of explaining, has brought us to this impasse, and Clive James has a lot to answer for. We have revelled for years in the apparently bizarre culture and habits of the Japanese, with the result that British businessmen – fed on images of shrieking naked men jumping into icy rivers to eat live squid, after being forced to drink eight gallons of salty water with prizes for the last to vomit or urinate – have developed a neurosis, almost a paranoia, that has made productive contact between the two nations – as industrial powers – a very rare thing indeed. Thus, before setting off for Japan (or as witless business colleagues and backers would insist on calling it, 'The Land of the Rising Sun', and occasionally 'Nipland', 'Japville', 'Slope City', or even, inexplicably, 'Chinkland'), I had a course of lessons in how to comport myself. Like some eighteenth-century debutante being prepared for her first ball.

All this business about bowing and shoes, and respect and not losing your temper, resulted in my being frightfully inhibited for my first few – unsuccessful – visits. I had been conditioned to see the Japanese as some bizarre, touchy, and dangerous species, whom to offend would lead to inevitable death. The accepted wisdom was that you treated Japanese businessman in more or less the same way you would a tiger, if you came upon it alone in a shady jungle clearing.

It was during my third visit to Japan, that I realised where we had – as a nation trying to do business – been going wrong. The fact is that the Japanese can be narcissistic, xenophobic, and chauvinistic – perhaps even more so than we are – and that, to them, everyone else is a 'wog'. A large, smelly, and very unattractive 'wog'. 'Geijins', in fact, is what they call us – which translates loosely, I believe, as 'wog'. For the first three visits it was the only word I could make out in their conversations. And I heard it a hell of a lot.

It doesn't help even to be ethnically closer to them than we are – like the Koreans or the Chinese. They will still hate you. In fact, they will hate you more. If you are not thoroughbred Japanese, you are 'Geijin', and not to be trusted, or liked.

It struck me, therefore, that all this bowing and scraping, sushi-eating and floor sitting, was a lot of nonsense: a waste of time, and a rank indignity. I reckoned that the only reason they were interested in me, if they were interested, was that I was different. And that it was our differences, not my ham-fisted attempts to be similar, that I should be focusing on. I reckoned the more different and eccentric I was, the more they would be interested in me. Just as a Texan oil baron in a Stetson, or a Jewish Hollywood executive, or a New York taxi driver, or a French footballer is more interesting the more different and eccentric they are. Everybody liked Jurgen Klinsmann, for example, but they thought he was boring because he tried so hard to be English. Eric Cantona, on the other hand, is called a genius, just because he does not try to be English, refuses to speak our language, and comforts himself in public with contrived Napoleonic arrogance.

So I stopped trying to ape them. I stopped wearing neat little charcoal suits and pretending to like their revolting food. And the more I protested my revulsion for sushi, the more they laughed – another crucial thing: they are going to laugh behind your back, no matter what. So make it easier for them, really give them something to laugh about.

The Apex secretaries, all women, were particularly friendly. The first thing they asked me was how old I was, and when I told them I was thirty-eight they positively fell about laughing, and squawking, 'Rook much older. Rook much older. Rook about a hundled!' And then they would look at my nose – a respectable proboscis, but by no means lampoonable in the normal state of things – and squeal, 'Nose rook rike Eiffel Tower!' before collapsing into manic cackling, which they always did with their hands cupped over their mouths to hide their smiles. But it was clearly not meant to be offensive, they even invited me along to an all-girls beer drinking session – in Japan the women do all the beer drinking for some reason – but just when I was looking forward to an evening of rare anthropological value, seeing Japanese women with their hair down, the managing director found out and stopped it. Instead I had to spend all night playing a sort of advanced Scalextric with him in a room at Apex given over to a gigantic track. By transposing 'l's and 'r's I am not seeking to mock my Japanese hosts, but merely to represent how their speech sounded to me, and to give a feeling of what it was like to be there. The transposition of these letters is not restricted to speech, but often happens with the written word too. When the first vacuum cleaners rolled off the production line they packaged one up and sent it to me. No time or expense had been spared in the glorious dressing of this product, but as I turned it over to admire the other side of the gleaming box, I caught sight of the words 'G-force – Cycronic Vacuum Cleaner'.

So anyway, the Apex people chuckled away, and I stopped bowing, and really relaxed. And we all had a lot more fun. You see, one of the absurd things about western businessmen going there and trying to pretend to be Japanese – to understand their working methods and to copy them – is that the Japanese are really only pretending to be Japanese too. They give you the performance about honour, and 'my word is my bond', and then they have their legal people shaft you before you've even left the room. Which, of course, is more of an American way of going about things. Not surprising, when you consider that the Americans taught them how to do business. It was at the end of the last war that the American army marched into Toyota and told them to stop building tanks, and start making cars instead.

'But we don't know how to build cars,' said the Japanese. And the Americans showed them how. Cut to the late eighties and what do the Americans do? They go back to the Japanese and say 'Right, now stop building cars.'

So while on the face of it you appear to have these fine, honourable people doing business the Japanese way, actually they are just small Americans with straight black hair, and a distaste for westerners.

Now, while I have propounded this unlikely sounding theory about being as different as possible from the Japanese, I should mention that it derives from and depends upon a crucial position. The Japanese will only do business with you if they have to. They would much, much rather do business with Japanese people. And they are not going to choose to do business with some big-nosed, smelly old Geijin, just because he conforms. So if they have to do business with you, well, you might as well be larger than life. They have only come to you because you are eccentric. They can get conformity in Japan. By the truckload. And they don't have to sniff your rancid occidental pheromones.

Apex were hugely enthusiastic from the outset of our dealings, and after the negativism of the British, and the dopey overreaching of the Americans, it was a joy to negotiate with them.

It was a company that had set itself up not long before, importing luxury Swiss watches and Filofaxes. It was they, indeed, who put Filofax on the map in Japan by marketing it as something the British military had used during the war, and they sold it along with a story about a British captain who had had a Filofax in his tunic pocket in the First World War which had saved his life when it took the impact of a .303 rifle bullet aimed at his heart. If they could do something similar with the cyclone – suggest, perhaps, that Florence Nightingale had used it to clean the sick bays in the Crimea – then that was going to be fine by me.

In fact, they thought the machine was wonderful. Unlike anyone I had met so far, they understood exactly what I was trying to do and knew exactly how to sell it. And within three weeks we had signed a deal by which I was to get front money of £35,000, plus design fees of £25,000 on completion of the drawings, and then a 10 per cent royalty with an annual minimum of £60,000.

The name 'G-Force' was first mooted at a lunch I had with the Apex chairman, Koyo Kanaya, on my first trip. We couldn't call it anything with 'cyclone' in the title, because Braun had already registered that name in Japan (for a product they never made) and G-Force was nice because not only did it refer to the technology within the machine, but it sounded a bit like GI, which they loved. Something to do with Elvis, I assume. There was never any talk of the negative aspects of the deal (not in English, and within my earshot, anyway), none of the 'who are you to tell us our business' crap that annoyed me so much in Britain.

They would just come up to me all the time and say, 'I ruv G-force, I ruv G-force', and fondle the handle lovingly, and look at it with stars in their eyes, just glowing with love. And why not? Taking pleasure in a product and what it can do is perfectly healthy. It is not obscene. There was nothing sexual in it, as far as I know. None of them took the G-Force home and tried to mate with it. They just appreciated it as one might a sculpture, with knobs on because they were so enthusiastic about its function. From chairman to salesman the response was the same, and as a result a bond developed between everyone involved that could result only in success. I thought I was in Heaven.

From the beginning of 1985 the G-Force became all-consuming. It had to be. I had lost Amway. I had lost Rotork, I was heavily in debt and had to survive. Quite apart from the importance of the money, I knew that if I had a product that was being sold successfully in Japan, and which clearly worked, it would lift the Amway stigma, and convince people that the cyclone had worked, and that we had not duped anybody. For not only was the Amway stigma making further deals impossible – 'Why did Amway drop out?' people would ask. 'Why did Rotork drop out?' – but I couldn't help wondering, as my spirits fell, whether there might have been an element of truth in it. I knew there wasn't, but my nerves were fragile enough to be susceptible to such doubts. I needed a success to help knock down the doubting Thomases. And I knew that if I could make Japan work then I had a fighting chance.

I spent much of the next year living in Japan, in stints of six weeks at a time, designing the G-force and seeing it into production. While it was mentally and emotionally draining, it was professionally quite amazing. They worked all day and all night. I could give a model maker a drawing at 8 p.m., and twenty-four hours later he would come back to me with a perfect working model – something that could take weeks in Britain. And there was none of the British attitude that makes a team sit down before any work is done and say, 'Right, how many problems have we got?' The only difficulty was that if there ever was a problem then, for the sake of honour, we had to overcome it without attaching blame to anyone.

In most respects the G-Force was identical to the Cyclon. They were very keen to keep the model lavender and pink, and I was delighted about it. The colours had been inspired by the time I spent in the South of France, when I would wake every morning to fantastic pastels in the fields. The light and colours of Provence had inspired the Impressionist painters, and it was only right that they should inspire the first Impressionist vacuum cleaner. Impressionist, because it was not a vacuum cleaner the way the world usually looked at it, but a vacuum cleaner the way it looked to *me*. No one had tried using pink in domestic appliances before, nor had they tried the pastelly, washed-out look. It would have been easy to laugh at – and believe me, many did – but if it worked it was going to be a major identifying point.

Once the Japanese were convinced that the colours were right, and were happy with the design, they displayed a perfectionism that put my own to shame. They would tolerate not a single weld mark, not a scratch or a fleck of dust, not even a fingerprint. It was all part of their love for the product, and their unique way of expressing their love. I would get phone calls in the dark hours of the Japanese night, with a man from the factory screaming down the line, 'Tellible ploblem with G-Force!' And I would drive over there to investigate, to find a dozen men weeping over the vacuum cleaner and crying, 'Rook! Rook! Rook what they've done!' And there would be a finger print on one of the moulded parts that I could not even see. They must have had some sort of stroboscopic light that could pick such things out. It is a kind of mania, but a kind that has not done Japanese industry any harm in the past. Once you get used to it, it becomes only another thing to admire. In the year I spent with the Japanese, I learnt an awful lot about design that would stand me in great stead when I set up alone to make the Dyson Dual Cyclone.

By August, 1985 I had completed the drawings, and in March 1986 the G-Force went on the market at a cost of £1200 per machine, and despite, or perhaps because of, its enormous price, it soon became *the* must-have domestic style-item for the fashionable man, or woman, about Tokyo.

Did they ever use it? Who knows. The Japanese, as a nation, prefer cylinder vacuum cleaners, and had never bought uprights in any great number. They don't really have houses, so there was no identifiable need for this full size cleaner, and there isn't much storage space for it in their tiny homes – which is why the uprights that had sold there had been ones with an attachable table top, so that when not being used they could be disguised as coffee tables. It may be, I suppose, that the fact that it looked so good was what made it attractive to a people who were not going to be able to shut it away.

Nor do the Japanese go for wall-to-wall carpet in a big way, and though I had included on the G-Force a special attachment for cleaning tatami mats, the suspicion in the design world was that this futuristic pink machine, half spaceship, half vacuum cleaner, just stood in the corner in most Japanese homes, and generated oohs and aahs. But it stood in a lot of corners. And though it took off only gradually, within three years it was making sales of £12 million a year.

If I was unhappy about anything – and I was not unhappy about much, for this success meant that I was able to pay my legal bills, and get on with my business – then it was that Apex had chosen to market the G-Force as a niche product, whereas I knew it was a fantastically viable mainstream one. Furthermore, this niching of the product, and huge retail price, was used to stiff me, in no uncertain terms, of a considerable amount of the money I was rightfully due.

The 10 per cent royalty deal I had negotiated was to be calculated as a percentage of Apex's sale price. By the time Apex had sold it to the wholesalers and the wholesalers had sold it to the retailers, and the retailers had sold it to the customer, it had reached this delicious price of £1200. Sadly, though, the wholesalers paid Apex only £200, and so my cut per unit was only ever £20.

The reason that this was so disastrous was that a wholesale price of £200 usually denotes a retail price of about £350, making my £20 not look too bad, and a reasonable reflection of the income potential of the machine. But by ending up in the showrooms at £1200 a pop, you see, the G-Force was never going to be a high turnover item, and at a vast unit cost with small sales, and me on a minuscule percentage (little more than 1 per cent), everyone was going to get rich apart from me.

I have had agreements of this kind with a number of companies, but have learnt now to negotiate better terms. A licensee will very rarely give you a percentage of the ultimate retail price, which is what you want, because, he says, he can have no idea what the ultimate retail price will be. By taking a percentage of the manufacturer's sale price, you relinquish all control over what the selling price to the consumer will be, and it is that price that determines volume.

In a number of deals I had made in the past (such as the Cyclon licence with Rotork) the licensee purported to be offering me a royalty on the wholesale price, which is better than nothing, but then slipped in a selling agent in between themselves and the wholesaler, so that my royalties ended up only half of what they should have been. In the case of Apex, of course, my royalty was reduced to a tenth of what it should have been.

In the end I only ever got the £60,000 annual minimums out of Apex (and Alco, who took over the licence in 1988). I was never even able to determine exactly how many units they managed to sell, because instead of properly enumerated sales reports all they ever gave me was little bits of scrap paper with lots of numbers written in pencil, and most of the words in Japanese, and even getting *them* was like trying to get blood out of a stone. As the years went by the G-Force seemed to be doing better and better, and yet they never, in their reports to me, admitted to be selling more than that bare minimum.

But negotiations with the Japanese were a nightmare. They were like sponges; they just sat their soaking up all my questions and never answering any of them. Their way was to constantly besiege me with question after question, to answer my questions with their own. I would talk to them for hours and hours, and never be any the wiser at the end. Eventually I was so frustrated that I called in an external auditor from Arthur Andersen, and sent him in to try and ascertain how many motors they were buying, which would tell me how many vacuum cleaners they were actually shifting. I even insisted on a Japanese accountant, hoping that he would at least be able to understand the little pencilled reports, and that they might be straighter with him. But he just went in there, had a cup of tea with the boys, and came out telling me what wonderful chaps they were, and that I shouldn't worry about it.

But whatever they really sold, or however badly I did out of the royalty agreement, it was that money that enabled me to extricate myself from trouble and begin all over again. And when the hassle became too much for me, and I needed a lump sum to set up with the Dyson Dual Cyclone, I was more than delighted to sell the Japanese rights off altogether, and leave them to it.

I would be back though, in time, to sell them my own machine. And then I would really have some fun.

The fact that after so much rejection I found my commercial salvation in Japan was at once surprising, and not so surprising. The Japanese are not brilliant, nor do they set any great store by brilliance. They are taught to conform from an early age, and while the young may revere certain elements of western cultural life, at the time I was out there, conformity was still the key. Interest in fashion, pop music, and western cinema was only just beginning and a boy in a leather jacket would still turn heads in the street – a group of them was a front page picture. Now you have a situation where the head of McDonald's in Japan can claim that the reason the Americans are so tall and blond and strong is that they eat lots of hamburgers, leading the young Japanese to forsake their traditional diets, and become prey, among other things, to the heart disease that was for so long unknown to them. They have also begun to experience unemployment, and the security of the company man, so firmly entrenched when I was there, and so refreshing after the timidity of the West, is no longer taken for granted.

But they retain those key elements in their psyche that made them such ideal partners for someone like me, and a product like mine. They are not inventive, in the way that we, the British, like to think that we are. They do not bumble along in the hope of making it big when some bright new idea dawns on the horizon. They believe in progress by stages, in the iterative development that I have described as Edisonian, the persistent trial and error that allows them to wake up one morning, after many, many mornings, with a world-beating product.

That is how they have crept up on the West. For so long we heard the choruses of 'Ho, ho, ho the Japanese can't make things.' We laughed at the toys they sold us, the cheap plastic crap we thought could never replace good, honest, Anglo-Saxon workmanship. And we laughed at the cars. God, how we laughed at the cars. Those early Datsuns, Toyotas and Nissans. They were a joke, weren't they? They were only ever the poor man's alternative to a real car.

But they were learning all the time. Improving little by little. And now they have the best technology, and the best design, and their cars are the best built and the most reliable in the world. In the old days of conformity there were no Japanese designers, and now that they are coming to grips with individualism, they are beginning to create beautiful things too. And the world is frightened. And all their success is born out of a theory of gradual development that is the very antithesis of the British obsession with the quantum leap.

In Britain we have laboured for years under the tyranny of expectation of a certain kind of excellence. For years, all that mattered was that you were top of the class, that you went to Oxford or Cambridge and got a first, that you were a genius. We placed all our hopes in quantum leaping, and as our industrial decline continued so the leap required grew bigger. It was going to take an awful lot to catch up. We put our faith in dreams of one brilliant idea that might put us back on top of the pile.

The Japanese always took the opposite view. They put no faith in individualists, and lived an anti-brilliance culture. And that was healthy. They know full well that quantum leaps are very rare, but that constant development will result, in the end, in a better product. And that is a mindset I share with them. I am not a quantum leaper. My initial idea back in 1979 may have looked like a major jump, but by 1986 when the G-Force was launched, seven years had passed. And five more were to pass before I produced anything of my own. It was all about gradual and iterative development. Ironically, I think that what the Japanese thought they were getting from this comedic, gallumphing geijin was a quantum leap of true British lineage. And that is probably why they liked it. But, in that sense, I was only pretending to be British.

And you know, this British inventiveness thing is a flag we like to wave, and one which many people pay attention to. But if you were to go round the different national patent offices of the world and have a look at who filed the most patents, it wouldn't be us. In recent research by the Design Council on 'Innovations Hotspots', Britain came eleventh in a league table of patent-filers, with 7.93 registrations per 100,000 of population, lagging behind countries like Japan, Germany, Taiwan, and even Switzerland. When I am going for a new patent I do not go looking for prior art in the British patent office, because I am far more likely to find it abroad.

We use our so called 'inventiveness', born of an arrogance rooted in some deep Edwardian cellar of our imagination where men like Caractacus Potts hold the future in their hands, as an excuse for our failure as an industrial power. In truth, the really strong industrial countries are the ones that have been doing the inventing. It just didn't look like inventing. Not only have they been inventing, which is only half the battle, they have been giving invention some respect. While part of our reverence for the idea of the inventor is born of our worshipping his crackpot image, at the same time it is that image that has belittled him in the eyes of industry.

Industrialists see inventors, and I saw them see it in me for far too long, as batty little people driven mad by enthusiasm for their madcap innovations. They are seen as difficult people, out of touch with the real world. Hence their constant imprecations that 'You are a designer Dyson, what do you know of engineering, marketing, or selling?' And they think inventors are deluded, arrogant, and backwards. How, after all, could an inventor come up with something better than their in-house engineers? If there were a better vacuum cleaner, wouldn't Hoover or Electrolux have thought of it first?

Industry's problems with invention do not end there. There is a short-termism, perhaps brought about by failure, that demands a fast return, an immediate whopping turnover, a quick buck. Design and research and engineering are not about that. They offer a long-term way of regenerating a company – or building one.

The easy credit offered, and easy money sought, by the Thatcher revolution encouraged selling, not making. If the banks and the City want instant returns then you go out and sell your old products harder and better than before, and you end up, as we did, with the most fêted advertising industry in the world, and bugger all else. (That this situation is not likely to be reversed in the near future can be seen in the fact that graduates leaving university are flocking to get into advertising, with firms experiencing applications from up to 2,000 students for every job, while fewer and fewer students are opting to study engineering at university. According to the university lecturers' union, Nafthe, nearly a third of 1996's engineering degree places went unfilled, and 2,000 engineering apprenticeships remained untaken. And, with their need for large workshop spaces and expensive equipment, it is engineering departments that are shut down first when colleges are forced to make cutbacks. Brunel would have wept.)

But advertising is the way to a very fast, very small, profit. In retailing we saw the coming to prominence of a mentality that wanted to sell boring, low-profit items at high volume, when the opportunity was there to create new and exciting products that could be sold at a high price, with a large margin, and make you much more money in the long run – something like the G-Force, for example. But again, that is high risk and long term. A risk, that is, in conventional terms. For I believe that it is the tunnel vision that sees money as makeable only by selling cheap things by the truckload, that is by far the riskier tactic in the end.

And so British engineers are the lowest paid in the world, and the least respected members of our companies. While the smoothies and the sharp operators have been taking the initiative, our engineers have become background boys, when it is really they who should be out there running the companies, as they do in Japan, like Mr Honda, and Mr Sony. Our engineers are nice people, not aggressive, and not over-ambitious. They are absorbers of knowledge, and easily trampled by the spivs. They will have to become negotiators themselves, and marketeers, and accountants and salesmen, if we are to regain a place at the top of the heap.

For the moment, we do not look like taking a real interest in research and development (the same Design Council figures that put us eleventh in the patent-filing table, put us twenty-seventh in a table of countries' growth in R&D spend between 1988 and 1992, with a net 'growth' of −0.9 per cent. South Korea came top, with a growth of 45 per cent. Spain had 7.6 per cent; Ireland 9.1 per cent; even Chile came out ahead of us). Not long ago I watched in horror as David Hunt, then minister for science and technology, rejected the Science Council's recommendations of tax breaks for companies that invested in R&D. Oh no, he thought, just stack 'em high and sell 'em fast.

I wrote to him to query his miserable decision. And he wrote back, telling me that such a tax break would result in distorted investment – that people would, in other words, start investing in R&D just to get the breaks.

'Well, exactly!' I wrote back. 'That is just the point!'

There is distorted investment now, in advertising. If I spend £1 million on advertising I get an instant return. But the same spend on R&D might take ten years to show a return, if it ever showed one at all. Naturally, everyone goes for advertising instead, and without encouragement, they will continue to do so for ever. And Britain will crumble into dust.

It all goes back to school, to that terrible philistinism that tells us that woodwork is for thickoes in sheds, and that making things is not respectable. Perhaps, with the City bubble burst, and the vapid materialism of the Thatcher years petering out, there is a little hope that we may turn the corner. But back in the eighties, when the rot was so firmly set in, that mentality closed many a door in my face. So I had to go to Japan. It was the only choice. And I'm sorry for it.

Alien invasion?

Back in the USA. Iona know the meaning of cleaning. Amway bring out their own product. We go to court. I am over a barrel. I roll off the barrel into court. I crack the commercial market at a blow, and head off to fry bigger fish.

With the G-Force knocking them dead in Japan, I was in a position to launch a new onslaught on America by a method very different from anything I had tried before. Instead of having to license my technology to a manufacturer, I now had an up-and-running commercially successful product which I could simply sell to an American company. The export route of electrical goods from Japan to America was, after all, a pretty well-trodden one.

The front-runner to sell the G-Force to the United States was a company called Video OEM which had made a lot of money exporting VCRs from Japan at a time when the market was just beginning to come to life. Like Alan Sugar's Amstrad, Video OEM did not actually make anything, although people assumed that they did – they exported products from ghost manufacturers in the Far East and branded them. It is a fantastically easy business to run, because there is no investment beyond the cost of your stock, and very low risk, because you are not selling anything new.

But in this, as in all areas of business, there is ample leeway to stiff the small operator. I should have been on the *qui vive* a little more vigilantly than I was for more shady practice, particularly since they met me in a suite at Caesar's Palace in Las Vegas, with marble walls and a great big circular bed in the middle, that would have made any Mafia don feel well at home. If I had been more alert I would have discovered that as soon as I began talking with Video OEM they had gone behind my back to Apex, and offered them £100,000 to guarantee that they would get the deal. Apex had accepted and pocketed the sweetener, and told me nothing about it. Why should they?

Not being privileged with knowledge of this little backhander, I was surprised to find, in my negotiations with OEM, that they were refusing to give me the front money I had demanded – front money, coincidentally, of £100,000.

Now I was not about to sign any deal without front money, close all other negotiations, and then watch OEM change their minds six months down the line, as everyone else seemed to do. I was on the point of calling the deal off when I got a call from Koyo Kanaya telling me that I was wrong always to demand front money, that he would personally guarantee that OEM were the right company and would not mess me around, and that I should drop the subject and get on with the deal.

So I did. It was Apex, after all, who were going to be making the machine, and if a personal assurance was good enough for them it was good enough for me. I was about to sign the contract when I discovered about the £100,000.

It was not the payment itself that annoyed me, so much as Kanaya's appeal for me to drop my own request for front money, when he was profiting by that amount, as long as I didn't ask for it. Apex could not do the deal with OEM without me, for although they manufactured the thing, they had bought from me only the rights to production in Japan. The rights to America were mine. So I told Apex, with a certain amount of righteous indignation, that I was not going to give them the deal after all, and that I would deal independently with the rest of the world.

And so I did, very soon hammering out a deal for North America with a Canadian company called Iona, run by an Englishman, Jeffrey Pike, with whom I had become friendly quite by chance after we sat next to each other on an aeroplane in May 1986, and both turned out to be reading the same novel by Fay Weldon. Having flunked English A Level all those years before, my fortune looked as if it was about to be made by a novel.

The only potential stumbling block was a non-competition agreement Iona had signed with another American company, Regina, that included an undertaking not to sell vacuum cleaners. Tricky. But not insurmountable.

I had been friends at college with a very talented interior designer called John Weallands, who had, among other foibles, a habit of washing his hair not with shampoo and water in the normal way, but with a powder that he used to rub into his dry hair, and then shake out. Some years later, when I was making the first cyclones, I remembered this dry shampoo of his and thought it might work as a carpet-cleaning principle, too. At the time, though, I did little more than include in my original patent a mechanism for distributing the powder with the cyclone.

In the intervening years a dry shampooing product for carpets, called 'Capture' and made by Milliken, had appeared on the market, and Singer was producing a machine that used it. This machine was being sold with fifteen bags, but that still wasn't enough. That inherent failing whereby the pores of the bag clog almost immediately with dust and impede suction was exacerbated disastrously by the cleaning powder. Naturally enough this excited me hugely, because it was clear that the cyclone was the perfect machine to use it.

Now it seemed to be the ideal way to get round Iona's non-competition agreement. All the machine would be was a vacuum cleaner with a function that allowed you to load in the powder shampoo, so that it was vibrated onto the carpet, brushed in, and then sucked up. But in America there have always been two distinct markets: one for vacuum cleaners and the other for carpet shampooers, and the production of the latter was a logical solution to our problem.

Iona agreed to license the cyclone for a dry powder machine called the Drytech, and we signed a deal on 30 July 1986. The company was saved, once again, but negotiations for a vacuum cleaner would drag on for much longer than that, and in the meanwhile I set about designing the Drytech for them.

I had a little staff working for me in the coach house now, a couple of designers, recent graduates of the RCA, an engineer and a draftsman, and we worked pretty solidly for the next nine months, developing the mechanics to vibrate the shampoo into the carpet, and incorporating that into an upright vacuum cleaner. By May 1987 I was happy with the finished product and headed off to Iona to see about final details.

There my troubles appeared to begin again. As the biggest retailer of vacuum cleaners in America, Sears held most manufacturers by the short and curlies. If they liked a product, fine. If not, you either redesigned, or kissed goodbye to most of your market.

They didn't like it. Or, at least, their buyer didn't like it. 'It's just too European,' she explained. Meaning, presumably, that it was too modern, too imaginative. European design was way ahead of American, and tended to look rather wacky by comparison with their lumpy old dinosaurs. My own designs, as I have said, tended to look more modern, more 'European', still.

'These bits of blue on it are just too way out!' she said. 'I want a sleek, slick look. I want it to look like a Ferrari.'

If she thought that, then so did Iona. They wanted a redesign.

Now I would have been prepared to back down on so much with Iona, but at this I baulked. They were desperate to kow-tow to the woman from Sears and were expecting me to play ball, and to do it her way. I was, frankly, shocked. I am constantly amazed at the way businessmen seem quite happy to treat designers in this way, an approach they would never take with, say, accountants or lawyers. They seem to perceive design as some sort of amateur indulgence, a superfluous frippery in which everyone can chuck in their opinions and to hell with the designer.

It was this attitude that led to Iona, in the face of my blank refusal, calling in an American design company to do a new design of the Drytech. Leaving them to it, I headed out to Aspen, Colorado, to give a talk at a design conference, and it was there, at two o'clock in the morning, that I got a call from Iona saying that their designers had produced a fabulous drawing which the Sears buyer was bound to love and would I please go and have a meeting with these people to work out the final design.

'No,' I said. 'I have designed you a vacuum cleaner which I think is the best possible design, and if you don't like it you can sod off. And if you are going to be kept in the pocket of that damn Sears buyer, you can also sod off. If you want to get another design team in then that is fine with me, but do not dare ask me to get involved with it. Now, I am going back to sleep.'

I was offended, you see. Hence the uncharacteristically strong tone. I finished my night's sleep, and in the morning I flew back to England, furious. Three days after I got home I got a phone call from Iona (yes, I will be vindicated in the end – what else would the story be doing here?)

'Err, James. We've changed our minds. And we want to do your design.'

Hand cupped over the mouthpiece I dare say I indulged in a gesture or two of self-congratulation, but I said only, 'Great. Why the change of heart?'

'We met with the people from Sears and showed them your design and one from our American company, and they had their own designer along with them and he said to us, "The Dyson design is brilliant, it's so European, you have to go with that one", so we thought we would. If that is OK, James.'

It was more than OK. And in June that year, the Iona Drytech hit the shops to my exact specifications.

At about the same time as I finished the Drytech, we had agreed broad terms for a vacuum cleaner deal, and Jeffrey Pike, Iona Chief Executive Allan Millman, and their lawyer Wally Palmer flew over to England to negotiate with me, booking rooms at a hotel in Bath. Unfortunately, my own lawyer had another deal going with someone else at the time, which was deflecting at least half of his attention and delaying the talks. The Canadians, reasonably enough, got fed up waiting around and sightseeing in the West Country, and went home, still keen on the deal, but insisting that we negotiate thereafter by phone and post.

So proceedings carried on for a while, with papers being sent back and forth across the Atlantic, until my lawyer, what with one thing and another, eventually fell ill. Whether it was because of overwork, or because he had not developed the resistance that I had to all the diseases that feed on vacuum cleaner licence deal negotiators, he took to his bed for a period of weeks and from then on, as he got slower and slower, drafts of the contract became increasingly difficult to wheedle out of him.

I say I had developed resistance. I lie. One night, in the wee small hours, Deirdre came into the bathroom to find me rolling about on the floor with the worst headache a man ever had. She called the doctor the next morning (why do we British always wait till the morning?) and I was taken to hospital where I was diagnosed, by means of a six-inch needle being inserted up my backbone, as having viral meningitis. I was laid up, then, for a couple of months, watching cricket on the telly, while my little team beavered, and my lawyer fiddled. Until one day the virus finally passed, in just a few hours.

In business things were not so easily solved, but the licence deal was creaking towards completion. By November 1987, we had a deal laid out on paper, and were licking our ballpoints and dipping our quills, in readiness for the exchange of signatures when, on the twenty-third, at about half past six in the evening, the sky fell in.

I was closing up the coach house for the evening, just turning the key in the lock, when Deirdre came out into the gloaming to tell me that Alan Millman (the Iona Chief Executive) was on the phone.

'Hi, James. I'm in a payphone outside Sears in Chicago,' he said. 'I've just been in there trying to sell them the Drytech. And there's ... well, there's a bit of a problem.'

'Is there a problem with the design again? Or is it the clear bin? I bet that's it, they don't like the clear bin because they think it's dirty.'

'It's worse than that, James.'

'They don't believe it works?'

'Oh they know it works, James ... They've got one already.'

'Whaaaaat?'

'The buyer's got a cyclonic vacuum cleaner just like yours in there. It's made by Amway.'

They license it, they say it doesn't work, they unlicence it, they get their money back, and then they bring out a dual cyclone themselves! I staggered backwards with the shock of it, and Deirdre noticed my skin drain of all colour. I was experiencing a terrible sense of *déjà vu*. It seemed to be just what had happened with the Ballbarrow. Quite apart from the fact that this put my whole licence agreement with Iona on the line, I felt at that moment that my closest personal property had been taken.

What was most unfair I felt was that I had invested all that money and all those years in research and development of my invention, and on patenting; I had had to borrow and pawn and risk the welfare of my own family and now some enormous organisation with more money and man hours than I could even dream of, were just going to get on with selling their version. They were out on the market before us, and, it transpired, they were claiming the credit for it. It would wreck the Iona agreement.

As soon as I had put the phone down, apart from a quick pause to roar like a wounded lion and smash a few close-at-hand domestic objects, I rang my US patent lawyer, Ian McLeod, and sent him on a mission to get hold of one of these things. Posing as a customer, he bought an Amway vacuum cleaner, and took photographs of a machine being demonstrated. These photos he sent to me by courier, and advised me, too, that at least four of my patents might be infringed. The offending beast itself arrived by post a few days later.

My first thoughts were, although it looked absolutely ghastly, it appeared to have my transparent bin, inside it was undoubtedly a dual cyclone, and it was sold with dry shampoo, yet another idea of mine. Hideous though it looked to me, I thought it was attempting the principles of my design, and looked very purposeful. God, I was angry.

Needless to say, I was by no means the only peeved party. Iona froze with terror, like a gerbil transfixed by the stare of a cobra. And I felt that cold tingle in my spine that told me my troubles were far from over. Just when I thought that particular chapter was closed, my legal battles in America began again, and, with them, the fear that my cyclone was doomed for ever.

Iona's first move was to seek legal advice on the likelihood of their succeeding in a law suit against Amway. Patent actions are always very hard to fight in America, because it is such a competitive culture – with laws that have grown up to protect that competitiveness – that anything that might prevent competition, such as strong patents, tends to be undermined, and relatively easy to challenge successfully in court.

We were, however, advised that we had a good case, and for a reason that I would never have guessed at. In America, you see, we could add to the alleged patent infringement a charge of 'misappropriation of confidential information'. And it was, apparently, the fact that I was claiming I had handed over information (as well as drawings and technology) in confidence, and trusted them with it, that could swing a jury my way. And so we could fight. But first Iona wanted to renegotiate.

'We'll look after the court case,' they said. 'But you will pay for it, out of your royalties. And, since the deal is not now nearly so strong as it was, you will be getting less than half of the annual minimum royalty we agreed. But the deal is still on, if you want it.'

What choice did I have? It was either accept that or go looking for another licensee, one who would be prepared to go into competition with Amway. I signed the revised deal with a heavy heart, and we got on with tackling the lawsuit.

Having learnt from the Ballbarrow case that out-of-town lawyers rarely triumph in America, we hired a lawyer from the town where the case was being heard. We (which is to say, Iona, Prototypes Ltd, and James Dyson) sued Amway on various counts, including patent infringement, misappropriation of confidential information, and importantly for me the damage caused to my reputation.

Of course, this is my telling of the story, not Amway's. Indeed, they steadfastly denied that they had done anything wrong and countersued for damages from me.

Nonetheless, our litigator, a very bright lawyer called Dick Baxter, was confident that we would prevail in the end, despite the fact that we had to fight several interim battles, including, to my amazement, one about whether our own lawyers would be able to stay on the case. They referred to me as an 'alien', apparently trying to turn the whole thing into a sort of *Star Trek* episode where they were defending the universe. All of this cost us a lot of money.

As the months, and eventually years, of the case dragged on I began to encounter other difficulties. Iona were not really going about selling the Drytech in the right way, I felt, and sales were not doing particularly well. Nor were they making enough effort, I thought, to get the Fantom (as the vacuum cleaner is now called) on the market. Worst of all, I was not making any money from the sales of the Drytech that they *were* making, because my royalties were all being gobbled up by the lawsuit. It seemed to me that the best thing for me to do would be to terminate the licence altogether. I was paying the legal fees anyway, so I could quite easily negotiate a new licence with someone else, and with a new company selling the products better than Iona, I could pay the legal fees with a portion of my new royalties. My lawyers advised that I had a good case for terminating, on the grounds that Iona were not using their best endeavours with the Fantom and, in May 1989, that is exactly what I did.

Iona, needless to say, were extremely miffed, and immediately filed a high court action in Toronto, suing me for $12 million for wrongful termination of the licence agreement. The whole thing blew up like a hydrogen bomb and, endeavouring to keep the thing out of court, we ended up sitting round a table for ages renegotiating.

In the end, we arrived at a fair and equitable settlement, which saw us splitting the legal costs between us, and agreeing to split any eventual winnings. Iona agreed to hand back to us the rights to a number of countries, and we were all the best of friends once again.

In time the project began to show a profit, and I was able to look around for further diversification. With products on the go in America and Japan even the stigma of the ongoing litigation couldn't put off the great Johnson Wax, who tracked me down after seeing a newspaper article about the court case.

'We've heard all about your troubles with Amway,' they said, 'but we'll be different. We just want to license your technology for the commercial market.'

Since Iona had licensed only the upright retail market, this was a great opportunity. They proposed a tank vacuum cleaner and a backpack cleaner (called 'Rocket-Vac') to be sold exclusively to industry and commercial cleaners. For romantic reasons, I insisted that we signed our deal in their Frank Lloyd Wright building in Racine, Wisconsin, which I suppose I thought was important symbolically. But symbolism or no symbolism, I wasn't about to turn down a fat cheque for £120,000, and on 29 September 1990, I flew out there and signed, and their lovely, completely seethrough tank cleaner was on the market in less than a year.

By late 1990, I was able to look about me and take stock. I was no longer in the kind of terrible debt that had plagued me for so long, I had the G-Force still going strong after three years in Japan, bringing in no more and no less than £60,000 every year. I had North America sewn up with the Drytech. And with the Johnson Wax deal my cyclonic system would now be available worldwide to all commercial cleaners.

The fly in the ointment? The lawsuit in America, rumbling like a volcano in the background, costing me about £300,000 a year for the last three years, worrying me and scaring my family.

But, hey ho. Life goes on. I still fancied a crack at the British upright vacuum cleaner market – the place where it had all begun, and the scene of my first rejections. By little and little I would circle back towards that market again, and prove all my British detractors wrong. I had a dry-shampooer, a pink and lavender oriental niche product, a back-pack and a tank. People were getting the point bit by bit. But when I tore the bag off my Hoover Junior and stuck a cardboard cyclone on it, I had bigger fish in mind. And it was time to fry them.

Freedom!

The last piece in the jigsaw doesn't quite fit. Can I go it alone?
Settlement at last.

By the time I got a call from Vax, early in 1991, asking if we could build them an upright vacuum cleaner for the British market – a notion put to them by Jeffrey Pike – I was already beginning to feel the world growing lighter on my shoulders. Royalties were rolling in now from our various licensees, as well as down-payments and design fees for new products. My little staff at the coach house and I were designing vacuum cleaners, and other bits and bobs, for our current licensees, and the Vax deal looked like the final piece in the jigsaw. Their offer was reasonable, with £75,000 front money, so I signed up and we began designing a prototype immediately. Within six months we had the model and all the final drawings complete, and we got them to Vax just before New Year, 1991.

But there was no sign of them starting production for a while.

Then I started to make enquiries.

'Oh, we don't like the design of the handle,' they would say. 'We think it's a bit weak.'

And so I would redesign the handle. And we would hear nothing for a while. And then they would find something else that needed fiddling with. After eight months like this – it was now July – it became clear to me that they could go on procrastinating indefinitely, and never go into production. I doubt that there was anything malicious in it, it is unlikely they would have signed up just to keep the technology off the market, but the faffing about and general lack of commitment was infuriating.

My mistake, I have to say, had been not insisting on a trigger date for the minimum royalties when I originally negotiated the deal. And you do not sign a licence agreement without a trigger date, otherwise it can run and run for ever without your ever getting paid anything. I had argued this with the chairman of Vax, Alan Brazier, and he had flatly refused to have a trigger date in the agreement.

'We'll be going into production as soon as possible, James,' he had said. 'Don't worry. There'll be no need for a trigger date.'

'Great,' I had replied. 'If you're going into production as early as possible, we can have a nice early trigger date.'

But he was having none of it. So when, after completing a major redesign that Vax had demanded, I again heard nothing until September, I rang Brazier and said simply, 'If you're not going to make the damn thing, I will.'

'You can't!' He squawked. 'We're the exclusive licensee.'

'I don't care, you're not getting on with it, and I'm bored of waiting. I'm going into production myself.'

'We'll sue you!' he threatened.

'You better do it quickly, matey,' I replied. 'I can hear those production lines cranking up already.'

It was then that Brazier made the great mistake of writing to us, in a fit of pique, and cancelling the agreement himself. Then Vax subsequently sued us for several million pounds. And we sued them right back, for several more million pounds, for not using their best endeavours. But we eventually settled up and parted company for good.

But for the moment, for two years in fact, I had two mega-lawsuits raging on at once. To distract myself I began designing a new tank vacuum cleaner for the retail market, for Prototypes Ltd, specifically with the British market in mind, which would subsequently be licensed to another UK company, Dyson Appliances, as soon as it could be started up.

With no capital, and most of our income going straight into the Amway case, there was no way I would be able to go into production without some outside investment. When I started out with the Ballbarrow I had approached a man called David Williams, whose plastics company, W.C.B., built all our tooling and then recouped the money in instalments as we began to sell, rather like a hire purchase agreement. He was now running a company called Linpak which, quite handily for me, was Britain's biggest plastic processor.

Williams and I thrashed out a similar deal for the vacuum cleaner as we had come to with the Ballbarrow, but the legal sparrows, as usual, bogged everything down with endless restrictive agreements and made an aardvark's lunch of the whole thing. As our legal fees, just to get a bit of tooling made so we could think about manufacturing, soared to £45,000 in a matter of days, I began to consider forgetting the whole thing and doing something else with my life.

Then a wonderful thing happened out of nowhere. But, as the Wizard of Oz tells us, that is often the way with cyclones. In short, we experienced the sort of release the Munchkins felt when that little wooden house, picked up by the cyclone, fell from the sky and landed on the wicked witch in the middle of a ditch. Which was not a happy situation for the wicked witch.

Or let me put it another way.

Leaving the lawyers to continue wrangling over the details of the agreement with Linpak, I had taken off for a holiday in Provence with Deirdre, where we planned to discuss our future. Perhaps it would be best, we decided, if I backed out of the Amway lawsuit. All this money that I was pouring into the Amway case I would much rather be using for more productive things. At that stage it looked as if the case, like the Jarndyce and Jarndyce case in *Bleak House*, could go on for ever, and subsume the lives of all those concerned. I am not one to give up, but there comes a point when you realise that you are not going to live forever, and I wanted to do more with my life than haggle over pennies and give endless legal depositions. Deirdre was often tougher than me in this matter, and would insist that we hang on and fight after spending so much.

One evening we were discussing these things over a glass of wine, listening to the crickets sing, and seeing the world in that mellow perspective that makes all your troubles seem so small, and all your battles the less worth fighting, when the phone rang.

It was Dick Baxter.

'Guess what?' he said.

I couldn't.

'We are talking, about resolving the case.'

However, no settlement had yet been reached when I was due to fly to America to make a further deposition. After checking in my baggage at Heathrow I was heading towards the departure gate when it occurred to me to phone Dick Baxter. I was gazing up at the boarding times on the computer screen when I heard him pick up the phone.

'It's all over, James. They don't need your deposition now. We've ...' But the last word was lost in a crackle of static. I didn't need to hear it, though, to grin with relief. No more legal fees.

And so I turned round, walked back to the check-in desk, retrieved my baggage and my ticket money, walked out of Terminal 4 into the bright English sunshine, collected my car and drove home, with Baxter's words singing in my ears.

It is safe to say that this was the greatest turning point in my life since the day I tore the bag off my Hoover. Coming at a time when my single largest problem was a shortage of funds to produce my own vacuum cleaner, the fact that I would no longer be haemorrhaging thousands into legal fees was like a gift from Heaven. That leak in the cash flow, that had only days before made me consider giving up altogether, was now finally plugged – like the fabled Dutch kid putting his finger in a dyke. Better still, Amway kept their product on the market and we became joint licensees as well. So we dismissed our lawsuit against Amway, they dismissed their lawsuit against me, and all of us, including Iona, got on with the business of selling vacuum cleaners.

With the lawsuit out of the way, I did not feel the same financial midget that I had before, and with the dealings with Linpak now getting so protracted, I decided to give up on them, and try again to produce the thing myself. Not that there was any need to take all the risk upon myself and borrow myself into penury again. Better, I felt, to use someone else's money, and give them a bit of equity in return. First call, naturally, was the merchant banks.

The response was incredible. Every single one wanted to know how much I was putting up myself; that was what they were most interested in.

'Listen,' I would say. 'We are ready to launch. All we need is £750,000 for tooling. I have already spent £1.5 million on patenting, and the patents are as tight as a full vacuum cleaner bag. And I have spent £2–3 million over the past twelve years on developing this system. As a result I have a full and illustrious product history in Japan and America, and there is no question either of the technology working, or of the customer response to that technology. We just need the last bit of money to get tooled up and hit the shops.'

'Fine, fine,' the bankers would say. 'But we put up this three-quarters of a million, how much are you putting up?'

'I just told you. I have already put in about £4 million, and the last twelve years of my life...'

'Yes, yes but what are you actually putting on the table now?'

This was the attitude I got from, to name only four out of eight or nine, Close Bros., Alan Patricoff Associates, Charterhouse Investments, and even 3I, who are supposedly revered as the most daring of venture capitalists. These damn bean-counters could not see past the cold cash. The valuing of money, now, here, where I can see it, over ideas, designs, experience, even money already invested, is yet another legacy of the Thatcher generation. The man with the readies is the man with the voice. Once you have spent your money, no matter what it has bought, you no longer have a voice.

There were, I must admit, one or two banks who were vaguely interested, but only as long as I did not run the business myself. 'You are a designer, Dyson,' they would cackle, 'what do you know about business?'

'Excuse me. But I have run a lot of businesses very successfully indeed. And for the last twelve years I have been running a Research and Development business, which, as you know, is the most difficult kind of business to run.'

'Not the point, Mr Dyson. We are the ones putting up money now, and that is what determines the issues.'

I was tearing my hair out as these doors were slammed in my face for the most obtuse reasons. The poor buggers were so wrong, to think that designers knew nothing about business, or about marketing, or about selling. It is the people who make the things that understand them, and understand what the public wants. It is men like these bankers who, by stripping the builders and makers of power, have run Britain into the ground.

I applied to the Welsh Development Agency, a quango that doles out funding for the Welsh Office, with a plan to build the thing in Wales. At first they gave me the old 'if there were a better vacuum cleaner Hoover or Electrolux would have invented it' line. But when they saw the prototype they loved it. I made my application through one of four large Cardiff accountancy firms insisted upon by the Welsh Office, at a cost of £20,000. As the drawings were passed on up the echelons, each successive bean-counter rejected it, and then fell for it on seeing the prototype.

Eventually it was put up for funding at a meeting with the Welsh Office while I was in Italy negotiating tooling prices, and was rejected out of hand by the then Welsh Secretary, David Hunt. It did not surprise me. Have you *seen* David Hunt?

Everyone else at the Welsh Office, apparently, was dead keen on the cyclone, but Hunt insisted that 'if there were a better kind of vacuum cleaner ...' and also that the project was seriously under-funded. Everyone else thought the project was adequately funded, and for months afterwards the Welsh Office kept hassling me to reapply. But I was adamant. Either they took it as it was, or left it altogether.

David Hunt was unmoved. And so I told them, as James Robertson Justice said to Dick Van Dyke in *Chitty-Chitty Bang-Bang* (when rejecting his proposal for Toot Sweets): 'Had yer chance. Muffed it.'

Balls to the government then, and balls to the merchant banks. I'd have to borrow after all. But £750,000, or thereabouts, was a hell of a loan to go asking my local bank manager for.

My first application to Lloyds was rejected out of hand by their head office at Swansea. But I was very lucky to come upon an unusual bank manager called Mike Page who appealed the decision on my behalf and got me my loan: £600,000 with my home in Chelsea and my home in Bath as security. I can only record, once again, my astonishment at Deirdre's preparedness, after putting up with so much already, to let our family homes be put at risk again.

All that remained to be done was to order the tooling and get on with producing the vacuum cleaner.

Hang on, though. What vacuum cleaner? I have got so excited talking about the filthy lucre that I forgot what this was all about. The lovely Mr Page sure as hell didn't hand over more than half a million quid without seeing what we were spending it on. And that was the first, the very beautiful, upright Dyson Dual Cyclone.

But when last I talked of vacuum cleaners, we were still planning to make a wet-dry carpet shampooing tank machine to compete with Vax. We were very enamoured of their market share, which was 800,000 machines a year, as compared to 800,000 cylinder machines, and 1.1 million uprights. The thing about their particular market sector was that we could really clean it up.

With conventional technology, wet cleaning was a nightmare. When cleaning dry you had to fit a bag into your machine, and when cleaning wet you had to take the bag out and then fit a float valve to stop it overflowing. You could only do one job at a time, and after a wet clean the palaver involved in tipping out the water, drying the machine, and fitting a bag, made the whole thing a nonsense. We knew that those 800,000 customers a year could be ours in no time.

But consumer tests had shown that people were finding it quite hard work to use, and while ours was a far superior product to that with which Vax had taken their third of the market, it was not really in the spirit of my original invention.

As far as cleaning carpets was concerned, we discovered that it was just as effective to simply sprinkle the dry cleaning powder on the carpet and then vacuum it up, a task that an upright vacuum cleaner could do perfectly well, and without all the drawbacks of a wet-dry system – such as leaving tide-marks on the carpet, and having to empty water down the loo, and all that.

Blinded by the Vax market share, we had drifted away from the original principle, and were not, in short, being true to ourselves. It would be far better to make a machine very similar to the G-Force, which had already proved itself. We could always sell a dry-cleaning powder with the machine – the success of Shake 'n' Vac had shown that even if people didn't believe our system could actually clean carpets, the public was already attuned to the idea of sprinkling powder on a carpet before vacuuming, just to make it smell nice. Shake 'n' Vac, after all, did nothing at all except leave a faint, nasty smell behind, and people had bought that.

With no figures to back up our feelings, it was a fairly momentous decision to make, sitting out in the coach house, to change direction like that. But we did. And that was how the Dyson Dual Cyclone was conceived. A gestation period similar to that of a human baby was to follow, until May 1992, in which the new model could be designed (and persuade the delightful Mr Page to do his thing). Time, as it were, for the foetus to grow fingers and toes.

The Dyson Dual Cyclone

Grappling with the octopus. Come over here if you think you're hard enough. We throw the dual cyclone over the balcony, regularly. No unnecessary knobs, but something special for the tools. Colour me silver. And a little mellow yellow. A bin with a view. And, finally, a design philosophy.

A vacuum cleaner designed entirely by me, incorporating innovations up to the very latest point at which my technology had arrived, to be produced and marketed and sold under my own exclusive direction was, to be frank, what this whole thing had been all about.

I had gathered around myself a small team by this time – whom I was able to pay out of the royalties from Japan and America – and we worked together in the coach house at the end of the garden, which had been so unpromising when I first moved in, deprived of power, water, light and heat, but was by now a rather impressive workshop and office which I had built and restored gradually over the years of development.

The team consisted of four designer engineers straight out of the RCA – Simeon Jupp, Peter Gammack, Gareth Jones, and Mark Bickerstaffe – all in their twenties, a marvellous bunch, whose presence made me feel as if I was freshly sprogged from the Royal College myself, and helped me to forget the wrinkles and grey hairs that the years of struggle had given me. And there was also Judith Hughes, who marshalled us all, organised everything and generally kept us in shape – resilient, resourceful, funny, ungetdownable, and blessed with an imperious voice that strikes terror into the strongest hearts, she is what would once have been called 'a brick' and, having made herself immediately indispensable, she is with us to this day.

This was not a collection of underlings with me bossing them about, by any means. We were a band on a mission to design a vacuum cleaner that could challenge the world, and it was bloody exciting. With this team, at last, I could put into unhindered practice all the things I believed, about the interdependency of design and function, about the way in which aesthetic perfection could be generated out of the engineering principles of the work, rather than being used to hide them, and about enabling the consumer to understand the technological benefits of new products, by using them to make the products fun.

A prime example of making a piece of technology fun, and then making the same thing again, but not fun, is the telescopic hose. When you push the yellow button on your Dual Cyclone handle today, and pull out the hose for space-age suction in all the irritating nooks and crannies and high-up places that the cleaner otherwise cannot reach, it all seems effortless and obvious – and I do genuinely believe that people enjoy doing it, customer feedback suggests that it is one of the favourite functions, and one of the things that has made the Dual Cyclone the first vacuum cleaner to be really popular with men. But no one could imagine the time and hassle that went into making that work so sweetly. It is all down to the instant changeover valve, so that you can just pull the thing out with a satisfying 'thwwupp' and suck all the rotting bits of human and canine epidermis from, say, above the door lintel.

But when, after my demonstrating it to them in 1982, Electrolux included my hose on a 1986 model of theirs, they had not bothered with the valve; they had just incorporated the hose so they could say they had one. Their sales department made great play of what they called, dramatically, 'above-floor cleaning', but to do this 'above-floor cleaning', you had to fiddle with the hose for nearly a minute to get it ready. They thought they had the feature, but they had lost the very core of it, which was its instantaneousness – it was supposed to make hose suction as easy as it is with a cylinder cleaner.

Then they claimed that they were the first to *have* a hose, the buggers, and put it in all their publicity. Well, I soon put a stop to that. But they had been able to take advantage of the fact that we were not yet in production with it in Europe (although we were in Japan). In falling over ourselves to make the changeover seal work perfectly, which was a hell of a job, we had slowed ourselves down hugely. They, not as bogged down by perfectionism as I was, could get something hose-shaped out on the market as soon as they wanted. And for us, afterwards, to try to show how much better ours was because of the quality of instant switch over, was not as easy as offering it to a public that had never seen anything like it. And Electrolux knew that.

But this fastidiousness of mine was to prove my strength in the long run.

Any little design improvement that you try to make will inevitably be used to exploit you by your opposition. For example, when Hoover were getting rattled by our success, they decided to claim that their machines had much greater suck than ours. They attempted to prove this by orchestrating a publicity stunt in which they presented a thing they called a suction gauge which they put over the nozzle of their hose, and then over ours. It covered the inlet completely and purported to register a pressure reading. The Hoover won.

Of course the Hoover won. For I had been worried, when developing the hose, that its size and shape, coupled with its tremendous power, represented a real danger to children, who might have an eye sucked out if they chose, as a child is bound to, to peer down it to see what was going on. And so I gave the nozzle not only bleed valves, but what is called a cod's mouth opening (it looks like a fish with an open mouth) and put that within a wider, prepuce-like casing, with slots in it, so that the point of suck could not be completely covered, either by an eye, or by a suction gauge. And thus we 'failed' their silly test. (At the time I was conceiving this I phoned Moorfield's Eye Hospital in London, and asked the nurse, to whom I was put through, how much pressure it would take to suck out an eyeball. After asking if this was a hoax call, she told me that it actually takes quite a lot of pressure – she knew this, she said, because she often put the nozzle of her own vacuum cleaner against her eye. Bizarre!)

The thing about inventing is that it is a continual and continuous process, and it is fluid. Inventions generate further inventions. In fact, that is where most inventions come from. They very rarely come out of nothing. So while it was the Dual Cyclone that was the basis of my first vacuum cleaner, as I went on to develop it over the next twelve years, and, crucially, in the nine months before bringing out the DC-01 (as it was to be called), dozens of other innovations were generated along the way.

Having gone up this blind alley, then, with the wet and dry tank cleaner, my little team and I were going full curved-turbine-fan ahead to produce an upright, and make up the time we had lost in that conceptual cul-de-sac.

Upstairs, which was the office, we designed every detail on computer, and downstairs in the 'factory', we made our models. It was a fantastic environment to work in, for it was just engineers and designers, and no one to mess us around. There were no salesmen, no advertising people, no marketing managers, to interfere and try to guide us in their direction. We had nothing to do but deduce our own dream product. There was no market research and there were no focus groups; it was, to be frank, a designer's wet dream. It was unique. The world just isn't like that. You were not supposed to do things like that, just go ahead and do it all on your own, and then order a million pounds' worth of tooling. It felt almost naughty. People just didn't know what we were up to, and we occasionally found a severe credibility problem, if no credit problem, such that when it came to buying tooling, or anything at all, we were expected to pay cash up front, to alleviate the worries of more conventional businessmen.

And yet we were to become businessmen ourselves, to metamorphose and begin crossing boundaries, as we ordered tooling and began to instruct manufacturers, following the path of my long-cherished dream that designers could lead business from the front. But before that, there was a product to design.

The basic body shape would be a quotation of the G-Force, but I wanted the new machine to look more aeronautical, more engineered, as opposed to the guts-hanging out, everything-on-display style of the pink machine.

In the first instance we contrived to tuck all the ducting away inside the body and make it a bit more discreet, less like a space-octopus wrestling with itself. We also made the cyclone and bin much more prominent, to make a greater display of the single most important technological advance.

We made hundreds of little technical improvements to the cyclone, and to the cleaner head, and at the same time concentrated on reducing the number of screws, joins, and parts in the finished design – this would concentrate our minds on the essence of the function, and force the form to follow it most efficiently, and also, most importantly since we never knew how much money we were going to have to put the thing in production, it could keep down the amount of tooling we needed (at about £20,000 a mould, any part we could possibly do without was rejected, *sans* ceremony).

All these stipulations were part of a dream I had – and had had ever since following Dan Dare through the pages of the *Eagle* back in the fifties – of making the product look like a piece of NASA technology.

Crucial to that idea, was indestructibility. We used ABS for the body, which is a plastic with a very high rubber (butadiene) content, and for the transparent bin a plastic called polycarbonate, the type of material used for shop windows in dodgy areas that is impervious to bricks and baseball bats (what Mr Blair might call 'zero tolerance' design).

In the drive for durability I had a great advantage in the year or so I had spent developing the two industrial cleaners for our licence with Johnson Wax (both known as 'Vectron', the tank version was a particular joy, with its totally transparent bin that gave 360 degrees of visibility for total cyclone-vision, and which looked like R2D2's younger and more sophisticated brother). An industrial cleaner has to survive being used for eight hours a day, every day, for the whole of its life, in environments much tougher and dirtier than the average domestic scene, and it was to that sort of specification that I constructed the DC-01, which is why it is very popular in commercial use itself.

I suppose every engineer is familiar with the standard hammer test, and we certainly spent plenty of time battering our machines, but we also had something much nastier in store. The ground floor of the coach house was marble, and the steps down from the office were cast iron. Many were the hapless dual cyclones tossed over the banister rail to bounce down the iron staircase and crash onto the marble. In retrospect it seems a bizarre extent to have taken our testing to, and perhaps a bit puerile. One of us would hoik the thing over the banister and then we'd all crouch down and cover our ears, like embattled trench soldiers, for it made a hell of a noise. I suppose it went some way to relieving the tension of so many hours on the job, but it certainly did nothing for the floor.

It was also at this time that I put together our first live test rig, a robotic arm that grasped the vacuum cleaner and pushed it backwards and forwards over the same bit of carpet – rather like a car mechanic's rolling road, twenty-four hours a day, seven days a week, for months on end. It presented an invaluable guide to the stamina of the machine, but, since it would vacuum away all night while we slept, and all weekend regardless of whether we were there or not, we were a little concerned about the fire risk.

Unable to afford a sprinkler system, we devised one of our own: a very long hose was trailed in from a tap in the garden, tacked to the wall, and across the ceiling to a point directly above the test rig. There, the remaining hose was coiled and attached, and the end firmly sealed. The tap was left permanently open. This way, we reckoned, if the rig overheated, or short-circuited, and caught fire, the flames would melt the hose, and bring the water spraying down to douse the inferno. Fortunately, we never did find out whether it worked.

Once you have ensured the stamina and strength of your space technology, the next thing is to do away with any gimmicks and gewgaws that might snap off or burn up during re-entry. There would, in short, be no silly knobs and buttons, such as air-fresheners and pile selecting dials. The design of vacuum cleaners, and most other domestic appliances has in recent years been beset by these pointless distractions purporting to offer futuristic advantages, which they patently do not. All those bits and bobs have more to do with lazy designers trying to make dull technology and poorly designed products look more interesting. The Japanese had insisted upon a pile selector, because they really are function fetishists, but I knew such things were unnecessary and would have nothing of the kind anywhere near my DC-01.

It was easier for us, as designers working apart from salesmen, to exclude the 'bells and whistles' because we were simply designing our own ideal product without worrying about marketing demands. When it came to talking to retailers, however, they always wanted to know where the height adjuster was. We would explain to them that we had designed a free-floating cleaner head that automatically adjusted to the pile of the carpet, or indeed to a stone or wood floor, but, for simple sales guff, I suppose the DC-01 appeared under-equipped.

We had no automatic internal flex recoil unit, for example, because it is quite simply quicker, on an upright, to loop the flex yourself onto the cleats on the handle, and it bypasses another frippery which can always go wrong.

And, of course, there was no vertical release pedal (which, in my experience, people always confuse with the on-switch pedal). Instead, we constructed the frame around a centre of gravity which meant that at 45°, the natural angle for cleaning, it would be perfectly balanced, and if you let go of it at any angle less than that, it would right itself. All you had to do to release it from the vertical was push the head down with your foot, for which we provided a little scalloped indent on each side (marked with a footprint lest one be confused). Each side, mind. For if someone like John Barnes or Chris Waddle bought one, we wouldn't want them to have to use their right foot, now, would we?

For further stability, the automatic hose would be connected to the base so that the machine would be pulled along after you, if you strayed too far while hosing, rather than just falling over. By the same token, two large wheels would make the Dyson easy to manoeuvre and turn, without scuffing, and make the climbing of steps considerably easier too.

All additional tools, such as car-cleaning attachments, brushes, and slimline nozzles for awkward crannies, would be integral, that is to say they would fit onto your cleaner so that they would not just be put away in a cupboard and forgotten, ignored because they were not in the right place at the right time, or, most likely, lost.

Perhaps the most important thing for that NASA look, however, was the colour. We wanted the body to look like it was made of machined aluminium, because that would best convey its nature as a crisp, high-tech product. Aluminium, of course, would have been far too heavy and far too expensive, but by taking an almost see-through plastic, and adding aluminium fleck to it, we were able to create a unique metal-effect plastic.

Aluminium is, in fact, a very good bonding agent and quite happy to go into the plastic, but it tended, in the early stages, to cause vein marks, like the marbling of fat on a piece of beef, where the waves of aluminium came together, and we only solved that by doing some flow analysis on computer to work out at what point the aluminium started to vein, and preventing it just before.

We introduced the bits of yellow for three reasons: because it emphasised the design, because no one else had ever done it, so we would own it, and because it made the product look fun. There was also something satisfactory in the way yellow is used for warning signs on building sites, and for hard hats. Even in nature, on wasps and tigers, yellow means 'Danger – keep away' and only added to the message of effectiveness: this machine was a predator.

Apart from anything else, the non-use of those tedious, homely blues and mulberries emphasised the engineered, high-tech nature of the machine. That bald, spangly look offers no concessions to domesticity, and while some consumers might have been put off by it at first, it was necessary to implant that feeling at the beginning.

As had been the case with the pink and lavender of the Cyclon and the G-Force, the silver and yellow came to be a major identification point for the DC-01. In the early days, when the public was only becoming aware of the Dyson, but did not know its name, people would often go into shops and ask if they had 'that silver and yellow one'.

In the beginning, our competitors sniggered at our colour scheme, but by 1996, when they had seen us swipe their markets, Hoover, Electrolux, and Miele all came out, simultaneously, with models bearing yellow features. Prevented from copying our technology, this was the best they could do. But the public wasn't fooled – they don't buy a domestic appliance for its colour alone, they buy it for its effectiveness, and they won't be parted from their money by colour association tricks.

That colour scheme was as close as anything on the machine got to be being done for 'designer' reasons. Everything was about function, and an over-designed look was the last thing I wanted – it is just that, as I will repeat to excess, the best looks come out of following the engineering. The ribs on the front of the handle, for example, were put there as a lightweight way of blending the shape of the ugly curve of the aluminium internal hose into the smoother lines of the body, and to make that point on the handle much stronger – the design byproduct of that is the suggestion of fin-cooling, a high-tech, motorbikey look.

The pre-motor electrostatic filter to the left of the cyclone, with its curved yellow fin, is there to capture – in tandem with the after-motor filter – the particles of carbon that come off the motor brushes as they wear down (to an effectiveness of 0.01 microns). These were pumped into the room by other vacuum cleaners. The 'design' effect is to have a little yellow fin, curved in reverse of the other curves, to break the symmetry. The way it slots in and out is for easy cleaning, but it has a satisfying similarity to the action of plugging in a video-game cartridge to its console, or loading a CD-Rom, for further high-tech credibility. Even the layering in the swing-out housing for the bin is as it is only because of the shape of the internal parts that slot into it – the fact that it looks 'art-deco-ey' has been noted, but was not why it was done.

I do protest too much, methinks. Back to the basics.

The bin, of course, would be transparent. This was perhaps the single most important feature. The most Brunellian thing of all. For it was this that would allow you to see the cyclone spinning, to see where the dirt was going, to understand how the thing was working. Many potential licensees had baulked at this idea, and Iona had produced tinted bins in America, because they thought it made the machine look untidy. Retailers often took the same view, and John Lewis tried to suggest that a tinted bin might be more seemly, when I first presented it to them. (We actually did produce a smoked plastic bin for them, which they tried in some of their stores early in 1994, but they came back to me not long afterwards, and said that they preferred the clear one, after all.)

But just as the Ballbarrow had stood out in showrooms because of both its utter oddness and its purposefulness, so the sight of a transparent vacuum cleaner full of rubbish would draw the eye of the potential customer. You see, it would have been very hard to convince the average person – who just wanted to buy the machine that will best clean his home – of this unbelievable, esoteric advantage that we were harping on about. He couldn't see it, so it might just as well have been the vapid sales trickery he was getting from everyone else. But if the customer sees a long line of pristine vacuum cleaners, and then this weird looking one on the end all visibly full of dirt, well, then it clearly works, doesn't it?

Another great bonus was what I think of as the 'German loo' principle. You get to see what you've done before you flush it away. It is always reassuring to know that the ten minutes you spent sucking around the sitting room wasn't wasted, and by seeing the vast amount of accumulated dirt in the bin for yourself, you know it was worth your while.

Better still, if you accidentally suck up something you don't want to throw out, like money, pen lids, stamps, gerbils, you will probably see it in the bin when you've finished vacuuming. You can even use it as a way of finding things you think you have lost. A lunch guest of mine in the South of France once thought she had lost her diamond engagement ring out by the pool. I vacuumed around the garden for a while until, after about ten minutes, I spotted the ring spinning round the cyclone. (Warning: do not try this at home.)

You can never tell what effect an original design feature will have on people, and it can be all things to all men. A journalist who came to interview me once asked, 'The area where the dirt collects is transparent, thus parading all our detritus on the outside, and turning the classic design inside out. Is this some post-modernist nod to the architectural style pioneered by Richard Rodgers at the Pompidou Centre, where the air-conditioning and escalators, the very guts, are made into a self-referential design feature?'

'No,' I replied. 'It's so you can see when it's full.'

There will always be detractors though, from anything innovative, and a few people just couldn't handle it. My favourite piece of wisdom on the subject, I think, was uttered by a member of the public whose opinion was solicited on an edition of the *Money Programme*. Asked by the interviewer what he thought of the DC-01's transparent bin, he said, in that typically British way, 'somehow it just doesn't seem right. Know what I mean?'

I have often, over the years, been asked what my design philosophy is, or my philosophy of invention, and I have occasionally tried to put it on paper for those who do ask. It is a difficult thing to reduce to simple points, because so much of it just exists in my mind, a weird concoction of things I have seen and learnt. But it might look something like this:

i) No one ever had an idea staring at a drawing board

So do not do this. I always rather liked Francis Bacon's analogy of the Spider and the Bee (I think it was Francis Bacon). A spider, he explained, works entirely upon himself, and from within himself, and produces only poison, whereas a bee works on raw materials, deriving his product from nature at large, and produces honey. (Or something like that. I probably failed whichever subject they told me that in).

At any rate, Bacon always got his ideas from walking in the countryside and observing nature, rather than sitting in his study. So get out and look at things, and when an idea comes, grab it, write it down, and play with it until it works. Don't sit and expect ideas to come. (Always bear in mind, though, that Bacon died of pneumonia, trying to invent frozen chicken.)

ii) Everyday products sell

Although it is harder to improve a mature product, if you succeed there is no need to create a market – something Clive Sinclair's C5, for example, could have done with. As before, thinking in a vacuum (forgive me) is not going to help. Try out current products in your own home, and make a list of things that you don't like about them – I found about twenty things wrong with my Hoover Junior at the first attempt.

iii) New technology

It may sound obvious, but many of the things that people write to me saying they have 'invented', interesting and useful though they are, are only modifications of existing technology, and can thus be copied by anyone under law. The thing about truly new technology is that it makes your invention patentable. And then no one can copy it.

You will find that in the case of almost anything you dream up, someone, somewhere, may have done something vaguely similar before. This being the case, your job, in seeking a patent, is to point out how original and unique what *you* are doing is, compared to what they did. This is often extremely difficult, particularly at the US patent office (as I have mentioned before), and patent officers can be very obstreperous people.

When you try to patent something it is likely to cost you £20,000. If, that is, it goes through first time. But that seldom happens. When I was trying to get one of my patents in the US, I had a particularly difficult examiner who kept having time off for mental problems of some kind. She would agree that what we were doing was unique – thus paving the way for the patent to be approved – and then we'd get a rejection letter from her six weeks later, and have to start all over again. It cost us $150,000 in patent attorney fees just to get that one patent through her.

Patenting being as expensive as it is, there is only any point in seeking patents in countries that are major consumers or producers, because you can get people for infringement either at the place they are making it, or where they sell it. I couldn't afford the luxury of patenting the cyclone in, for example, Mexico.

Proving that you have new technology can be extremely difficult. I have mentioned 'prior art' before, and for most inventions you might come up with there is quite likely to be a bit of it, lurking somewhere, in some form or another. Nobody needs to have tried building it, they just have to have had the idea.

Prior art does not even have to have been patented, only published. The tragic tale of the windsurfer is a good example. The original idea was developed by some boys from California, who just stuck a mast on top of a board. The problem was that every time the sail went over, the board went over too. So they introduced a rig with a universal joint, and came up with the wishbone as a means of holding the sail, rather than, as in other boats, a rope. They developed this marvellous craft in the good old Edisonian way, and made a huge success of it. And then someone challenged the patent. It turned out that some irritating bugger had written a letter to a yachting magazine, ten years before, explaining how you could have a mask with a flexible joint at the bottom, and he had included a sketch. He hadn't patented it, he hadn't solved all the little problems, he hadn't made it work, but that's prior art. The magazine published it, and ten years later it killed the patent for the windsurfer, and everyone was allowed to copy it.

(It was a similar thing that rendered me powerless when my hose appeared on the Electrolux. When we filed our original patent for it, we discovered that some twit in America, back in the 1920s, had put a hose on the back of an upright vacuum cleaner, but had never made it work, and had never gone into production. And yet that was enough to undermine my patent for an operationally perfect version, sixty years later.)

The terrible tyranny of patents, however, is that the costs do not end when you get your approval. Thereafter you will be charged enormous sums to renew your patents every year – up to £2,000 per country per year in some cases. And this is money that you, as a small inventor, are unlikely to be able to spare, because you will not have turned your invention into a profitable business yet. In Britain it is not as high as in some countries, but it can still be up to £400 a year.

I believe that an invention is a piece of creative art, like a book or a song, and *those* don't require annual renewal fees. If I cannot afford an annual renewal fee – which is simply some spod stamping a piece of paper – why should the patent office be able to steal it from me? The legal establishment argues that these fees are an incentive to stop people sitting on technological breakthroughs. But that is patent rubbish. Quite literally. The whole thing is clearly stacked in favour of the big companies, to whom the fees mean relatively little, and against the small innovator.

This is, I believe, a human rights issue. And I am, at time of writing, taking the DTI to the European Court of Human Rights over it.

iv) The Edisonian principle

Engineering is a state of mind, or at least a method of working. You *can* become expert on anything in six months, but steer clear of projects that require too much maths, and stick to empirical things. You can achieve major breakthroughs by a bit of lateral thinking, and this approach will often lead to new inventions being born of each other (just as, for example, the Dual Cyclone came out of the Ballbarrow).

Keep testing and retesting and believe only the evidence of your own eyes, not of formulae or of other people's opinions. You may have to fly in the face of public opinion, and market research. They can only tell you what *has* happened. No research can tell you what is *going* to happen.

v) Constant revolution

Not an imprecation to espouse a Marxist-Leninist theory of history, but constantly to rethink and improve every aspect and function, never being satisfied until you have solved *every* problem. Do that, and you can be sure of consistently and reliably outperforming the opposition. The thing about solving functional problems at every level, and to as high a degree of perfection as possible, is not only that it will result in greater consumer satisfaction, but that it will lead to further patents.

And further patents are crucial. A patent only lasts for twenty years, and that is not as long as it sounds. Look at the way Qualcast, and everyone else, pounced on the flymower as soon as Flymo's patent expired. Now if I had stopped with my initial invention I might be in a similar sort of danger. But by continuing to improve my technology over that time, I have now accumulated over 100 different patents on the machine, many of them cyclonic improvement patents, which will lengthen indefinitely our period of exclusivity.

The only way to keep possession of your invention is to keep strengthening it.

vi) Expressive design

I think we have established that it is what is inside that is important. To start thinking from the outside is to doom the project from the outset. If your first thought, as a computer designer, for example, is that keyboards ought to be cruciform, dimpled, and purple, with fluffy bits on the corners and a slight smell of rose-hip, then you have probably not come up with anything useful or patentable.

But once you have established your technology, then you can produce a design that accentuates it. (Perhaps that is what they were going on about all those years ago at the Byam Shaw Art School, when they made us start in the middle, and wouldn't let us draw outlines.)

Good design, generated out of the function of the thing, will explain why it is better, and why it should be bought. If it looks 'the business' or 'the bollocks' (I interchange these two synonyms to suit my audience) then it will present the impression of its own effectiveness.

One of my great heroes, Alec Issigonis, who invented the Mini – a postwar design classic – in 1959, believed that design was about integrating new technology to improve function, not simply about styling. His space-saving placement of the engine, and an oil supply that served both engine and gearbox, were as important in its success as the way it looked – a look which, of course, accentuated its technological advantages.

'If you style a car it goes out of date,' he said. And a production run that lasted more than thirty years proved him right.

Products can only begin to be beautiful when they work well. And then you can allow the form to follow the function. *Then* be different for its own sake. Then make it orange and red, or pink and lavender, or silver and grey. Go further, there is nothing wrong with making the consumer laugh. That is why we had publicity pictures with us riding on the Ballbarrow, and with Deirdre and Sam and I pushing DC-01s round the garden. A product can have a humanoid quality. While all the ribs and fins tend to make the DC-01 look like a piece of aeronautic equipment, they also make it look a little as though it were breathing, and that is accentuated on the G-Force with its pink colour and the curves of the tubes. The DC-02, of which more later, has also been described as looking like a big bug. And as you pull it around the house behind you it can sometimes seem, out of the corner of your eye, to resemble some twenty-first century robo-pet.

Conventional looks do not make a product more marketable. How is the poor customer to know it is different from the rest, if it looks the same? If I had followed the existing vacuum-cleaning idiom, then my lovely technology would still be sitting in a warehouse, unseen, unappreciated, and unloved (unruvved, even).

vii) Stamina and conviction

Painful but true. Breaking the mould will upset people. Challenging sitting tenants will be tough. It will take longer than you ever imagined. Ten years of development? Do you fancy that? And then negotiations on a knife edge, a shoestring, and hanging by a thread? It will take balls.

viii) Total control

From the first sprouting of the idea, through research and development, testing and prototyping, model making and engineering drawings, tooling, production, sales and marketing, all the way into the homes of the nation, it is most likely to succeed if the original visionary (or mule) sees it right through.

As I have often said, I aim not to be clever, but to be dogged. And my doggedness had got me, so far, to a point where I had my very own cyclonic vacuum cleaner at last.

On 2 May 1992, I found myself looking at the first, fully operational, visually perfect, Dyson Dual Cyclone. We carried it around on our shoulders like a Five Nations hero at Twickenham for a while, and then took reels of photos of it in moody lighting all over the house. It was a humdinger, and we knew it.

I was thirty-one years old when I tore the bag off my Hoover and stuck a cereal packet in the hole. 2 May 1992 was my forty-fifth birthday.

16

A little more luddism

Three-quarters of a million and it's yours. 'Dyson' – a nice ring to it, don't you think? Italians have the best tools. There's a welcome in the hillsides. And then someone actually buys it.

Lovely though it was, a handmade vacuum cleaner, costing around £40,000 a time to produce, was never going to make a big splash on the mainstream domestic appliance market. All that remained was to get the thing into production, market it, and sell it. All.

Before I could go ahead and order the tooling that would get the show on the road, I needed a war chest. Yes, I had the £600,000 from Lloyds, but the tooling alone was to cost £900,000, and product launches never go according to plan, there can be any number of unforeseeable problems and delays. It is best, if possible, to be prepared. Besides, I had an idea where I could get the money, and there was more than one reason for doing it.

I was fed up with Japan. Apex (and Alco, who had taken over the licence in 1988) had never, in the end, paid me more than the minimums, and I had spent the last six years flying backwards and forwards between Japan and England, fighting for their little scraps of paper and their pencilled figures. Their methods of negotiating had ground down my resistance until most of the fight was wrung out of me.

And the effects were becoming physical. Quite apart from the fact that all the travelling was keeping me away from my family and making me unhappy, it was making me ill. (What my children remember best about the time is all the crazy Japanese gadgets I used to bring back for them. I suspect that in an attic somewhere there is a pile of old watches and video games and robots and miniature technology of varying degrees of silliness, all defunct now, standing as a monument to the time I spent away from the people I love.) I need to sleep a hell of a lot, you see. I am no Maggie Thatcher. Ten hours a night or the whole day is useless, and so I used to suffer terribly from jet-lag, which I came to realise was cumulative. I was flying out to Japan (or North America) at least once a month, sometimes twice, and as the lost hours built up, I was becoming more and more tense and irritable, short-tempered and bad at concentrating.

The only way to cope was by taking Temazepam. But I would wake up at three in the morning thinking it was ten o'clock, and have to take another one to knock me out. At first it seemed to be helping, and then I began having to take it at home. It messes with your mind in the end, all that. I was even losing the ability to count.

For the piddling £60,000 a year, which was never going to change, it was simply no longer worth dealing with them, and so I sold up to them completely. Which is to say, I gave them all the rights to production of my technology in Japan – a paid-up royalty in other words – for the tidy sum of £750,000.

That amount was not as much as I should have got, but I was in a hurry to get into production, and if Britain was not going to stump up then it was my only option. It was a major wrench for me at the time, quite a rite of passage, because the Apex deal was what had made everything possible, but at least the sale meant I could now tackle Britain with confidence.

A company had to be set up, of course, and as the actual money from the Japanese sell-off would not come through, they reckoned, until the following year, it was set up with a share capital of only £2,000.

You can look it up at Companies House if you like, it is there in the book – Dyson Appliances' share capital was and is £2,000. (Actually, I have a feeling it is now £2,222. But it would be far too boring to explain why.) I suppose the value of those shares is now nearer £300 million. That is a growth of, what, almost 500,000 per cent in five years? Very tidy.

But the amount of money you put into a company to start with is perceived, by other businesses, as an indication of your confidence in it. So when we were trying to get tooling made, or hire an advertising firm, or some other kind of contractor, on the never-never, they would look us up, see that we were only worth £2,000, and think 'Ey up, this doesn't look a safe bet.' So we always had to pay cash up front.

But the forming of the company, and the company name, was crucial. I was about to go up against these big multinational companies, and my great advantage, in a jungle ruled by faceless conglomerates, was that I owned this product myself and was personally responsible for everything I sold to my customers, and so I made this clear in the name of both company and product. And, as I intended to design other products too, they would all be closely identified with me personally. Dyson, though not a particularly common name, was disyllabic, and had a nice ring to it (well, I would think that, wouldn't I?) It was also fairly obviously British.

With a company set up, borrowed money behind me, and a humdinger of a product sitting in the coach house, I set off to Italy in the spring of 1992, to order my tooling.

I had first encountered the joys of Italian tooling when I was helping Rotork with the Cyclon. After their first failed efforts to use English toolmakers I had, as I have mentioned, approached Zanussi. And what Zanussi had done, after taking the contract, was to spread the work among various subcontractors around their headquarters in Oderzo, near Venice, in the foothills of the Italian Alps.

It is a huge job, you see, to make even one mould (they can weigh up to 2000 kilos each), and since we needed about forty, no single company could take the job on alone. This time, though, I bypassed Zanussi, and went to the smaller contractors directly, signing up seventeen or eighteen independent toolmakers by the end of June, with each one making a couple of pieces for me.

Now, toolmakers are like builders in many ways. Whatever they quote you for the work, they are sure to start increasing that price every time you make even the smallest change to your order – it is practically built in to their financial planning. Even if the changes you make result in the tool you require being smaller and simpler, you will probably find that they double their price. And you have to expect that.

At that time, however, I was up against the wire and could not afford a penny over the £900,000 the work was already set to cost. I made clear to the designers that once the orders were made I would not allow a single change, and that any alterations to our original requirements would have to be made by ourselves, once we had the tooling in England – and so the Italians never got a chance to raise their prices over the estimate, which didn't make me terribly popular.

Having said all that, the Italians are quite fantastic to work with. Where an English toolmaker, like an English builder, will respond to any request, or to any change of method, or to any apparent difficulty, with that deep intake of breath, the tutting, and the shaking of the head, the Italians' response is to salivate. If you ask them, 'Can you make it bigger?' or 'Can you do it in this way, which has never been tried before?' they say, 'Of course!' and positively drool.

By the end of November, which is quick work in tool building, all my little Italians were ready. A minor hiccup presented itself in the form of an Italian lorry drivers' blockade, and a strike at Italian customs, but we had our trucks slip out backwards through Austria and they arrived in Britain about Christmas time.

The tools were to be set up in Wales, where we had arranged to have the moulding done by a newly established American company called Phillips Plastics. It was an ironic choice of partner, because Phillips had set up their factory with £2m of aid provided by the Welsh Development Agency – the same people who had so recently refused to fund my own efforts. I can only assume that they chose to fund Phillips and not us because Phillips was American, and the

Welsh office loves to boast about how many American and Japanese companies it attracts. Who would want to invest in a British company? It was a particularly unfathomable decision because a condition of the grant is that its recipient does not, by its nature, endanger any jobs elsewhere in Britain. Now at that time 60 per cent of all vacuum cleaners in Britain were imported, so we were not stealing any British jobs, but Britain had loads of plastics companies, any of whom might have suffered by Phillips' arrival.

But, not being one to let sour grapes stand in the way of business, I gave Phillips the contract to mould our parts in their brand new factory, and also contracted them to assemble the vacuum cleaners from the parts they made, which was a nice little sideline for them, and made life easier for us.

The Welsh workforce was good and efficient, and with the tooling installed after Christmas we saw the first DC-01s roll off the production line at the end of January 1993.

It was time for the public to make up its mind.

The first thousand-odd DC-01s to be birthed in Wales had been spoken for back in July 1992 by Isaac Wolfson's Great Universal Stores, the largest mail order group in Britain, which incorporates Brian Mills, Choice, Janet Fraser, and Kay's catalogues, among others. They are prevalent mainly in the north of England and are a way for people to buy things on drip, in very small instalments.

Making the first sale of DC-01s was almost as exciting as seeing the first ones come off the line. I had driven up to Manchester, a city I had never seen before, with the vacuum cleaner in a great black carbon fibre coffin with steel buckles, like the kind of thing rock bands carry their equipment in, to meet GUS's chief buyer, Brian Lamont.

It was no laughing matter, this meeting. I have tended to belittle salesmen in the course of this book, but mail order accounted at the time for 20 per cent of all the vacuum cleaners sold in Britain, and GUS had at least half of that. Lamont, a dapper chap with an unfortunate surname for someone professing financial acumen, was a man I simply had to impress.

He was also a man who took his job very seriously and our talks went on for hours. He didn't believe, to begin with, that the thing could work as a dry-cleaning machine for carpets. But I had taken with me some of the dry-cleaning powder, called Zorb-it-up, and he suggested that I went out and bought some Ribena, while he found a bit of carpet for a proper demonstration.

Eventually finding a carton of the stuff in a petrol station, I returned to his office, poured it on the carpet, sprinkled the Zorb-it-up on the carpet and then vacuumed it up, leaving not even the hint of a stain.

'Hmmm,' he said. 'Well it's obviously a very good vacuum cleaner, James, but tell me one thing: why should I chuck out a Hoover or an Electrolux from my catalogue, which I know will sell well because they are established names, and replace it with this unknown Dyson thing?'

After six hours of talking, and driving around Manchester looking for Ribena, I was in no mood to be messed around. I lost my temper, and did what I always do when that happens: I told him the truth.

'Because your catalogue is boring, Brian. That's why.'

And he laughed. 'You've got a cheek,' he said. 'OK, we'll do it.'

Lamont was the first buyer to say yes to us, he took about a thousand. (He had a weird stipulation, though: we were not to mention the 900 m.p.h. cyclone in the promotional material, because housewives, he feared, would be frightened of it!) For all the Dual Cyclone's wonderfulness, it was a remarkably brave decision, particularly since he was going to stick it in the catalogue on the basis of a promise from me that we would have them ready by January. (Catalogues such as GUS's take a fair while to produce, so you have to agree an order at least six months before you expect to see the product on the pages.)

After this success we managed to secure a deal with Littlewoods to appear in their catalogues, and while others, such as Grattans, professed to have enough vacuum cleaners already, we had enough orders to busy ourselves with production.

At that time I was not keen to try the high street retailers because I didn't want our competitors to get wind of our impending launch any earlier than was necessary, but just before we went into production, and with the tooling heading towards Wales from Italy, we did arrange an order for 250 vacuum cleaners with John Lewis, whose buyer, Ian Thompson was very excited about the machine.

And after that, things began to really move.

After the launch, I went to see the people from the Eastern & Southern electricity board shops, who became the first multiple to take us on. (E&S only agreed to take us on though, if we put out some television advertising in their catchment area. We had to pay cash up front to the agency that made the ads, because of our low financial credibility, but we had no choice. The E&S deal was extremely important for us. More of that advertising campaign later.) Other board shops followed, like South Eastern Electricity, Scottish Power, and Scottish Hydro, although SWEB, the south-western bunch, our local electricity board, demanded such ludicrous discounts that we never appeared with them.

Then, in April 1993, came a big order from Rumbelows and things looked fairly sweet for the future. It was Curry's and Comet that we really needed to get into to make an impact, but they were interested only in the big names, and for the moment we just had to sit on our initial successes and develop a good base from which to approach them.

We hardly expected a threat to that initial foundation-building to come from our own manufacturers.

'This week's highest new entry...'

Phillips fiddle us about, thus providing a fillip. Our own factory. Sales soar despite reticent retailers. We finally manage to impress Curry's and Comet. We climb the North Face of the Eiger. We hit number one in no time at all. And it's goodbye from Hoover.

Phillips Plastics was a brand new subsidiary of a large US company; ours was the only moulding job they had; and their factory was otherwise empty; all the equipment was brand new; and with our forty or so mouldings we represented an extremely big job. We were providing jobs in the area, justifying their receipt of the WDA grant, and giving the factory something to do. They were even getting an additional profit from assembly of the product. It was a lovely deal for them.

Sadly, though, their quality control system was utterly hopeless. We had to have up to five of our own inspectors on site in Wales at times to keep an eye on them, for without our overseeing the work, there was real danger of sub-standard machines finding their way onto the market – a terrible thing for a company's reputation at any time, but potentially quite crippling in the first few months of its life.

We kept the standards high by our own efforts through the first half of 1993, and sales began to move well until, on 27 May, by which time we had sold maybe 12,000 vacuum cleaners, the factory at Wrexham was paid a visit by the head honchos from Phillips in

America. At very short notice they asked to see me. I was in London at the time, and could only spare them an hour. The Americans came, they saw, they shafted.

'We want to double the assembly cost,' they drawled. 'And we're gonna add 16 per cent to the price of the plastic parts, too.'

'One thing at a time, boys,' I said. 'Why do you want to double the assembly cost?'

'We're losing money on it.'

'So you're saying that you are a moulding company, at heart, and that you want to mould parts, not assemble products. Is that right?'

'Exactly.'

'And you certainly don't want to go on assembling at the old price, because you're losing money?'

'Perfectly right.'

'Fine, I'll assemble it. Then you needn't lose money doing things you don't want to do, and frankly are not terribly good at. Right, now about this 16 per cent on parts.'

They looked aghast. 'You'll never be able to assemble them yourself.'

'That's my problem. Don't worry about that.'

And so off they went, looking rather sheepish, and a few days later I got a letter saying that since they were not going to be doing the assembly (which, as I said, was a nice little profit on the side) they didn't want to do the moulding either. I am sure it was just done in a fit of pique, and that they were only trying to scare me into letting them assemble it at the inflated rate. But they reckoned without one thing: I had had my fill of being turned over by American sharp practice and, at this stage in the game, I was not going to let them even consider it.

Long, weary intake of breath. 'Right. Fine. OK. I'll find someone else to mould it,' I said. But I was thinking, deep down, 'Christ, what a nightmare.' And then they really stiffened my resolve by showing themselves to be the utter bastards I was beginning to suspect.

'By the way, Mr Dyson,' they said. 'Instead of the 16 per cent increase for mouldings, we're going to add 32 per cent as of now, so there will be no more deliveries at the old price. And we intend to back-charge you the difference from the new cost of the mouldings on all your previous orders, all the way back to January. And we are going to back-charge you double the cost of assembly all the way back to January, too.'

Have a nice day.

It was blatantly unfair. But the most important thing, when we'd terminated our relationship with them, was to get set up in production somewhere else as soon as possible.

First of all we had to move the tooling – our tooling, remember, made in Italy at a cost of £900,000. But to give Phillips time to find other work, and us to find someone else to do our moulding, we offered to move it out in stages. And that is when they decided to hold us to ransom, insisting that we paid up before we moved a thing.

'Listen,' I said. 'You can hold us to ransom just as easily with one mould as with forty. Since we can hardly make the thing with a bit missing. Let me move out most of the moulds, and I'll pay you every penny I owe before I move the last one. You just write and tell me how much.' They agreed, and to this effect we signed a very carefully worded deal, with an incorporated tool-removal schedule as well as a production-order schedule, which allowed us to move our tooling out gradually while they carried on moulding for us on the equipment that was left.

But when we arrived to move the first thirty moulds in the initial stage of the tool-removal schedule, they refused to let us in, and prevented us from reclaiming our property, in absolute breach of the agreement.

Once again, a court action was called for. We rushed off to the high court in London to apply for a court order to make Phillips let us have our tools, and they showed up with £71,000 of dubious invoices. The decision of the court, finally, was that we should pay the £71,000 into court pending a further hearing, and that Phillips should give us back our equipment instantaneously. As for the £71,000 I have only recently settled with Phillips, and I got my money back from the high court just the other day.

(Court action again. Am I really such an aggressive, litigious person?

I don't think so. But I often wonder to myself whether there is something about me that invites all these lawsuits. I shirk away from fights in most areas of life, but in a straightforward question of rights, like this was, it is sometimes the only way. There is a system out there and sometimes you have to use it to defend what is yours.)

When we did finally recover all the tooling – in June, after a very boring, expensive and time-consuming case during which, worst of all, we had had to cease production – we found that Phillips had damaged it. Not only had it not been oiled, or looked after, but they had actually vandalised it by cutting all the hoses and wires. Pathetic. We made all the suitable repairs, though, and prepared to ship the stuff to a company called EM Plastics in Portsmouth, who were to take up production.

Yet still there were setbacks in store. In the twenty infuriating days that the court took to reach its decision, EM had been offered work by someone else and were no longer interested in us. We had to store the tooling somewhere safe, which we did at a small tooling outfit called Electromagneil, and then find a way back into production quick.

We soon relocated our tooling in various places, such as Chess Plastics in Droitwich, BM Plastics in Birmingham and places in Hemel Hempstead, Portsmouth, Germany, Holland, Italy and France. And determined to set up production in a factory of our own.

With the help of a brilliant property manager, Rob James, who found the ideal spot for us in two weeks, we moved into a 20,000 square foot former Royal Mail depot, called Bumpers Farm, which we rented at £3 per square foot on a three-year lease. It was a strange place to work in at first, because it was surrounded by eighteen roller-shutter doors, by which the mail vans could make their tyre-screeching egress, which meant that in winter it was very draughty, but in summer we could work with all the doors open, which was lovely. (By December it would already be too small, so that we had to put up six portakabins and four containers out back, as well as a 10,000 square foot tent, for a goods inwards area. It had two huge peeks visible from miles away, and the local taxi drivers used to call it Madonna!)

It was on the night of Friday–Saturday, 27–28 June that we had everything travelling down the M5 to Chippenham and, quite amazingly, we had production started four days later. With fourteen people on the line, assembling the parts that were coming from all over Europe, we were at least making a few vacuum cleaners again after that frustrating fallow period. After a couple of bad months at the beginning, we had been in positive cash flow since March, and now that we were making it ourselves, under our own total control, we were making far better products, more of them, and much quicker. (I remember a great cheer going up all round the factory when, a couple of weeks after moving in, it was announced that production had hit 100 a day.)

And so it was that on 1 July 1993, I cradled in my arms a Dual Cyclone – first dreamt of on the way home from work, fifteen years before, on that rainy night in October 1978 – built by my own staff, at my own factory. Amazing.

Sales continued to climb, via the outlets we had managed to find, but still there was no glimmer of interest from Comet or Curry's. The buyer at Comet wouldn't even answer my phone calls. These two were crucial to our success, and yet they wouldn't take us because we were not a familiar enough name.

It is received wisdom in the appliance market that brand is important. But I knew that myth could be exploded. Brand is only important when two products are identical; it is not important if one of the products has better technology or a better design than the other. Hoover had traded on their name for too long, which was easy as long as all the products were the same – theirs was identical to the Panasonic or the Electrolux so why not buy it?

That brand dependence was quite simply shattered when the Dyson came along, because it gave the consumer, for the first time since men wore top hats in town and rode horses to work, the choice of something better. And suddenly the customer had something other than brand name to look at. We even went so far as to make our own brand name not very clear, which emphasised the point. If you are selling cornflakes or cola then branding is all important – it ought to mean nothing when you are selling technology.

But, still, in Curry's and Comet they would always say, 'Personally, we like the cyclone system, but Vax has just brought out a new upright and we're going with that, because they're a bigger brand.'

And the big brands would do anything to maintain that unfair advantage. They place demonstrators in shops, who are their own employees, and paid by them to push their product. Yet they are usually dressed up as employees of the store, and pretend to be bona fide sales staff.

I remember once, when I was still having difficulty with the retailers, Deirdre and I went into a shop in Edinburgh to see what would happen if we tried to buy a particular brand.

'Actually, I recommend the Hoover,' whistled the diminutive sales lassie.

'Sorry, I have gone off Hoover since the free flights farrago,' I replied.

'Och, dinna worry yer wee sel' abba tha',' she said. 'Everyone was compensated in the end.'

'No, I want an *Electrolux*, please.' (The words nearly choked me.)

'The Hoover's better.'

'Electrolux.'

'It's no' very reliable. Now, the Hoover comes with a no quibble guarantee and...'

'Listen, do you by any chance work for Hoover?'

'Well, as a matter of fact...'

I wasn't surprised: she was a crooked old woman. And she smelt of Hoover bags, to boot.

Not only do manufacturers plant their own stooges, I discovered, but they sell their cleaners to sales staff, at discounts, to convert them to their product. When I tried this it was described as 'a clever trick', as if to insinuate that it was underhand, by people who had been at it for years. The only clever thing about it was that the retail staff liked my product more than any of the others, bought it in large numbers, and then sold it with greater conviction.

Some staff, though, remained in the thrall of the fat cats, and with things going smoothly at the factory, I took to making incognito calls on some of our retailers. Initially I was worried mainly about people going in and asking for 'a hoover', and being presented automatically with a Hoover. (I needn't have worried – Hoover boast that 80 per cent of customers walk into a shop asking for a 'hoover'; what they mention less often is that only 17 per cent walk out with one.)

It so happened, one winter's day in 1993, that I got wind of something called 'switch selling' – a practice by which a customer goes in to buy a certain product and is sold another that is more favoured by the shop staff – going on at John Lewis in Bristol.

Win some lose some, I would normally think to myself, except that this was happening to some of my dearest friends and relations in the West Country – none of whom, I felt, deserved to go home with anything less than a Dyson. I decided to pay an incognito visit.

'I am interested in an upright vacuum cleaner,' I said on arriving at John Lewis, trying to look as little like a vacuum cleaner manufacturer as possible. 'What about this one?' And I pointed at the Dyson.

'No, mate,' said Gary (names have been changed to protect the guilty). 'You don't want that English thing, all designer gimmicks and fragile as a woman's love. What you want is this one, the Sebo. That's quality *German* merchandise, that is.'

'Why do I want that?'

'It's got better plastic,' said Gary.

'What plastic is that then?' I asked.

'No idea, but it's better than the Dyson.'

'Who told you that?' I asked, all sweetness and light.

'The Sebo rep,' he said.

'Well . . . Gary,' I said, squinting to read the name on his John Lewis store badge. 'In case you are interested, the Sebo is made of high density polythene, like washing-up bowls, and it costs £600 a tonne. The Dyson is made from ABS and polycarbonate, which costs £3,500 a tonne. It costs us, in other words, six times as much, and we use it because it is indestructible. Dyson is a local manufacturer, Gary. Dyson has attracted customers into John Lewis to buy a Dyson, and you are telling them to buy a Sebo, which is made of inferior quality plastic – never mind that it uses vastly inferior technology – and to cap it all you are using *German* as a positive adjective. I have a vested interest, by the way. I'm James Dyson, and I made this bugger myself.'

This said, Gary skulked off to find the Under Manager (who has since become a friend, and made John Lewis Bristol the most successful John Lewis outlet for Dyson). He suggested I come down to the store in two weeks to do some staff training. I took a Sebo with me. I told them why I chose to use polycarbonate. One of them felt challenged by my harangue, and went off to fetch a hammer.

I invited her to hit the Dyson. She did.

'No, *really* hit it,' I said.

And she set about it with increasing viciousness. The hammer blows just continued to bounce off.

'Hit the Sebo,' I said.

It shattered at the first stroke.

Sales continued to grow throughout 1993 and 1994, but until we could get into Curry's and Comet we still had 50 per cent of the market excluded to us, and as we weren't in the independent stores either, that was another 15–20 per cent closed off. It was a real chicken and egg situation: to get into those shops we had to prove that we could achieve very high sales, but as long as we were only available to 30 per cent of the consumers, that was pretty difficult to do.

Market research in the vacuum cleaner industry is carried out by an independent company called GFK Lektrak, to which all manufacturers subscribe, and which publishes a regular hit parade of sales. As the year wore on we progressed to tenth place in the table, and as we rose up the chart we kept going back to the big two retailers.

Finally, towards the end of 1994, we were able to show Curry's that in the outlets we were in we now sold five times better than any other model, and at the fifth time of asking they finally conceded that we were a major sales force, and agreed to start ordering, with Comet

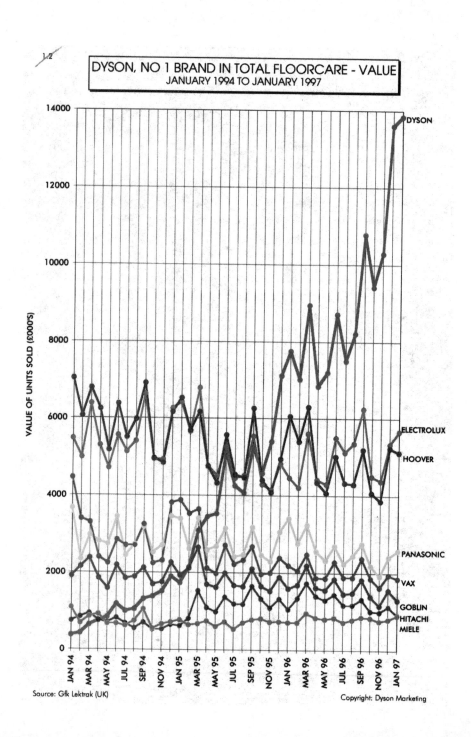

1.2

DYSON, NO 1 BRAND IN TOTAL FLOORCARE - VALUE
JANUARY 1994 TO JANUARY 1997

VALUE OF UNITS SOLD (£000'S)

14000 — 12000 — 10000 — 8000 — 6000 — 4000 — 2000 — 0

DYSON
ELECTROLUX
HOOVER
PANASONIC
VAX
GOBLIN
HITACHI
MIELE

JAN 94 MAR 94 MAY 94 JUL 94 SEP 94 NOV 94 JAN 95 MAR 95 MAY 95 JUL 95 SEP 95 NOV 95 JAN 96 MAR 96 MAY 96 JUL 96 SEP 96 NOV 96 JAN 97

Source: Gfk Lektrak (UK)

Copyright: Dyson Marketing

following soon after, and both getting behind us well by the start of 1995.

Their reluctance had been threefold: we were too small, they felt, to compete with their multinational regulars; our product was so different and unusual that they feared being made to look foolish; and in an industry where everything is about discounts and price-slashing, our being double the price of anything else made the idea of high sales seem ludicrous. What they wanted from a vacuum cleaner, in short, was a big name on the front and a few colour choices. We offered no big name, no colour choice, and a little point-of-sale label explaining our difference from the rest, expecting to sell by technological advantage and original design alone.

But once they had taken us on, the sales graph went North Face of the Eiger (see graph on opposite page). Curry's and Comet began to promote it more and more as they realised that customers weren't bringing them back; they agreed to take our point-of-sale labels, that explained our difference, and they ordered more and more as they realised that the customers who bought Dysons went home feeling they had made a discovery, which they demonstrated to their friends, who in turn came in to buy them.

What we were doing, to put it another way, was selling Mercedes or Porsches in Ford Escort quantities – and all Hoover could do was call it 'a passing phase', and describe the Dual Cyclone as 'a niche product'. In June, we got into Argos, and by September we had hit the number-one slot, selling more vacuum cleaners than anyone else despite costing twice as much as most, and going from tenth place to first in a matter of six months.

If we were a niche product, what were Hoover?

A crack in the floorboards?

Say goodbye to the bag

The Dyson Dual What? The value of editorial, and the right smell. A little bit of advertising never hurt anyone. Bad advertising. Good advertising. The importance of overseeing all aspects of business yourself, and never, ever, giving a penny to agencies.

Now, many people express surprise that the Dual Cyclone is the biggest-selling vacuum cleaner in Britain. They do not have one, they say. And they have never seen one in anyone's home. I wish my competitors were that naive. I wish, for my sins, that GFK Lektrak did not publish the evidence of my success – for the other companies all get those statistics too. I would so much rather outsell them without their knowing, for they would not fight back as hard, with their shabby air miles stunts and miserable freebies, not to mention campaigns that mention us by name and seek to knock us.

Hoover, for example, started sending out brochures to retailers saying they had better suck than us, and using as proof that poxy suction guage which I described earlier. And Sanyo went as far as to place an advert claiming more suction power than a Dyson. That was extraordinary. Not only because it wasn't true, but because they were using us the way Porsche are used in adverts by other car companies: as a benchmark for power and excellence, as an icon from which to try to extrude a little kudos for themselves. It is an old advertising method, but I have never seen a huge company (like Sanyo) try to rub kudos onto itself from a young upstart (like us). In a comically self-defeating way, Sanyo only indicated how quickly we had become the Porsche of vacuum cleaners.

Yet a lot of people, on hearing that Dyson outsells every other brand in the market, by volume as well as by value, and that the DC-01 and DC-02 occupy the number one and number two slots respectively, often ask, 'Why have I never seen one, then?'

But think about it. There are 22 million homes in this country. If we sold a million vacuum cleaners in Britain (actually, we have now sold about one and a half million, but that makes the maths a bit too complicated for me), that would leave twenty-one out of every twenty-two households without a Dual Cyclone (sad, dusty places though they would be). You could visit twenty-one homes, representing perhaps the dwelling of fifty friends, and still not expect, statistically, to see my silver-and-yellow beast. Add to that the fact that the buying market is predominantly twenty-five to forty-five years old and you have a further restriction of the homes in which you might be likely to have seen one. And how often do you go into a white goods showroom? And, when you do, how often do you look at the vacuum cleaners? If you do, then you will see one Dual Cyclone among forty other machines. How do you know that the one which is clearly the most beautiful, sexy and effective (as well as, very possibly, the most expensive) is also outselling the other thirty-nine?

We have not sought to make a feature out of our position in the market. For years, the best reason Hoover could think of for buying their product was that it was number one. I, rather pompously perhaps, take the view that that is no reason to buy something. Buy it because you like the design, or think it is a good idea, or have heard it is a good vacuum cleaner.

Hoover had thought that by saying 'We are number one' they would appeal to the conservatism of the British consumer. But I don't think that the British consumer behaves in that sheep-like way when it comes to buying products, whereas retailers and middle-men do. Hoover believed, in their own marketing, as much as in their knocking of us, that they could appeal to a mentality that says, 'This new thing is not to be trusted.' But that is because they are a very conservative company, and the fact of their being number one impressed *them*. But the public was just not interested in a conservative company beating its own chest. Once we had exploded the myth that brand mattered, which didn't take long, it would have been both hypocritical and pointless to run adverts about the all-conquering hugeness of our market share.

We also scooted to number one so silently because our profile was raised more by editorial coverage than by paid-for advertising. Apart from being cheaper, this is much more effective, because it carries more of the weight of objective truth than a bought space. But in terms of visibility it is less popularising, while being more efficient in selling to those to whom it is exposed, because those prospectively in the market will be drawn to it. It is also out of your control – you cannot make journalists write about you, and I have never tried. And, when they have, I have never sought to influence what they write and have never asked to see their copy before publication. They take me, or the products, as we are, and I have to hope they like us.

It is one of the virtues of having such a strange-looking product, however, that journalists are more likely to take an interest in it. Something genuinely different has a humanity, even a humour value, that another clone model from Miele or Panasonic will never have. A journalist's job, particularly in the area of design and technology – but also in the field of business – is to find things that are going to be exciting in the future and then get there first, or as early as possible. They also seem to be unerringly good at it. And one story can generate a groundswell of editorial coverage that gives you the kind of accreditation that advertising never can. Advertising can only take you so far, you see, until the consumer realises he is being sold something.

We have been very fortunate in that journalists were very quickly onto the Dual Cyclone, tried it themselves and then wrote business stories, initially, and then ultimately product stories that explained why we'd got rid of the bag, and the value of doing that. It was this, more than anything, that explained our technology, and gave people a reason to go out and buy it.

I had already experienced the power of the press when I launched the Ballbarrow. I had no money at all to advertise then, but one small press release led to the enquiry from Graham Rose of the *Sunday Times* which I mentioned a while back, and that totally launched the product, generating an avalanche of copy, and getting the product onto *Tomorrow's World* and the *Money Programme*, which in turn gave the Ballbarrow further coverage in parts of the newspapers (such as news and general features pages) that I would never have dreamt of.

For an example of the power of unpaid for newspaper coverage in boosting sales, you need look no further than the Hoover flights scandal of 1993. That hoo-ha also proved very conclusively that there is no such thing as bad publicity. For what the whole business did was to give Hoover untold amounts of column inches and television space. And every item was introduced by a phrase such as, 'What is so extraordinary is that a company as powerful, well established, respected and successful as Hoover should have done this to consumers.' The main message conveyed in all that, to the buyer of vacuum cleaners rather than the seeker after freebies, was that Hoover is a 'well-respected', 'successful' etcetera maker of vacuum cleaners. If you examine the figures for that period you will see that Hoover's sales soared at the very time their folly was being most loudly mocked in the media. (They claim to have lost something like £45 million on it at the time. I do not believe them.) It was a short-term gain, however, because they did irreparable damage to their reputation in the long term. Think 'Hoover' today, and you think 'free flights scandal'.

The thing about advertising is that it doesn't always work. It is a large investment that is only too easy to make and has no guarantee of return – people will either take it or leave it. We had a huge mountain to climb, for example, with the Hoover name and the fact that it had become a generic term in the minds of so many people. A huge advertising spend could have made the Dyson more famous, but it needn't necessarily have made it sell. Only the objective power of editorial was able to do that. Anything advertising can do, true journalism can do better.

OK, having pooh-poohed advertising and said it doesn't have the power of editorial, I have to admit that you can't just launch a product and hope that people write about it. But I had certainly not planned any major advertising campaign when, as I have described, E&S showrooms demanded that we advertise in their television regions (Anglia and Southern) as a condition for stocking our machines.

Faced with having to produce an advert, I assumed, as I am sure everyone does, that I would have to employ an advertising agency. They had been big news since the early eighties, and it appeared to be the way such things were done. I had two very good friends who were in the business, Al Randall, a photographer and film-maker, and Georgia Loizou, a stylist and producer. Al had made ads for BMW, among others, and I had even worked with him a while back, when I built a robotic dog for a dog food commercial he was making. I asked their advice, and they introduced me to a company called Evans, Hunt, Scott.

I met Ken Scott and I liked him; Hunt was a nice chap, too. After that I went to the agency to discuss my requirements with an account handler. He, in turn, put the job to their 'creatives', who split into teams of two and produced a set of story boards for a thirty-second commercial.

They were all terrible, but time was running out and I was forced to go with one of them, which we rejigged a bit using an idea of Al's. It involved footage of a real cyclone in America cut in with footage of the cyclone spinning in a DC-01, with a voice over, by the late Simon Cadell of *Hi-De-Hi* fame, which talked about something to do with 'harnessing the power of the cyclone'.

The end result, I felt, was deeply unsatisfactory: it treated the cyclone as a gimmick, made the product indistinguishable from all the other rubbish on the market, and did nothing at all to explain the advantages of the technology. It only cost £32,000 to make, but it was £32,000 down the toilet. Except in so far as it satisfied the demands of E&S. When it was all over I went to talk to Al again.

'This agency business just isn't going to work for me,' I said. 'I don't want to talk to account planners, and account managers and these other assorted suits. I need to talk to the "creatives" directly, and explain to them what I am trying to achieve. But they won't come to meetings because they are "creative".

'And the fact is that they are not creative at all. They are doing the very worst thing you can do, which is to sit there staring at a drawing board trying to come up with an idea out of nowhere. You need dialogue to create. Of all the creative jobs I have encountered it is advertising people who make the most song and dance about creativity. And, you know, they are not creative at all. When I think of the real creation that my designers are involved in, and compare it with these "creatives" who are earning so much more to just sit around in the Groucho Club and be generally useless, it makes me vomit. I can't go on supporting an industry like that, I'm afraid.

'What I need,' I said, my harangue over, 'is someone who is not in an agency at all, to just sit down with me, so that we can talk it all through.'

Al understood completely what I was after, and soon produced a huge Yorkshireman by the name of Tony Muranka. I sat down with Tony in the factory in Chippenham and we talked for a week, all day every day, about the whole philosophy, all my objectives, and everything that we thought we needed to say.

It was clear that we had to explain adequately what was wrong with the bag, in order to say what was right with the cyclone. Merely to proclaim the Second Coming of the vacuum cleaner would not be enough. This was a radical improvement of an existing product, and people had to be told why the old one was flawed. It would be no good to say, straight off, that the Dual Cyclone gave you '100 per cent power, 100 per cent of the time', because people were not aware that their own vacuum cleaner didn't do that already. By explaining that the bag killed the suction, however, we could plant the seeds of the idea that improvement was needed.

And so it was that we came up with the 'Say Goodbye to the Bag' campaign.

It's pathetic really, to look back and think that two grown men could sit in a room for an entire week and come up with a campaign, for a product with so many technical advances and advantages, that focused on the one thing it *didn't* have.

As a marketing ethos, 'Say Goodbye to the Bag' has been criticised as insufficiently 'proactive', a word I hate. Why don't we tell people how the machine dry-cleans, how it climbs stairs, how it has an automatic hose action? The answer is twofold: you can't sell more than one message at a time, or you lose the belief of the consumer, and we had to establish, beyond all question, that our machine overcame a problem that *all* other systems suffered from.

People said that to focus on the mucky bag was unromantic. But we thought it was rather sexy, and in a wonderful advert by Tony Muranka and his brilliant copywriter, Ken Mullen, and photographed by my friend Al Randall, that ran in *Marie Claire, Interiors*, and the *Evening Standard*, among others, we featured 119 different cleaner bags lined up rather like pants on a washing line, to show what ludicrous things they were, each with the word 'goodbye' written beneath them in a different language or idiom.

Our first television commercial after the meteorological effort was a nice, simple affair in which a woman, not a model, not skinny or glamorous, but a woman-next-door type, approached the camera and said, 'Look at this. A vacuum bag. Did you know that it clogs? So much so that after vacuuming just one room you can have lost 50 per cent of your suction.'

She then tears it up, chucks it away, and says, 'The new Dyson has no bag, so you get 100 per cent suction, 100 per cent of the time. Better get rid of this.'

She vacuums it up with the Dyson, and you see the pieces spinning round inside it. And the voice over says, simply, 'The new Dyson vacuum cleaner. We've said goodbye to the bag.'

Not designed to win advertising awards, just to sell vacuum cleaners. It is always hard to say how effective these things are, but it certainly led to sell-outs for our mail order stockists.

The most fun thing about the ad was that Miele complained about it – as they were to do ever afterwards. They informed the Independent Television Commission (ITC) that the Dyson could not possibly have picked up the large pieces of paper from the bag. But the ITC ruled in our favour, because not only did we prove that the Dyson could do it, we proved that it had, live, on that advert. It was early evidence of the lengths Miele were to go to, to do us down. And also, of course, of how inadequate they must feel about their own machines.

A further telly ad, for the cylinder model, or DC-02, had a bit more fun, with a mime artist playing a besuited man trying to find the bit where the bag went, and then resorting to hiding it under the machine and skulking off.

And that was about it for advertising, apart from a newspaper and magazine advert which took our determination not to skirt the dirt issue to the extreme, with a great pile of rubbish – picking out particularly the pollen, viruses, dust mite faeces, and pet hairs – and the legend, 'The evidence against vacuum cleaners with bags keeps piling up.' This took the German loo principle to its extreme, and epitomised the honest approach we always took to what our machine did.

The final pieces in the Dyson advertising jigsaw were our brochures and point-of-sale tags. Once people had enquired about the Dyson in a store they were given a fold-out triptych showing the machine, with every element of its construction explained, and every benefit enumerated. There were no superlatives, and no persuasion, just facts.

Finally, came the story leaflet. It was a small booklet, modelled on the size and shape of Beatrix Potter books, and the most inspirational idea of Tony Muranka. He reckoned that if people were being asked to spend £200 on this vacuum cleaner which was invented, engineered and designed by one person, who was personally accountable for every one that was sold, then they had a right to know who I was. The fact that I was British, and just a bloke down in Malmesbury making and caring about vacuum cleaners, was a selling point that it would be useful to make clear.

So we produced this little booklet that told, in a couple of hundred words (nicely written by Tony's friend Nick Rootes of the Rootes Cars family), the story of the Dual Cyclone and . . . well, the story you have just been reading yourself. And we persuaded our retailers to hang one on every Dyson in their shop, with the result that all the sales staff read it, and knew a bit about it, and that customers, even if they had come in for something else, would end up bending over the vacuum cleaner to read the story.

We never did do all that much advertising. I think our total spend so far is still less than £2 million, which is not much when you consider that Renault, for example, spend £20 million *every year.*

Ever since those early experiences I have made it a golden rule to avoid employing an outside advertising agency or marketing team. In the British age of advertising, it is still all too easy to take that road, and it is a tragic waste of resources. Occasionally, though, now that our success is assured and our coffers are full, the big agencies come to me, plugging their minimal talents, and only reinforcing how right I was to have ignored them for so long. Nothing underlined this for me more poignantly than Saatchi & Saatchi's undignified pleading for a contract with Dyson. Having told them repeatedly that I was not interested, they still sent me their proposal for a television advert. 'It is *the* way to advertise your vacuum cleaner,' they said. 'We have come up with something quite brilliant.'

It involved a man tipping some gunpowder onto a carpet in two separate piles, then vacuuming up one pile with a Dyson, and one with another vacuum cleaner. The man then lights the bit of carpet which the Dyson has cleaned, and nothing happens. He then puts a match to the other bit of carpet, and it blows up. Bang!

And people are paid for this sort of thing. Talk about monkeys and typewriters.

That idea did absolutely nothing to explain why a Dyson was different from its competitors. It was just another tired example drawn from an ancient idiom, some ponytailed plonker trying to be witty about something he doesn't understand. It was a campaign that could be used for any cleaning product on the market, and which, in only very slightly differing shapes and forms, frequently is.

The problem, to speak briefly in general terms, is this. When marketing began to emerge as a separate and identifiable skill, some time in the fifties, it quickly came to be considered as a distinct managerial area, and ultimately the area around which all others in a company should gather to determine their movements. This was fine, for marketing was still something that began inside the factory and was a process that continued all the way to the consumer, and kept producer and user in delicate harmony. But then it started to move away from its roots. Marketing became more portable, agencies sprang up that did nothing else, and gradually, and inevitably, marketing and advertising became detached from design and production.

The 'creative' who drew up the gunpowder idea had probably come hotfoot from selling lavatory paper, by way of six months working on depilatory creams, and subsequently went off to devise ways of promoting cheese. How on earth could he know how to sell vacuum cleaners, particularly ones unlike any anyone had ever seen? The modern marketing man has neither the time nor the inclination to learn about the creation and manufacture of the things he is meant to be making more attractive to the consumer. He simply applies his all-purpose skills to selling more of what already exists and the world gradually bores itself to death. In a piece in *Marketing* magazine in December 1995, a columnist of theirs, Jeremy Bullmore, a non-executive director of the Guardian Media Group and WPP Group, explained the ramifications of this sad situation in terms far better than I ever could:

> ... Who is it that gets neglected? The inventor, that's who. The designer, the engineer, the chemist, the brewer, the boffin. The people obsessed by the product; who will willingly accept that the sizzle is important, but who get their kicks trying to make an even better steak.
>
> Car companies used to be run by people who loved cars. They knew how to make cars themselves, and were always trying to make them better. Retail companies used to be run by people who loved shops, and a hundred and something years ago, George Safford Parker was nutty about fountain pens. As businesses got bigger and more complex, these obsessive, impractical, product-driven enthusiasts couldn't cope. They had to be helped by money men and lawyers and marketing persons with advertisement agents.

From that moment, the status of the maker in this country has been in decline. And the rise and rise of marketing persons, through no fault of their own, has done nothing to help . . . It might even be, I think, that the erosion of our manufacturing sector, and the rise and rise of our service sector, is in part connected with the de-coupling of making things from marketing things.

In other words: if you make something, sell it yourself. And so we did. And absolutely nothing went bang. Except, of course, everyone else's market slice.

Genetic engineering

To the cyclone, a sister. Out on the pull. History repeats itself, in the nicest possible way. I saw a Dyson – where? There on the stair ... The Dyson Absolute. The Dyson De Stijl. The Dyson Antarctic Solo. And hints of further exploration.

With the dominance of the DC-01 – which became the best-selling upright on the market by value in October 1994, and by volume in February 1995 – well and truly established, the time was ripe to go cylindrical.

The world is divided, you see, into two sorts of people: pushers and pullers, divided at birth and in nurture, and unswervable from their chosen path. We are, quite simply, genetically predisposed to favour either an upright or a cylinder. These predispositions can also tend to cluster in nations and continents, influencing their followers by the million. On the mainland of Europe, for example, the populace is quite fanatically cylindrocentric – determined for all eternity to drag the body of its vacuum cleaner behind it, while waving its giant wand in front. Japan is the same, but in America everyone is, of course, ramrod upright. (I have always assumed that America is the most upright-friendly country because it was the first country to have fitted carpets – for which a beater, rather than a sweeper, is more suitable.)

In Britain there is an almost exact fifty-fifty split in this matter, although there is a predominance of cylinder-fanciers in London and the South, while uprights become more prevalent the further north you go, until you get to Scotland, which is entirely upright-minded. After geographical bias is accounted for, one's ultimate preference is determined by the behaviour of one's mother. If she pushed, you will push, and if she pulled, therefore also pull you. While the actual DNA breakdown has yet to be properly understood, the gene is thought to pass directly through the mother (with 90 per cent of upright users coming from upright mothers), though this may have something to do with a lack of statistics for vacuum-cleaning fathers – of either bias – before the sexual revolution. But in an age when the aristocracy is in decline, and the House of Lords is on the way out, I think the vacuum cleaner is a fitting emblem of the future – eschewing as it does the feudal prejudice of primogeniture, and passing itself on through the distaff side.

Since it was crucial to tap in to this other 50 per cent of the market, the options were either a cynical exercise in eugenics, or the production of a cylinder model. I had always planned a cylinder cleaner, of course, but it was important to let the upright bed down in the public imagination first: people can only handle one new product – one new message – at a time. Furthermore, the upright market was going to limit me very much to Britain (Iona, remember, are looking after the US). If I was going to look further afield, then it was time to prepare the world for the DC-02.

I knew, right from the outset, that the technology could work in a horizontal position – that there was no problem with the cyclone lying down – because I had whipped up a crude model just for fun, back in the early eighties. At that time I had identified the only real difficulty that I would encounter – namely, that in removing a horizontal bin one risked leaking dust onto the floor. Even then I had solved that problem, by constructing the body around a hinge, so that you broke it like a shotgun, and the open mouth of the cyclone bin pointed upwards as you opened it. When it came to production this hinged body would be a major identifying point, because all other cylinders were exactly the same shape, and tended to look like plastic handbags – horrible stylised boxes, designed with no attempt to be expressive of function, in fact barely admitting to being machines at all, but hiding their true nature, embarrassed of it, and opening, of course, to reveal another crummy paper bag.

Round about the time I was planning the DC-02, I was at the RCA degree show – for I had since become an internal examiner on their product design course – and I went around offering one or two of the graduates jobs, as is my habitual wont. One of those whom I recruited was a brilliant engineer and product designer called Andrew Thompson, who had graduated with an ingenious folding bike and deserved a first, which he didn't get. I immediately latched on to him as the man to help me with the cylinder, and the two of us got down to work together straight away, soon being joined by the whole team: Simeon Jupp, Pete Gammock, Alex Knox and Mark Bickerstaffe.

Although I wasn't conscious of it at the time, it was very much a case of history repeating itself: Andrew was working for me in the very same way that I had worked with Jeremy Fry twenty-five years before. Who knows, maybe I even sympathised with his failure to get a first for such a good design, just as I felt I had been unlucky in getting a 2:1 for the Sea Truck.

At the stage that Andrew joined me, I had got no further than a bread board, and the fun and games lay ahead. The cylindrical market was going to be an even better market to attack than the upright one because, while an upright is a beater ('it beats as it sweeps as it cleans'), a cylinder vacuum cleaner can only slurp. In the old days, in fact, they were known as 'suction cleaners', and the truth is still that a cylinder vacuum cleaner lives and dies by its suck. The last thing it needs is a paper bag inside it cutting off its lifeblood.

In most other respects, though, the technology was the same as in the DC-01. We had realised that the pre-and post-motor electrostatic filters ought to be more visible than they were, so as to remind people to replace them occasionally – so we placed them on either face that shows itself as you open the cleaner to empty it.

With the help of a young aerodynamics graduate from Bath University, Connie Yuen, we set about creating an even spacier design than the DC-01, and we succeeded, generating even more excitement over the pure design, in the trade and in the press, than we had before.

Although there is usually a single great development at the core of any revolutionary design or invention, I am a great believer in the autogeneration of inventions out of each other, a kind of asexual reproduction of the product gene, if you like. It is usually when you actually come to design the product that some of the most interesting things happen. The thing that really excited everyone about the DC-02, for example, and got it so much press attention, even after that of the Dual Cyclone had been pretty exhaustively covered, was its ability to sit on stairs, and even to climb them.

Again, it is the humanoid quality that creates a humour that journalists – and, more importantly, consumers – cannot resist. It is also a design concept that is meaningful outside the specific idiom of the electrical appliance trade: by means of nothing more than a right-angle on its underside, which had never been used before, it does this great little anthropomorphic thing of clinging onto steps as you climb them.

We arrived at this idea only by low-grade lateral thinking. Cleaning stairs was presenting more of a problem than it had with the upright, because you can't put a stretchy hose on a cylinder – the DC-01's hose, remember, can easily stretch to the length of your average staircase, so you can leave the cleaner at the foot of the stairs and clean each step with the hose.

It was clear that the machine had to be able to sit on stairs, for what most people seemed to do was to balance their cylinder cleaner precariously on the step, which was by no means satisfactory. So we devised this structure that could wrap around a stair of any size or shape, and keep its centre of gravity nicely tucked into the point from where it hung, for absolute stability. We made up a number of models of the shape, and found that it worked. Not only that, but we discovered that with a few minor alterations it could be persuaded actually to bump up the stairs behind you as you pulled the hose – it really was going to be like a little domestic pet.

Other improvements on the norm included a giant handle across the whole body, rather than a piddly one at one end that meant you had to bend right down and do your back in; a double-jointed wand that allows use in any position and so reduces strain on your wrist; and a special compartment for additional tools (a thing that was going to be bumping up stairs all the time couldn't have them clipped to its outside, now could it? It had to be like the nose of an Apollo spacecraft, stripped for re-entry). All these, of course, were subsidiary to the simple fact of its cyclone technology.

Well, again the stockists made a bit of a song and dance about it. The cylinder market is not so top-end loaded as the upright market, and where the DC-01, at £200, was a little more than twice the price of others, the DC-02, at the same price, was at least three times as expensive as the average cylinder. I remember at least one buyer refusing to stock it and saying, 'You've got too big for your boots this time, Dyson.'

As it happened my boots fitted just fine: the DC-02 launched in March 1995 and eight months later, in November that year, it became the number-one cylinder cleaner by value, and then in March 1996 the best-seller by volume. Bingo.

In the year or so after the DC-02 joined the 01 at the top of the league, I began to launch the odd variation on the silver and yellow theme. My technology was acknowledged now as the best, and I felt strong enough to move away a little into other areas of colour, but it was with the DC-02 that these departures would work best, because it really looked so different from everything else.

In July 1996, we brought out the DC-02 Absolute, in which the large wheels, the shroud around the inner cyclone, the hose, and the cleaner head were purple, while the rest was coloured in the silver-and-yellow tradition – and various elements of the design were dramatically enhanced by it.

But the Absolute was more than just a colour change. We had already established that we had the cleanest expelled air on the market – because it wasn't sent back into the room via clogged and smelly pores – and hundreds of asthmatics had written to say that it had changed their lives. But there was more we could do.

I approached an air-conditioning company that had been working with bactericide screens, because recent outbreaks of Legionnaire's Disease had shown that the bacteria breed in air-conditioning systems. While an absolute filter traps bacteria, we knew that they could still breed on the filter itself, and leech out into the room. By incorporating a 'Bactiguard' bacteria-killing screen to the filter, and bonding to it a HEPA (High Efficiency Particle Arrester) filter, a system which was tested at the chemical warfare establishment at Porton Down, we developed a filter that as well as removing pollens and other health-threatening particles that stick easily to the lining of lungs, would capture and kill dangerous viruses like salmonella and listeria.

And that was the Dyson Absolute.

The next departure was our DC-02 De Stijl, with a wackier colour scheme still. My son Jacob, who is also a designer, had sprayed one of our models in the red, purple and yellow colours of the De Stijl modernist movement, a group founded in 1917, with links to the Bauhaus and the Constructivists, who used colour to highlight struc-ture, and, indeed, eschewed all decoration apart from colour. He had been inspired by a De Stijl chair that we had just bought, and sprayed up the model as a present for his girlfriend, and then did one more because we all liked it so much. Over the next few weeks everyone who came to the house and saw it seemed to love it, and so, late in 1996, we brought out a limited edition of 20,000 DC-02s in the De Stijl colours, drawing even greater attention to the unique structural and geometrical forms of the vacuum cleaner. At £249, it was a bit more expensive than the standard models, and looked too 'designery' for a mainstream product, but made an excellent addition and comp-lement to the line.

The final addition to the family, so far, came with Dyson's spon-sorship of Sir Ranulph Fiennes' solo expedition to the Antarctic in October 1996, and was known as the Dyson Antarctica Solo. An upright model replaced the yellow parts with light blue ones, while the cylinder model did the same and then went further, replacing the silver body with a white one, colours that proved enormously popular with the public and sold out, despite Sir Ranulph's ultimate abortion of the mission through illness.

The venture had begun with a book by Ran that he sent to me inscribed with the words, 'from one British pioneer to another', which was extremely flattering, not to mention being a fascinating and exciting book.

He had latched onto me after being sent to Minehead by his wife to buy a new vacuum cleaner. Pointed towards the Dyson by a sales assistant, he at first said that he didn't want a British one, but he read the story leaflet that was attached to it, and was converted. It turned out to be the most expensive vacuum cleaner I ever sold.

Soon after I got the book, Ran phoned up and said he wanted to come and talk to me for ten minutes about his forthcoming expedition to the Antarctic. I wasn't sure what to make of it until the ninth minute of our meeting, when he told me that his last expedition had raised over £1 million for multiple sclerosis. From then on I was hooked. For three years we had been doing nothing but running a business and making money for ourselves, and had begun to wonder if we could do something different. In that sense, Ran's timing was immaculate. Having lost both my parents to cancer, I was keen to do something for cancer research, and the association with Ran appealed to me enormously, not only because I could see that it was a great way of raising money for cancer, but because his approach was so much like my own: he did what he did not by flashes of brilliance, but by working very hard, for long periods, in the face of great hardship. I preferred to raise money by sponsoring that sort of activity than some one-off stunt.

First of all I gave £1.44 million to Breakthrough, the breast cancer charity – funding research, rather than care, because research was my own area of expertise – and then we produced 100,000 of these Antarctica Solos, persuading everyone who stocked it to give a part of their profits to the appeal. To their great credit, they were all delighted to do so, in sums varying from £5–10 per machine.

*

Genetic engineering, then, and a little cosmetic surgery, helped to open up new markets, but there were still boundaries to be breached. With the DC-02 we were now ready, if not to walk on water, then certainly to cross it. And, beyond that, to look to the final frontier, to make the ultimate manufacturing statement and, nature being the cyclical thing it is, to bring it all back to where it began.

Coals to Japan?

And the award for best vacuum cleaner in a leading role goes to ... if I can only get this envelope open ... the DC-02. The Dual Cyclone passes into myth. Mr Rutter and Hoover make a terrible confession. Japan – the final frontier. To boldly go where no man has gone before. Dysoning down under. Le Dual Cyclone. Achieving simultaneity with America. Vacuum cleaners yet to come.

Not long after the launch of the DC-02, we started to win awards. There was no doubt that the design establishment had already taken a liking to us, it was just that the gongs didn't start coming until we had the cylinder model. Before that, though, the upright technology, in the form of the G-Force, had been getting a different kind of recognition. It became the only domestic appliance to go on permanent display at the Victoria & Albert Museum, when it was put into their new Twentieth Century Gallery in 1990. It was also put on permanent display in the Design Museum at Butler's Warf, in the Boymans Museum in Rotterdam, and at the Science Museum in London. And it won the 'Best Design' award at the World Design Exhibition in Nagoya in 1989.

The DC-02, however, did the real award-winning. It won the *Daily Mail* Ideal Home award in 1995, and in the same year the Chartered Society of Designers' product design award. Then in 1996 it won the Industrial Design America prize for best product and the DBA-Marketing Week Evershed's Grand Prix trophy and Consumer Product Design award. Not to mention a Design Council award for product design and one for having won the DBA-Marketing and having been shortlisted for the European Community Young Company award for Innovation and Design, which I also won, subsequently, at the end of January 1997.

Quite apart from award-winning, we were making storming advances in production. In August 1995 we had to move out of the Chippenham factory, where we could not get production above 30,000 machines a week. A fantastic new factory was designed for us by my old tutor Tony Hunt, and a whizzkid architect called Chris Wilkinson, but we expanded so fast that we had outgrown it before it was even built and had to move in to the factory at Malmesbury that I have already described. Wilkinson and Hunt were back, though, in the autumn of 1996, to drawing up plans to treble the 90,000 square foot factory space by extending over more of our twenty-acre site. And so fast are we growing that we have had to move into organic furniture.

When we first arrived I wanted everyone to have enormous tables, so I set about making them myself from 2-foot by 2-foot box section, which could be cut and welded in less than an hour to make a frame for a 12-foot by 4-foot table top consisting of two work tops laid back to back. We now have 180 of these, and every time we have ten new employees we just whack up another one. So often does this happen that we have a chap called Derek for whom making tables for new staff is practically his entire job.

It was not only we who knew how fast we were growing. In 1996 the Marketing Council listed Dyson Appliances as one of ten UK companies in a state of hypergrowth, as our turnover swelled from £3.5 million in 1993 to £85 million in 1996, and we were officially recognised as the fastest-growing manufacturing company in the country. Needless to say, our ancient, creaking rivals were not happy. As we progressed towards our present 42.5 per cent, February 1997, share of the total vacuum cleaner market by value (Hoover has 13.6 per cent, Electrolux 14.7 per cent) the fatties would try to belittle us at every significant watermark we passed.

When we became the bestselling upright by value, Hoover said, 'Ah yes, but we sell more machines.' And then we overtook them by volume, too. (We now have a 42 per cent share of the upright market by volume, and a 55.8 per cent share by value). And exactly the same pattern was repeated in the cylinder market. Today we have not only a 25.2 per cent value and 12.3 per cent volume share of the cylinder market, but occupy the number one and number two slots of the whole market combined, with only the DC-01 outselling the DC-02.

Any other tricks up the multinationals' sleeves? But of course. In March 1995 Hoover claimed in their advertising that they were number one, and yet we were clearly outselling them. Their justification for the claim? They had sold more over the past twelve months than we had. Our objection was their use of the present tense. They should have been made to say, 'we have been number one.' But the Advertising Standards Authority ruled against us, as it has continued to do in nine cases out of ten.

With Hoover beaten in both markets by both volume and value, they then circled their wagons at the last bastion – brand share. With their vast number of models they could still, for a while, say that they, as a company, sold more vacuum cleaners in total than we did. We first passed their brand share of the value of the market some time in 1996, and at the very end of that year we finally passed them by volume, selling more vacuum cleaners in total, with our two very expensive models, than they did with their scores of models and cheaper machines.

To finish the figures, I can record a worldwide sales turnover of vacuum cleaners built to my patent of £2 billion to date. Last year's turnover at Dyson was £85 million.

Oh, vulgar, vulgar, vulgar, vulgar. The money is not the point, at all. The point is that we beat off all the big manufacturers, we won prizes, we made good things that people wanted, and we passed into a sort of folklore, so that the big boys started to wet themselves with worry. Miele have complained about almost every advert we have ever made. Everyone has copied our colours and unpatented features; Electrolux have brought out as close to a replica as they could manage, and Hoover have been hopping around like fools trying to say the right things.

I enjoyed particularly a *Money Programme* feature in which Hoover's VP Europe, Mike Rutter, was pushed into the front line to try to make an attack. 'We've been in the British market place since 1919,' he said, as usual trying to make play of having been at the forefront of technology eighty years ago. And he went on, 'During that time we have seen twelve to thirteen shooting star competitors who've made a short-term impact and disappeared. Dyson are yet another of those examples.'

Yoohoo, Mike. Still here.

The Managing Director of Electrolux was wheeled out as well. 'From test work we have done, there is nothing new about this product. It is certainly no better than Electrolux products.'

That is presumably why they have been trying to copy it ever since.

Then the presenter of the programme explained that, 'We wanted to show the independent research figures demonstrating the sales of all machines. Whilst Dyson agreed, sadly Hoover, Electrolux, and Panasonic refused.'

Can't think why.

Was Hoover going to respond, they asked. And Mr Rutter explained that they would be bringing out a yellow upright. And then came his *tour de force*.

'There are two reasons for taking new technology,' he said. 'The first is to put it into your product range.' That was the only one I could think of. And I was dead curious as to what his other reason would be.

'The other is to take it off the shelf to make sure nobody else uses it.'

Eh?

'I do regret that Hoover, as a company, did not take the product technology off the shelf, take it off Dyson. It would have lain there on the shelf and not have been used.'

If anything typified the attitude to new technology of major British manufacturing companies it was this. It is something you take off the inventor and hide away in case anything ever changes and you have to wake up and do a bit of work.

And so the folklorification of the Dyson continued. Carl Gardner, the editor of *Design* magazine, told me he had heard people using the phrase 'doing a Dyson', to mean designing, engineering, manufacturing, and marketing one's own invention. There have been questions in the House based on its success (Nigel Jones, Lib-Dem for Cheltenham, in a science budget debate, 2 February 1995. Cf. Hansard, Volume 253, No. 43, p. 1300); Tony Blair has called it an inspiration to young British designers, and even Prince Charles commiserated with the tales of my early woes: 'It's a classic British story,' he said. 'Nobody ever pays attention to the best ideas.'

And in the press the two vacuum cleaners seem to have become objects of fascination that stand outside their natural place in business or design stories. The best example of this, or at least the funniest, came in the Dear Mary column in the *Spectator* on 24 February 1996:

> Q. How can I enliven my dinner parties? I am always rigid with nerves when guests arrive and can't think what to say to anyone. – P.W., Shaftesbury.

> A. Why not stimulate your guests on arrival with a demonstration of a Dyson vacuum cleaner? A surprisingly small number of Britons have any experience of this super-sucker and people are always delighted and enthralled to witness the huge amounts of detritus that can be wolfed up by the drunk cyclone machine and then displayed in its see-through frontal chamber. The demonstration will set any party swinging as guests anticipate the great pleasure in store for them for the rest of their lives – or at least until the novelty wears off – of using a Dyson machine in their own home and seeing their own detritus despatched in such a gratifying manner.

But of all the fantastic, and once unimaginable successes of the cyclonic vacuum cleaner, there is one that stands alone. It is a painful paradox, and it has been a constant source of irritation to me, that when you try to sell a British product abroad, you come up against a wall of nationalism. The Germans, the Japanese, the Americans, are all suspicious of foreign manufacturers and make every effort to keep their business at home. And yet when I try to sell in my own country, I meet the exact opposite response! In Britain nobody wants British manufacturing at all. They'll get all weepy over British beer, or whisky, or cheese, but try to sell them technology and they want German, Japanese, American. Our bad name in manufacturing is quite literally ubiquitous. But British technology can make great leaps, and early in 1995 I proved it.

When the DC-02 was launched, I sent a brochure to the makers of G-Force in Japan just out of politeness really. I knew that Japan preferred cylinders, and thought they might be interested. Next thing I knew, a great delegation appeared at the factory. Twelve of them came together, and I could only assume that they were after the drawings, for their deal entitled them to make their own version of it. To that end, I had even prepared copies of the drawings for them to take away. And then they surprised me more than they had in all the years I had been privileged to experience their peculiar foibles.

'We want to buy DC-02.'

Buy?

'Yes. Buy. You make, we import.'

And that was it. The world's most competitive market cracked like an egg. Or like the shell of a Sebo vacuum cleaner.

There was the odd delay due to their fanatical perfectionism, which, it was nice to see, was still light years ahead of my own. They took some samples away with them that day, and came back complaining about fingerprints. They really can pick things up from 1,000 yards that you couldn't find with a microscope. But we began a policy of wiping every component that came in, covering everything in the factory with plastic bags and issuing everyone with white gloves, and they were soon satisfied.

I have still never seen a Japanese person unwrap a new domestic appliance in their own home. I can only assume that they put on a pair of white gloves first, and then lift it from the box like a midwife extracting a baby, put it on a table covered with white linen, and then, after squinting closely at it for a while, rest their hands on their hips and say, 'Aah, no fingaplints.' Otherwise how could they know the fingerprints were ours?

Once we had our cleanliness problem solved there was no stopping them. They renamed the thing 'Mr J.', which was rather nice, and we had to translate the little storybook into Japanese, and then they agreed to take 200,000 vacuum cleaners a year (which they would sell in Japan at about £300 each) in a deal worth £30 million a year.

Originally, they tried to make the Mr J. a bit smaller than the DC-02 – because the Japanese like small things – and they came up with a couple of models. But they decided, soon enough, that they preferred it the way it was and in July 1995 we began shipping. As far as I know, we were the first (and are still the only) significant exporters of electrical appliances into Japan. It was the Japanese who had invested in me when nobody else would, and it was they who had the humility and the foresight to come to Dyson Appliances and become our first international customer.

It is a sobering thought, when you drive into Malmesbury – which was last at the cutting edge of technology in AD 1006, when a Benedictine monk attached a pair of wings to his back, jumped off the Abbey tower and became the world's first recorded air crash casualty – to think that this quiet little medieval town in Wiltshire is the place where the myth of British technological inadequacy is finally being laid to rest, and that from here, vast quantities of vacuum cleaners are being sent thousands of miles across the globe to the very home of the electrical appliance.

With the confidence of now being an exporter to Japan, I began to reckon that if I could command a 20–30 per cent share of the market in Britain, then there was no reason – vacuum cleaners being a pretty global product, and not really differing from one continent to another – why we should not be equally successful in other countries. It was, quite apart from anything else, our moral obligation to go out and do that for the sake of Britain, to change the way the world thinks about our ability to manufacture.

But I was not keen on simple export. We had conquered Britain by conducting ourselves, and our business, differently from everyone else, and to succeed abroad we would have to do the same. It was no good just finding distributors; we would have to set up our own subsidiaries in any country we chose to move into. The advantage of this, apart from allowing us to bring our whole philosophy to the new territory, was that when we brought out further products we would have the mechanism already set up to sell them abroad. But if we signed up with a vacuum cleaner distributor somewhere, and then started making, say, toasters, we would have to start all over again from scratch. The disadvantage of the approach was the time and money it would cost to set up. We couldn't have just anybody; it had to be someone who understood, and could operate, the Dyson way.

My first thought was to try to move into France. It is next door; I have a small farmhouse there which I bought when the Dual Cyclone money started to come in, and the people are stylish with a good history of design appreciation, from the Eiffel Tower and Citroën to Concorde. The market is not as big as Germany's, but I think I understand the French a little better, and the market there is certainly as big as Britain's.

Early in 1996, however, when I was making the first tentative steps towards setting up Dyson France, I got a call from a man called Ross Cameron. Cameron was an Australian who had seen a presentation of mine at Johnson-Wax in Racine, Wisconsin, and been instrumental in setting up my deal with them for the commercial market. He had since become their manager of global technology, and was phoning to tell me that they were about to stop producing vacuum cleaners, which would mean an end to our association. He was, he said, very disappointed that Johnson-Wax was giving up on vacuum cleaners, which were his first love, and he was also heartily sick of travelling the world all the time. I immediately came up with the obvious solution.

'Why not start up Dyson Australia?' I asked.

A couple of days later Ross rang back to say 'OK.' He is that sort of man, not one to mess about. He left Johnson-Wax almost immediately, setting up Dyson Australia in March of that year.

Ross was exactly the sort of dogged, stubborn achiever that we needed to represent our company. When I first met him he had been in the process of building a house at the bottom of a very steep slope, down which the builders refused to carry the bricks, claiming it was too difficult and dangerous. So Ross, with the help of his two young sons, carried every single brick for his house down that slope himself, by hand, working at it steadily every single morning before showing up for work at Johnson-Wax. Quite apart from his good technical background as one who had worked as an engineer for British Leyland in Australia, this was a man who could build things. And companies are built, not made.

I was vindicated in my choice. Dyson Australia has been up and running for a year now, as a warehousing, marketing and selling operation, and Ross positively lives and breathes it. He has a small team of four or five sales staff, and runs a service at weekends on his mobile phone from his private strip of beach in a Sydney suburb. And, I am glad to report, the Dual Cyclone is doing brilliantly in all the stores.

Dyson France happened a little more slowly, as things in France are wont to do. I wasn't about to move in there with my eyes closed and give my business to the first person who came along. I had to find the right person.

I started off by selling direct to stores in France, and very quickly got into Darty and Boulangère, the French equivalents of Curry's and Comet – which shows again how much better other countries are at accepting change and revolutionary technology – as well as the Conran Shop in Paris (which was handy for publicity because *Elle Décoration* goes there a lot) and the famous Galeries Lafayette (who gave us another prize, I seem to remember). Initially I was shipping to France direct from Malmesbury, and invoicing from here as well.

But although we did very well, without advertising and sales support we were never going to crack it. Then, late in 1996, I appointed a Frenchman called Meyer Brecher as directeur générale de Dyson France and we were off again. I have some French title that makes me effectively company secretary, so that I am ultimately responsible, but M. Brecher runs the show from our new offices in the Creteil district of Paris. We had been planning to go to Lille, the so-called 'Gateway to Europe', but opted for Paris because of the abundance of universities which would furnish us with the raw young graduates that Dyson has always depended on.

There was an initial setback with the staff, in that when the five trilingual graduates we selected to run the office were sent back to England for training in Malmesbury, they liked it so much they refused to go back to France. And they all now work in our export division. And are quite brilliant. But the next time we got our crop of graduates we didn't give them so much as a sniff of the Wiltshire air, and they are all now working with M. Brecher in a similar warehousing and selling operation to Dyson Australia, and the product, as in Australia, is now taking the market by storm.

What else is there to say? Britain is about to go 100 per cent Dyson; Japan has jumped on the bandwagon; Australia is on the way, and from France all Europe is about to open up to the all-conquering cyclonic army. Oh, well I suppose there is still America to clear up. But that is not our job, thank God. It is the one place we have been able to conquer without the burden of having to sell it ourselves, and without me having to spend my life on an aeroplane. Iona has every angle covered. After our initial difficulties, and those occasional contretemps, our relationship with Iona settled down into delicate harmony and firm friendship. In 1992 the Fantom was finally launched into the US, and Iona even changed its name to Fantom Technologies, which was some indication of its commitment to the product. For a couple of years it sold unspectacularly, and then the company re-launched it using infomercials. It sky-rocketed in the 1994–5 season, becoming, I have been told, the most successful product ever launched by television shopping channels. A nauseating method, but productive.

Why let Fantom do it, and not do it myself? Well, it has a lot to do with the fact that I have plenty on my plate as it is, and that there is really no need. Last year Fantom made sales of $100 million, which is not bad, and we got 5 per cent of it, which is better than a slap in the face with a wet hoover bag, without having to have any input at all. Best of all, though, we have a sister company, and like any family relationship we have had our ups and downs. We have been together for eleven years, and now that they trust our design and engineering skills, and we trust their manufacturing and marketing abilities, that relationship has bedded down to one of mutual respect. And there is something reassuring about having another company, on the other side of the world, that is in the same position as you are, with the same technology, and experiencing the same birth pains.

I can't possibly blame Fantom/Iona for taking ten years to trust us – it takes an awful lot to put the future of your company in the hands of another man's technology. The full fruition of our relationship was symbolised by their launch of the Fury in 1996, which is their version of the DC-01 (the Fantom was considerably larger than that), and the fact that they are about to do their own DC-02. And when we bring out the DC-03, Fantom will bring it out in America at the same time. As in all the best relationships, we will have achieved simultaneity.

The DC-03? I have jumped the gun. For the DC-03, like the DC-04 and the DC-05, is still in the future. And the future is yet to come.

A new philosophy of business

As often as I am asked about my design philosophy, I am cross-examined as to how I run my business. People see the numerical and financial success of the product and want to know how it was done. It is never enough to say that it is down to the qualitative difference of the vacuum cleaner, and to be fair, there may well be more to it than that. But a business philosophy is a difficult thing to distil out of the daily workings of a company, because you never really know how you do it, you just do it. It's like asking a horse how it walks. I thought, perhaps, if I tried to explain everything we do that other companies probably do not do, then people might be able to work out the philosophy for themselves.

Everyone who starts work at Dyson makes a vacuum cleaner on their first day

This is true from the lowliest member of staff to a non-executive director like former trade minister Richard Needham who joined us in 1995 to advise on export. Quite apart from being fun, making you feel good, and reinforcing my conviction that anyone can do anything, it means that everyone in the company understands how the cleaner is put together, how it works, and why, because of its design, it is better.

Everyone then takes it home and uses it, so that they can see its benefits in its natural environment, and get a grasp of the company's *raison d'être*. They have to pay £20 if they want to keep it forever, though. That's another thing worth knowing: you don't get anything for nothing! The idea is that everyone understands the whole product, even though they may only be working on a small part of it. It is, in fact, a core element of the next point:

A holistic approach to design

When we moved into a new factory in Malmesbury in 1995, we commissioned a rising star, Chris Wilkinson to make some alterations internally and externally that transformed the building, including a jaunty tubular and sheet tension structure to provide shade to the offices.

Deirdre designed the lilac, lavender, and purple interior colour scheme, and we designed and built the high-tech office tables that I have already described. We also bought Vitara chairs, designed by Antonio Citerio, at great expense (£400 each) for every employee. A chair, after all, is the most important piece of furniture in the office. At Dyson we care about people's bottoms.

The offices are open plan so that everyone can communicate easily and feels part of the same team. The graphics and engineering people are in the geographical centre of the office, and that reflects the centrality of design and engineering to the whole operation. But there are no department boundaries or borders or walls, fences, ditches, moats, ha-has, or minefields: freedom of movement and of expression is total.

I hope, in this way, to make everyone design conscious, and to feel encouraged to make creative contributions.

Engineering and design are not viewed as separate. Designers are as involved in testing as engineers are in conceptual ideas
Elsewhere in industry, designers just design the look of the product, and maybe sketch the odd part. Then engineers design the mechanics of the product. Test engineers do the testing. And model makers make the models. And machinists machine things. At Dyson, uniquely, we see no barriers between these disciplines – everyone in the department does everything. This way, everybody understands the implications of what they are doing, and enjoys total creative freedom. And it goes further.

Everyone is empowered to be creative and knowledgeable
Or at least to feel that creative contributions are encouraged. In practice, of course, most ideas come from within whichever department they are supposed to come from, but not always. The idea of putting our helpline number on the handle of the machine – we are the only company to do this – came from Jackie on the service desk. And, when we were having trouble getting the motor seal to seal properly every time, someone else from the service department, a chap called Pete, discovered that if you did up the screws in cylinder head manner (in a prescribed order) that they would be 100 per cent effective.

No memos – ever
First of all, memos are just a way of passing the buck, avoiding the issue, and abdicating responsibility. Secondly, memos only generate memos, then memos responding to the memo responding to the memo, and then ... I could go on but it would be as boring as a memo. Thirdly, and most importantly, however much they multiply, nobody ever reads them.

Dialogue is the founding principle for progress. Talk to people, they listen. Monologue leads only to monomania. Memos are also tacky, soulless, and get lost. I would rather people did less, if it means doing what they do properly, and a memo, though quicker than a conversation, is far more likely to lead to a misunderstanding.

By the way, computer messages are the pits – and e-mail is even lower. The graphics are so appalling I just can't get interested enough to read them. I am considering banning those as well.

No one wears suits and ties

Every company needs an image. The smaller and less established you are, the more important that image becomes. And it is not a nebulous, intangible thing – like a reputation for ruthlessness, or for charm, or for efficiency – but a real, concrete and visible thing that people can take away with them, like a souvenir implanted in the brain, that keeps your company, and your way of thinking, locked in their mind – even before they have seen what you are trying to sell – crystallised in a simple, comprehensible motif.

Now it may be that the not wearing of suits has taken on an importance for me that is greater than it really is. It should not, after all, become a stricture, because that is to make the practice as much a uniform as the miserable outfit it is trying to avoid. The fundamental principle is this: I do not want my employees thinking like businessmen. I do not want them sitting round a table with me, or with anyone else, and coming out with the same old crap as you would expect from a businessman. As soon as they start thinking like businessmen they will think that the company is all about making money, and it is not. I have no time for businessmen; they are the suited pen-pushers who have always endeavoured to stifle creativity. And while what I choose to wear is entirely up to me, and not open to question, I have chosen also to discourage my employees from wearing suits, because it seems to me the best way to instil in them my own heartfelt conviction in the theory of difference for the sake of difference.

A man in jeans and a T-shirt has nothing to hide behind – and will not feel compelled to hide behind conformity in anything else. He will be less likely, therefore, to come out with conformist remarks. We want people really to think about the business and come out with radical remarks – it is merely an offshoot that you provide people with something to recall about you, that instantly tells them what sort of company you are. For me, personally, it has become almost symbolic of my difference, of my not putting on airs and graces. The old cliché that springs unsupressably to mind is all about getting what you see.

I first got obsessed with this idea in the mid-eighties (it was, in fact, a friend of mine in France, Diane Bauer, who also looks after some of our affairs over there, who first put the idea into my head. I happened to mention on the way to a meeting, that I hated wearing suits. She looked astonished and said 'then stop wearing them.' And so I did). It was after a meeting with a company called Millikan, the largest private company in America, when I had to give a lecture to a panel of twenty-four people. Now, in business circles on the east coast, you were simply not taken seriously unless you wore a traditional IBM suit with a sober tie – but I walked into the board room without one, took off my jacket and tossed it on the floor and told them that ties make you go deaf in your old age.

'It restricts the motion of your larynx,' I explained, 'and is known to hasten the onset of deafness.' And at that, twenty-four of the most powerful men in America immediately took off their jackets and ties, and relaxed. They are a funny lot. If they go into the office on a Saturday they will always, without fail, wear jeans, trainers and ghastly lumberjack shirts – it is just another kind of uniform, as soulless and restrictive to creative thought as a suit.

I read once about a company, I think it may even have been IBM, that issued all its staff with T-shirts bearing the company logo. Torn between showing loyalty to the company, appreciation for the chair-man's generosity, and not wanting to appear too casual, they all put the T-shirts on over their suits. The same mentality is reflected in their quaint ol' tradition of mufti day, when everyone goes to work without a suit, one day a year, and gives their daughter a dollar for charity. Not a tactic that would squeeze much of a donation out of us.

It may be that I attach too much significance to this, for you never know what really makes people behave the way they do. But from the evidence of institutions that depend on uniforms – primarily schools, armies and prisons – it seems that they have been developed merely to encourage conformity and discipline. If I were organising a military campaign such things might be useful...

I am not a fanatic about it, and there is always the odd misfit. New employees tend to wear suits and ties out of habit, but they go after six to eight weeks. The suits and ties that is, not the employees – I don't take it *that* seriously.

A suit is like a biker's leathers, or a fireman's protective kit: it is merely protection. People wear one because if you look the part, if you look efficient, look sober and reliable, people will assume that you are, and you can get away with being inadequate. Show up for a marketing meeting in your underpants, though, and you have to be pretty damned impressive to pull it off.

I'd rather the qualities of my employees shone through in what they did, rather than what they wore. That is why I employ brilliant young graduates with no experience at all. I want free-thinkers who can take the company forward, and have revolutionary ideas.

My own justification for not wearing a suit is the same. I want people to make their judgements about me for deeper reasons than what I wrap myself in to keep out the cold. And then, of course, it becomes embroiled in this culture of difference. People come to see us and go away thinking of people who look relaxed, behave efficiently and think differently, and they think to themselves, as they undo the inside button of their shiny green double-breasted suit, and pluck up their matching trousers at the knee to stop them creasing, as they take their seat on the train home from Chippenham, 'Now there is a refreshing company.'

To be totally honest, I did wear a suit to work once. It was the day Prince Charles came to look round the factory, and it was not, before you leap to conclusions, done out of toadying royalism. Deirdre insisted that I wear the armour so that HRH wouldn't feel out of place.

A café not a canteen

We operate in two shifts at the factory, so lunches and breaks are taken from 10.00 a.m. through to 7.00 p.m., and since there is nothing in walking distance, we clearly needed our own restaurant. It was also important to create a kind of social focus, or at least the sort of atmosphere where employees would find it easy to get to know each other.

I couldn't bear the thought of a 'canteen' or anything at all resembling mass catering – I wanted something a bit more Conranny, with the nearest thing to fresh Italian food that we could do in the South of England. I am not the sort of swollen-gutted, eructating business-luncher that sets off in the limo for four hours of beef and claret every day at noon, and comes back to do little more than gurgle and fart all afternoon. I eat on site like everyone else, and I needed a nice middle-class lady to make pastas and salad.

It so happened that there was an antiques shop in Malmesbury that was also a delicatessen. Judith Hughes, my PA, latched onto it like a shot as a source for lunches – reinforcing my own long-held belief that antique dealers are usually gourmets. Taste in food and taste in objets d'art clearly walk hand in hand across the palate of life. And it was the existence of this deli-antiquery that inspired the formula for our café – a place that would be run by antique dealers who liked food. A lace dealer called Jane appeared to run it for me, and recruited more dealers to help: good, wholesome, vegetable-biased, unfried food was just around the corner.

The staff were not, as you might expect, by any means chuffed. They wanted pasties and chips, bacon and eggs, pies and chips, sausages and chips. Not fusilli, pesto sauces, aubergines gratin, rocket salad, cherry tomatoes, fennel, steamed fish, snails, kiwi fruit, carrot and orange soup, or fruit salads. But after only a few days Jane was doing 450 lunches a day for a delighted staff, who were going back to work unbloated, free of the tyranny of cholesterol, their skins luminous with health, their organically fuelled bodies trim as a *Baywatch* lifeguard. And Jane was hunting for more antique dealers.

If you are ever in Malmesbury, by the way, I recommend the kedgeree.

Encourage employees to be different, on principle

This is part of my anti-brilliance campaign. Very few people can be brilliant. Those who are, rarely do anything worthwhile. And they are over-valued. You are just as likely to solve a problem by being unconventional and determined as by being brilliant. And if you can't be unconventional, be obtuse. Be deliberately obtuse, because there are 5 billion people out there thinking in train tracks, and thinking what they have been taught to think.

If you go in and be illogical, then half the time people will laugh at you, and half the time you will strike up something interesting because you have stopped everyone else from thinking logically, which has failed to provide a solution. Be a bit whacko and you shake people up a bit. And we all need shaking up.

Methodologically it even makes a bit of sense, in that, to bastardise a dictum of Mr Sherlock Holmes, when you have eliminated the logical, whatever remains, however illogical, must be the answer. So why not start there? I probably only think this because I can never be *bothered* to think anything through logically, but we'll let it go. At any rate, to be different is something we try to instil in all our staff, because, for the reasons given above, we don't want people behaving like businessmen, but behaving like normal human beings and treating the customer as a friend.

Don't relinquish responsibility once the sale is made

For as long as their Dyson is under guarantee our customer has the unique and, though I say so myself, rather charming, entitlement to phone the hotline on the handle and, if necessary, a brand new machine will be delivered by first thing the next morning, totally free. And, once the guarantee is over, the customer is ever afterwards entitled to ring the hotline and the machine will be picked up immediately, repaired by us, and returned by courier.

We do not use some outside engineer who arrives when he feels like it, asks for a cup of tea, scratches his bottom for a while, and then says, 'What you need is a new vacuum cleaner. This one's finished.'

It may sound like an expensive service for us to run, but real service, like real innovation, is what people want more than anything, and people are so delighted when they discover that we will immediately send them a new machine that their call of complaint becomes a call of gratitude. They phone up steaming because something has gone wrong with their very expensive vacuum cleaner (although it rarely does), and end up deliriously happy because they are about to get a new one.

Employ graduates straight from university

The basic reason for this is that they are unsullied. They have not been strapped into a suit and taught to think by a company with nothing on its mind but short-term profit and early retirement. We are trying to do things differently from everyone else, so it's easier to teach fresh graduates this new way, and enable them to challenge established beliefs, than to retrain someone with 'experience'. Sometimes some of our staff do lack knowledge, but there is now a cadre of experienced and talented managers, and this combination provides an extraordinarily energetic and intelligent stratum of managers, which is what gives Dyson its strength.

I began employing graduates because I was so appreciative of the opportunities given to me when I was younger by Jeremy Fry. He, after all, had taken me on when I was still an undergraduate. And as soon as I had graduated he gave me *carte blanche* on the Sea Truck project, and entrusted me with running the business from the start. I enjoyed, and benefited from, the responsibility of learning things by doing, rather than being taught by superiors. That was what made me feel I was a pioneer.

So when I first set up Prototypes Ltd to develop the vacuum cleaner, I started employing engineering graduates from the Royal College of Art – and we now have about twenty RCA graduates in Malmesbury. It never occurred to me that they wouldn't be able to do everything brilliantly. And they did.

When I began building Dyson Appliances I employed fresh graduates for graphics, marketing, production, tooling, and export. And their enthusiasm, intelligence, inventiveness, and resource has been the most emotional and rewarding part of the adventure. They're getting old now though – the average age of our employees has just hit twenty-five.

Our competitors sometimes say, as a way of belittling the company's achievement, that all we are is good at marketing. Well, all our marketing has been done by Rebecca Trentham, from a standing start as a languages graduate from Oxford, and all our products have been designed and engineered by new graduates.

The atmosphere and spirit generated by these young people learning the business for themselves, is something we would never have got by employing old hacks to teach them.

Not to forget, of course, that the young unemployed are cheaper to employ than most, which was a great help in the early, cash-strapped days. But their pay rises fast – if not as fast as they would like.

Meet the staff as equals – they are

Although during the course of daily life I speak to most of the staff at one time or another, I speak to them, as a group, about once a month. And, because we have expanded so fast, I now have to do that in three goes: talking with the morning shift at 1.45 p.m., the evening shift at 2.05 p.m., and the office at 5.00 p.m.

I talk, by and large, for about ten minutes about anything from marketing issues – such as what our competitors are doing, and what we are doing about it – to management changes, how our overseas subsidiaries are doing, advertising campaigns, and property purchases. When, for example, we became involved with Sir Ranulph Fiennes' solo expedition to the Antarctic, I introduced him to everyone and he gave a small talk, which probably made a nice change from listening to me wittering on.

We also address the kinds of social issues that I am sure most good companies do, such as the canteen, shift changeovers, and pensions. And then the staff fire at me whatever questions they like, although we also run clinics for that, which are a better forum for the less extrovert individuals, and a suggestions box for the positively retiring, whose letters are always answered personally.

I do spend a lot of time walking around the factory, but it is a mistake to live under the illusion that one is therefore communicating – for it is usually the same people who approach and ask you questions and offer their opinions. The advantage of the soap box occasion is that you are setting aside time especially to communicate aspects of the business that all the staff should know about, and other things that directly affect their welfare. It is eyeball to eyeball contact, and there is always a very palpable atmosphere: sometimes very positive and upbeat, and sometimes difficult when news is not so good.

The meetings offer a good time to reaffirm our philosophy – and I think it is fair to call it a philosophy rather than just a 'company policy', for it is not a way of 'doing' that we impose on anybody, but a way of 'being' that I find is generally most productive. For example, it is often in these meetings that I remind people that the assembly lines need not be in a hurry. Speed is not important, and neither are numbers. The only thing that is important is doing everything carefully, thoroughly, and vigilantly. New assembly workers, used to the methods of other manufacturers in the market, have sometimes become accustomed to a mentality that works at full speed all day to achieve mere numbers, at the expense of care and quality.

Feedback from the floor, when it concerns production, usually centres around the quality of components fed to the line by sub-contractors. It is a crucial melting pot of ideas, that enables us to share with the assembly staff our management experience and efforts with the subcontractors, at the same time as they describe the end results of our efforts. So useful is this proving, that we have arranged, in future, for subcontractors to attend the meetings. Hope they can take it.

The final assembly is done entirely by hand

There is very little mechanisation in our assembly lines, which is rather unusual. It allows us total flexibility to lengthen or shorten the line when we need to, to add or remove people, or to add new lines at a moment's notice, change the assembly method, change the design of the product. It does mean that we rely more than others on the skill of our assembly staff but it allows us that 'Can Do' attitude to change that is anathema to British manufacturing otherwise. And we do take a pride that the work is done by hand, and say so when we can, rather than pretend that everything is built by robots, and is therefore somehow better.

Everything in the factory is, in fact, done by hand, because we do not keep the tooling here, or manufacture any of the components, thus keeping nasty, heavy, dirty machinery out of the place, and making it feel more like a craft workshop – albeit a very modern one – than a factory.

We do spend a lot of time supervising our many subcontractors, but our skills are in designing and making vacuum cleaners, not in the processes of making components. In our cleaner, quieter, more pleasant factory we are all able to concentrate our minds on engineering, testing, and quality control, which is what makes our customers happy, and our business the success that it is.

We pay our staff well

In addition to very good rates of pay (which have resulted in most of Malmesbury and the surrounding area beating a path to our door) we pay a flat premium, on a weekly basis, that is subject to full attendance, as a reward for reliable and loyal staff. Everyone has life insurance and a company pension, twenty-two days holiday a year, paid sick leave, and leaves early on Friday. The café is heavily subsidised (a lunch of top continental cuisine, healthy as a walk in the country, still gives you change out of two quid) and we run a free bus service from Chippenham.

Japanese influences

To the outside world some of our ideas may appear to be rather Japanese in their conception. But that is only because they are not very British. We have none of the corny Japanese ideas, like the exercises or mantras, foregoing of holidays and chronic presenteeism (though we do run football, netball, and squash activities) but I have noticed one or two things in our approach which, while we were not aware that they were particularly Japanese, have certain similarities.

I have mentioned iterative development as part of innovation, and that extends to the workplace. Like the Japanese, we are never satisfied with the product, and are always trying to improve it. We take any complaint very seriously, even if it arises out of the customer's own error (such as failure to read the instructions), and solve the problem. Customer feedback is our way of foretelling and directing our future, and we spare no expense in acting on that feedback.

We are aware – as the Japanese are – that the strength of our business does not lie with the quality of the director's and senior managers, but with the quality, effort, intelligence and, above all, enthusiasm, of everyone else.

We are fascinated, to the point of obsession, with the product. We do not, perhaps, attain quite the delirious object fetishism of the Japanese, but are determined that whatever we produce should be perfect, as well as exciting and beautiful. It is this that allows us to maintain ownership of our product, and without it we do not have a business.

Dealing with suppliers

There are four straightforward requirements that we have of our suppliers: that they should provide (a) what we order, (b) at the time stipulated, (c) in the correct quantity, (d) to the quality stipulated.

I wish.

The thing is that if they let us down in any of those areas, not only their future business with us but, more importantly, our business with our customers, will suffer. The trouble is that suppliers seldom see beyond our role as the cash provider for whatever they ship – 'right, Dyson, we've sent off a truck load of bits of plastic to your gaff, where's the money?'

They are not all like this, of course. But it only takes one to stop the whole production line, and that, in turn, demoralises the staff.

We have some very good suppliers, with whom we have shared the success of our business, and I try to make the best of them the watermark by which I select and judge the others. A good example of what I look for is the attitude of Adrian Hill of Belpar Rubber. Back in November 1992 he flew over to Italy, when the tooling was finished, to help me assemble the first off-tooling samples – he had made all the rubber parts, and was so keen to make sure that they all worked properly, cared so much about his own business fulfilling all that was asked of it, that he insisted on being there himself when they were first put to use. Belpar is a very successful small family business, and has been a major supplier to Dyson ever since.

As we grew, we realised that we had to work constantly with our increasing army of suppliers to improve both quality and technology. To this end I am grateful to a man called David Brown, of Motorola in Swindon, who in September 1995 introduced me to a quality scheme of theirs called Sixth Sigma. Under this excellent programme, which involves us redesigning parts as required, and suppliers altering their production methods to accommodate us, and going through a rigorous checking process themselves, we have worked with them to reduce rejects to 6 parts per million.

We depend on our suppliers, and they know that. Many of them put their faith in us in the early days, trusting us to succeed, and believing that our initially small orders would become reasonable. They have adapted well to our spiralling demand for extra products, and to changes in design, and it has been good to share our success with them.

We have a similar relationship with our retailers, most of whom were initially asked to put their faith in a small company, with the promise of greater things to come. Although shops and mail order catalogues are our immediate purchasers, we are very much attuned to the existence of the consumer as our ultimate customer, and depend on the skill and enthusiasm of retail staff. We encourage them to buy and use the vacuum cleaners themselves, and to attach our point-of-sale labels to the machines so that the people who walk into the shops get a picture of the whole story. We in turn are aware that we must support them with promotion and advertising.

And that, from the comfort of our bottoms and the state of our digestion, to the quality of our parts and products, is how we do things at Dyson. And I think it is a good way. It has worked for me, at least. A note of caution though: it wouldn't count for diddly if our vacuum cleaner had a bag.

The future:
cleaning up the planet,
and a way forward for Britain

*Helping you breathe more easily. The Recyclone. Why we are not as brilliant
as we think we are. Taxing our way to success. Revolution begins at school.
Why it's all her fault. Finding new ways to skin a fatcat. Engineers leading
from the front – not just an Eastern promise. Making industry sexy. A new
national anthem, and the end.*

The future for Dyson Appliances, the future for me, personally, and
the future of this country will all, with a bit of luck, be similar in at
least one way: they will all be about making, and investing in, exciting
new technology and design.

 While establishing my company has involved an awful lot of 'business'-type work on my part, I intend, as the years go by, and as the
infrastructure that we are building beds down, to go back to spending
most of my time in the hands-on business of designing and engineering new things. The company cannot rest on its laurels, and apart
from the development of the export side there is only one way to go
forward. There will be no stock-market flotations, no sell-outs (though
impressive offers have been made) and no endorsing of other manufacturers' products with the Dyson brand (though there has been at
least one serious approach). No, we will go forward by developing
more and better products. The DC-03, DC-04, DC-05 (though I am
beginning to get a bit tired of the numbering system) will be at large
fairly soon, and after that will be things beyond vacuum cleaners –
new technology in areas that our competitors can only guess at.

And then, of course, the country must follow suit. Business must forget the advertising agencies, and the market research, and the short-term benefits of a stack 'em high sell 'em fast mentality. Britain must put designers at the forefront of a new industrial revolution: government, manufacturers, venture capitalists, whoever has the money, must invest heavily in new design, and new technology. We must employ more engineers and more designers, and be prepared for slow returns. Be ready to make not a penny for four years, five years, six years ... and one fine morning we will wake up to an era of real, and very rapid industrial growth.

A piece of new technology that could do an enormous amount for everybody, but will require a bit of initiative from either governments or manufacturers if it is to succeed, is the cyclonic filtration system that I have devised for diesel exhausts. It is a gloriously simple device that I first started looking at nearly ten years ago. I have done my own tests, and after half an hour of driving around at normal speed in a brand new diesel-engined Ford Transit van, the cyclone had collected half a cupful of black soot. That carbonaceous soot is the vilest, most poisonous stuff imaginable: carcinogenic particulates that give us acid rain, ruin our cardio-pulmonary health, and kill our children, not to mention dangerous trace elements that kill us slowly through the food chain.

GKN Technology expressed a vague interest in it in the early stages, but there was a problem, they said, with disposing of the soot, because it is so vile you are not allowed to just dump it. A far better solution, I suppose, is to just dump it in all our lungs? For that is what has been happening for years.

I tried to license Eminox, the company that make most of the vertical exhaust systems for big trucks. But they only make exhausts, not engines, and they make whatever exhaust systems the manufacturers tell them to – so it wasn't their problem. And Turner & Newell, another big name in exhaust systems, were equally disinclined to look at it, while the car manufacturers don't care because (a) they don't have to, and (b) no one else uses diesel filters.

Car manufacturers pursue a very sheep-like existence, you see. They do nothing for years and years, tweaking the odd thing here and there, and then when something like ABS, or airbags, comes along, they all do it at the same time. There must be some sort of cartel, or else a kind of collective unconscious, operating. At any rate, none of them would stick their neck out.

Attempting to fund the thing myself I applied three times for a DTI smart award grant. Three times they refused. I went to see Chis Patten, then Minister for the Environment. He came back to me some time later to say that the vehicle manufacturers had assured him that there was no point using my filter, because they were going to be bringing out much cleaner diesel systems in the future.

They didn't.

Then came a push to say that diesel engines were much greener than petrol engines, which they are not, and the price of diesel was kept disastrously down, and the filter was all but forgotten. Now that we are coming round again to the realisation that diesel is filthy perhaps there is hope – though I find it best to try to forget that Britain was one of the last countries to pass unleaded petrol legislation, because we wanted to protect our motor industry from having to make a change.

The diesel filter cannot succeed without government legislation. I cannot put millions of pounds and hours into developing the thing, and then have no one buy it. It is what I call a 'preaching product' in that before you can sell it you have to preach the need to clean up diesel exhausts. If there were an existing product that did the job, then I could introduce a better one to challenge it.

When Clive Sinclair made his C5 he had to go around trying to tell people that they ought to be going out on Saturday night to meet their friends in a low slung plastic coffin with an electric motor. They didn't listen to him, and he lost millions.

Let government only invest in it, or make it a legal requirement, and we can start cleaning up diesel's act. But government, in hock to wealthy motor manufacturers, refuses to do anything because they want proof that diesel is harmful – an attitude that typified their approach to the BSE crisis as well as Virginia Bottomley's refusal to ban smoking in public places. There is proof, and there have been tests. But the only tests the British government (and I speak of the Tory government of the last eighteen years) would accept would involve strapping a hundred babies to exhaust pipes and driving around for five years, while another hundred babies grew up in a field somewhere. There is no possible reason for such defensiveness and scepticism in this particular case, though, because the solution is so cheap and easy. This invention is not one with which I am trying to make a killing. It is one with which I am trying to stop people being killed. And, as an indication of the condition of Britain, it is really rather depressing.

Not depressing at all, however, is the Recyclone.

About a year ago I began to start thinking about what would happen to all our Dual Cyclones when they came to the end of their natural lives. It was early to begin thinking about it, I know, because even the oldest ones are no more than three or four years old, but all things are mortal, even cyclones.

It seemed terrible, after all that had gone into each one, that they should just be thrown on a landfill when they die, and so it occurred to me that we should offer to take back all our vacuum cleaners at the end of their lives, and recover whatever is recoverable. And then it occurred to me that *everything* should be recoverable. And so we did, and it is. All you have to do when your Dyson dies – which should not happen for a very, very long time – is to call the hotline number on the handle and we will send round the undertakers free of charge.

We talked to a lot of recycling people, and then to a number of our suppliers, and set up a system whereby the machines will be reverse assembled, stripped down to their component parts and then all the reusable parts put into storage. The rest of the plastic is then washed and pelletised, and washed again, and then melted down and reformed into parts once more.

When there is enough recycled plastic, and enough reusable parts, we will begin production of an entirely recycled vacuum cleaner that will be identical to the original in all respects, except, of course that the silver parts of the body will not be silver. They will be green. They will be packaged not in the usual box, but in a reusable canvas bag, that can be used as a sports bag or laundry bag, or whatever, and all the literature, the instructions, and the storybook, will be printed on recycled paper. And it may sell at the slightly higher price of £220.

We are, in fact, just about to launch a limited edition of 400 Recyclones, made of the recycled parts of all our old test models and the early rejects. Although it will be some time before we can begin major production – because of the toughness and durability of the Dyson – the fact that so many of our machines are used commercially, and in industry, where life-spans are much shorter, means it shouldn't be too long before we can get a small output going.

While other manufacturers sometimes try to attain a small 'green' cachet by saying that 'our parts are recyclable', they are paying only lip service to fashion. We will be the first to collect our own products from people's homes, recycle them ourselves, and then sell an entirely waste-free product. The world's first recycled vacuum cleaner.

I just hope people copy this one.

After the soon to be launched DC-03, 04, and 05, there will be other and different products. But they will not be 'copycat' products – that is no principle by which to work. We are in the business of developing new technology and new products, and of recruiting bright young graduates to help us do exactly that, so nothing will come out that is not both innovatively designed and conceived around a brand new invention. It is an ambitious attitude for us to take, and is bound to slow down our growth, but though it is slower, it will send our roots deeper than the quick development of a huge portfolio of old technology that we have merely redesigned. And it will be much more satisfying for body and soul.

What those further products will be I can hardly reveal, or even hint at, given the predatory nature of my competitors, but whatever we do, we will always take the hardest route, through iterative development, and the more time-consuming route to export domination that I have already described. And, as the company develops more and more experience, and finds more and better personnel on the commercial and export side, the less of a hands-on role I shall take there, returning gradually to the test-rig, and the bread board, and the workshop, and the throbbing heart of the company.

That's enough about me. You can hardly have failed to gather, from the pages you have read, that British industry – and, by extension, Britain itself – is not in a very good way. If we are to make any real attempt to effect the kind of growth we need, then we will have to make radical changes. We will have to take the long, hard, and initially expensive route to success that I have been pursuing these last twenty-odd years. There is no miracle cure, and it is a foul medicine to swallow, but the best medicines always are.

A good indicator of the health, inventiveness, and solidity of a country's industry is the number of patents it files each year. In Britain, we always boast about how inventive we are. We are deluding ourselves. As I have said before, in the most recent research on world patent activity, the UK comes eleventh. We simply do not have any ideas any more, and the long-held conviction that we do is a worrying sign of our national complacency.

There are still, I am sure, a number of inventive individuals, but it would appear that corporate applications for patents are few and far between. This can only be because we eschew at inception the pursuit of iterative development. The Japanese and the Koreans understand the importance of continuous active development, and of never letting up. They appreciate only too well that small step-by-step improvements add up, in the long term, to massive improvements which, in turn, generate patents, and thus ownership of technology.

The British, however, do not relish this approach, preferring to admire the brilliance of a quantum leap, and to pin their hopes on that kind of advance. But those of us who are involved in R&D know that such leaps are few and far between, and are dependent on nothing more than the vicissitudes of Dame Fortune. We should admire and reward not flash-in-the-pan tub-thumpers but dogged persistence, and prevent money men from stamping on R&D before it has a chance to make a breakthrough.

For Britain to compete again on world markets it is imperative that tax legislation takes into account the riskiness and long-term nature of R&D. At present we have very distorted investment because of the demand for fast results. To introduce tax incentives for research and development would solve this problem at a stroke, and while it might initially cost the government money, the fact is that in the long run tax revenues would be increased through the increased profits resulting from the higher prices our new, technologically better products would command.

At present, R&D expenditure receives the same treatment as advertising spend, an absurd situation which loads investment precariously at one end of the manufacturing process. Double taxation relief on research expenditure is the way forward – already there are 100 per cent allowances on the cost of research buildings, so why not encourage investors to spend money on the research itself?

With the situation as it stands, Britain has a large and successful advertising sector, said to be the best in the world. Is that something to be proud of? It just means that advertising fees are ludicrously expensive, that companies invest an absurdly high amount in advertising, and that advertising men get paid infinitely more than engineers and designers.

Is it a good thing that bright university graduates flock to get into advertising rather than manufacturing companies? This last year, university applications to study engineering were down by 30 per cent. But the rot sets in much earlier in our children's education.

When I was at school I was made to choose, at thirteen or fourteen, between arts and sciences, perpetuating for ever an idea of the two things as mutually exclusive. With the rapid expansion of interest in the new design and technology GCSE, the problems are beginning to be solved, but there is still a long way to go.

The problem is that schools (and as a result schoolchildren) tend to view industry as a boring, Dickensian money-making activity. And at the same time middle-class parents think of accountancy, law, the civil service, medicine, and teaching as the only worthwhile careers. Industry does not help its cause by appearing so boring, staid, conventional and obsessed by profit and loss. And it has made a thoroughly rotten job of inspiring young people – not surprising when it languishes at twenty-seventh spot in a world chart for initiative.

Industry should do better to make clear, and schools to understand, that manufacturing is about making things that people want and which work well, and look good. Creating these things, and bringing them to the market is a hugely exciting thing: it is a fun creative activity and involves high-risk gambling based on judgement and intuition; it creates jobs and, as a byproduct, money.

In industry the stage is always changing, and the players must do the same: you can never rest, never sit still, always thinking, inventing, and creating, finding new ways to challenge established beliefs and prejudices and ways of working. Compare that with the staidness and sameness of the professions and you see how easy it should be to change the way young people think about their future.

In turn, the education system must work to break down the barriers between disciplines – which at present mean that a student who learns how a turbine works does not learn how to build it, and the student who learns how to build it does not learn how to make the thing it powers look interesting. Perhaps physics A Level, the most notoriously boring of subjects, should be changed to incorporate a more practical approach, and be a little less mathematics based. Taking cars to bits, or building working prototypes would be much more fun as well as more inspiring and worthwhile.

By the time they got to university, students would be ready to benefit from a more creative and practical approach to engineering, in which the highly academic courses that have been driving them away in their thousands, have been revamped for a brighter industrial future. For new products to be generated out of higher education, rather than just theoretical knowledge of scientific details, it is also imperative that design be made a part of all such courses.

Much of the blame for the miserable low-point that British industry has reached can be laid at the feet of Margaret Thatcher. Her period of rule and of crippling the nation's industry, covered almost exactly, and quite ironically, the long period between my first invention of the cyclone filter, and the appearance of the DC-01. (If you consider the first part of John Major's premiership, when he had taken over but not yet won an election, as really the last year or so of Thatcher, then the period of the three Thatcher terms 1979–92 covers exactly the same period as the invention-production route of the Dual Cyclone.) As such, I feel myself in a unique position to grumble about her.

I have for a long time carried an image of Mrs Thatcher in my mind, marching around and swinging her handbag like a weapon of war in the direction of industry, making these wild proclamations:

'Inflation is the greatest of all possible evils!' she cries. But I have never had a good explanation as to why this should be the case. I can see that inflation erodes savings, but if you are borrowing money then inflation reduces the size of the loan – and since enterprise always involves loans, inflation is good.

'Interest rates must be kept high!' she bellows. Presumably because she wants to keep inflation down as part of her frantic monetarist fever. But high interest rates make enterprise – based on research and development – impossible, because most companies will just not borrow in periods of high interest rates. Instead, they earn packets by putting money on deposit, and the ones with no money can't borrow, with the result that you have nil investment.

Now, businesses involved in R&D, and businesses experiencing rapid growth, are the two kinds of enterprise that most need to borrow. But Mrs Thatcher's low inflation/high interest policy resulted directly in a lack of new business start-ups, a heavy decline in R&D expenditure, phenomenal under-investment in industry, and fat-cat companies sitting on piles of cash. The only kind of investment that could be risked was in advertising, because the fast returns kept down the period of borrowing at these terrible rates of interest.

The Hansons and the GECs earned vast profits from their cash piles, asset-strippers made profits from takeovers and sell-offs that could create interest-earning cash, and while it was all wonderful for the city, where cash in the pocket became the *raison-d'être*, it was death to industry, engineers, and scientists.

The final insult of the Thatcher era, for me, was the George Soros disaster: we had got ourselves into a position where a single man could take billions from the British people by currency speculation, and then be treated as some sort of a hero, rather than being locked up in the Tower. He doesn't make anything. He doesn't employ people. He doesn't create any wealth for Britain. Is this the kind of behaviour that the City admires so much?

If so, it is because we have lost sight of the things that matter. The true purpose of industry has been forgotten, and takeovers, shares, profits, and prices have become more important than building, and creation, and jobs. Seldom, on the business pages of the newspapers, are R&D, design, engineering, or investment in new products given a mention; only tales of the fluctuations of share values seem to be of interest.

Newspaper coverage we can take or leave, but the funding imbalances are positively criminal. Where the Design Council gets £2.4 million a year from the DTI, the Imperial War Museum gets funding of £40 million a year, a new gun museum in Birmingham gets built at a cost of £44 million, and the Arts Council gets £1.8 *billion* each year, not a penny of which gets spent on design, going instead on opera houses and wings of art galleries. It is a source of constant horror to me that Terence Conran has had to fund the Design Museum entirely out of his own pocket since its foundation.

A new industrial revolution depends on our ability to innovate and design, and yet we spend our money on commemorating the past.

Maybe Tony Blair will be different. He at least took an interest in a young designers exhibition at the Business Design Centre in July 1996, and the fact that Cherie noticed my jacket had different-coloured buttons may mean there is some design consciousness in the family.

I suppose that the most depressing thing about all this is that I am by no means the first to say it. Short-termism is such a well known national illness that it could almost be called short-termitis. And yet nobody does anything about it. That, if anything, is the recurring theme of this book.

Let us now, at last, plan for the long term.

Let us encourage engineering through channels political and educational, as well as through business and industry.

Let us, please, invest in research and development for future profit.

And let us reduce our spending on advertising, so as to refocus business, and make it into something product-oriented, and R&D driven.

There will be lower profits for a while, but if companies that make the sacrifice are rewarded with tax concessions, then we will all be better off in the end.

If we need evidence that the approach I have outlined works for nations as well as for companies, we need look no further than our own fear of the East. I do not vaunt the oriental suppression of individualism (though even there old clichés are becoming redundant, as design of great flair and originality begins to seep out) but the patience that has gone into their economic growth is quite outstanding.

And it is not only the Japanese. Korea is making massive inroads into their dominance. Daiwoo, LG, and Samsung are investing huge sums in R&D, and financing courses at the RCA, where they are placing many Korean students, and for the moment they are happy to be making annual net profits of no more than 1 per cent, while establishing themselves in markets, and reinvesting in their future. And we are helping them. We fund their factories in Wales and the Northeast, allowing them to pursue their own iterative agenda – yet we do nothing to help ourselves!

It may be that it is down to the engineers to take control themselves. Honda and Sony are two companies, started just after the war, that consistently pursued a strategy of gradual technological development, until both were world-dominating market leaders. Both companies were founded and owned by engineers; both built themselves up by innovation, leaving others to play catch-up in their wake, and both had to start from scratch, a far worse scratch even than Britain is at now, from the ashes of postwar Japan. For years both had to cope, as British manufacturers will have to, with worldwide low esteem for their country's manufacturing quality. But they turned the tables on the rest of the world, and revolutionised the way their country was perceived.

Whenever I have tried to suggest that our own manufacturing businesses ought to be run by engineers and designers, it has made me very unpopular. I suppose businessmen are worried that if the builders run the business there will be nothing left for them to do. But why should companies be led by accountants, lawyers, and salesmen? Accounts are important, of course. Keeping score always is. But team leaders have to provide inspiration – as in football or cricket – not just balance sheets.

When I went to the venture capitalists for funding (they call themselves venture capitalists, but it seems to me to be a lot more capital and a lot less venture) they would not back me *because* I was a designer. Well, while I might not understand all the intricacies of accountancy, at least I make it my business to know and understand what people might buy, to understand the technology that might be able to produce it, to know how it could be made, and what it would cost, and what customers would be prepared to pay for it.

So why not empower the engineers? Why not bring them up to run industry? If creation is to be at the centre, then so must the creators be. It may be risky, but if we don't do it, we will slowly die. Die of the British disease.

If the engineers themselves take the responsibility for the taking of those risks then mistakes will not be feared, only learnt from. But that is rarely the British way – one only has to look at Clive Sinclair and see how his one failure, the C5, is constantly thrown back at him, rather than congratulated for its attempt, and revered for its bravery. Mistakes are an important part of the learning process of R&D, and only companies led by engineers will move on positively through them, rather than pulling up at the first sign of trouble.

The Japanese are not the only ones to whom we should look for example. Britain does have its great companies. Over the past twenty-five years JCB had provided a fantastic model to follow. It is a private company that practises iterative development as a way of improving its products, and operates the very holistic design approach that I employ myself – in front of their headquarters, for example, they have two JCBs reared up and wrestling with each other like a couple of dinosaurs. They are globally competitive and have managed to stay ahead of Japanese giants. Psion and the hi-fi manufacturers Linn are two more British companies that have achieved great success by intensive R&D.

I would also have to say that Richard Branson is to be admired, if only because he does things differently, is a fierce competitor, and provides an inspiration to many businesses. It is just a shame that he doesn't actually make anything. To an extent, revering him is not so far from the reverence of Sock Shop, Tie Rack and Marks & Spencer that has kept us a nation of shopkeepers these last few years while BMW come in and buy up Rover so that Britain no longer owns a volume car maker, and British Aerospace sell the Hawker division to Beachcraft (USA) so we don't make a commercial aeroplane either. Much more of this, and we will forget how to make things altogether.

I could lay some blame with the engineers themselves. They should be more assertive; they should resist being pushed into the role of backroom boys. They tend to be nicer, gentler, more creative people, and cannon fodder for the sharp-suited City boys. Their problem, I think, is that in any discussion about the future of a company, the accountant can prove his point with historical figures, the salesman with marketing data, but the innovator has no proof. He has only his vision of how the future will be, and you can never prove that. I cannot begin to number the meetings I sat in where chairmen and directors and MDs refused to see the value of a bagless vacuum cleaner, or the merits of a hose on the back of an upright. I couldn't *prove* anything; I could only give them my vision.

Look how Britain ignored Frank Whittle with his jet engine, or Barnes Wallis with all his ideas – it is part of our self-mocking folklore.

How often does that kind of negative thinking go on every day in British companies?

And, by the way, engineers being at the front does not mean the end of management. Why stick to the same jobs all our lives? Why should a couple of years of training in our late teens determine for ever the course our lives take? Where is our sense of adventure?

If engineers want to be in control, and they must want to be, then they must be given reasons to be confident about manufacturing their inventions themselves.

I came upon this confidence myself only by chance, by seeing what Brunel, Buckminster Fuller, and Issigonis had been able to do, and then meeting, in Jeremy Fry, a man who was doing it in the modern world. I saw how he was pushing his own engineering and design through to their fruition by running his own company, building his own factory and taking that holistic approach to innovation that had brought greatness to those few forebears.

And so, classics trained son of a teacher that I was, I was provided with the inspiration to try something different. In the not too distant future, children might be given a better opportunity to come by that inspiration themselves. If, as I gather is planned, the design and technology GCSE that I mentioned becomes compulsory in schools, then children will be exposed, at a constructively impressionable age, to the idea that industry is about making better-designed products. They will be encouraged, as embryonic designers, to take an informed and broader view of industry, and maybe, just maybe, be tempted away from the safe, middle-class professions, and experience the excitement, adventure, and control that only comes with making things.

That is the most I can hope for, that my own story, the non-secret of my success, will inspire other people to go out and make things, just for fun at first, and, if they find that they have made something they love, to go further, to make it better, and keep hold of their dream, to show the rest of the world that in Britain we are making things again. That way, with enough people doggedly pursuing their wildest hopes for the future, day in day out in the face of no matter what discouragement, Britain can again become the kind of country that I thought it was when I read the *Eagle*, marvelled at the Mini, and ran at night across bridges built by Isambard Kingdom Brunel, afraid of what might be catching me up from behind.

It is a Britain our children have never known. And it may be just around the corner.

afterword

There were times when I wondered whether anyone would be allowed to read this book. Shortly before the book was finished, I again became involved in a lawsuit with Amway Corporation. I am not at liberty to divulge much about the current proceedings (they are still ongoing), except to say that the publication of the book was threatened by the suit. Fortunately, we were subsequently able to go forward with publication, even whilst we continue to sort out in the American courts what I am permitted to say about my experiences with Amway and what I am not. So, the less said the better.

In the nine months since my book was first published the international side of the business has expanded. Dyson have founded another subsidiary in Germany and have made distribution agreements in New Zealand, Turkey, Belgium and Sweden. It appears to me, that feeling threatened by our success, our competitors have joined ranks in an attempt to block our progress. Dyson is currently being sued by six multi-nationals ganging up together, who claim that our advertising campaign in Belgium is based on falsehood, even though the same advertising has run successfully in the UK and Australia. Our message has always been that vacuum cleaners with bags lose suction, a fact even acknowledged in the small print of our competitors' instruction manuals. Perversely, their campaign has only succeeded in strengthening my resolve. It shows that these bag manufacturers have run out of ideas for making any genuine improvements to their own vacuum cleaners.

Electrolux has declared war on Dyson. They are taking me to court for defamation because I criticised the efficiency of their new Powersystem vacuum cleaner, launched in March, which features a cyclone backed by a huge nappy filter, which might as well be a bag for all the clogging it causes. They have also released misleading comparative data to endorse their products. So now I am having to countersue Electrolux. Tests showing results biased against Dyson were published by Sweden's best-known consumer test magazine. When we went to the same laboratory we got completely different results.

It's a new salutary lesson to learn that when you've overcome the problems of launching a new product and it meets with some success, you have only won the first battle in a war. Once you start to threaten established multi-nationals sitting on fat market shares, the big boys will come gunning for you.

I have realised, however, that I have firm support where it matters most, which is with the people who have helped me make and develop the Dual Cyclone and with the public who have bought it. Many people I have met at lectures and book signings, have told me that my story has given them hope, even though my tale is not a sweet one. My experience shows that creativity alone is not enough to succeed. You have to be as dogged in solving the commercial problems that you meet, as you were in solving the creative challenge that turned your idea into reality in the first place. However, I hope my story has shown that the adventure can be rewarding and worth taking the risks to achieve success.

In recent months, Dyson have won design prizes in the Czech Republic and Japan as well as the Prince Philip Designer's Prize and an Oscar from the French book *Inventions of the World 1998*. Winning these prizes renews my belief that, with perseverance, good design will win through. As a member of the Design Council and a Trustee of the Design Museum, I am able to put forward new ideas for promoting creativity in industry. The people who have the influence to make change happen are beginning to listen. The current British Prime Minister, Tony Blair, recognises the need to foster creativity in schools and industry. His ideas for highlighting the importance of design in education and society must be put into practice. The Design Council's Millennium Products scheme, which will show examples of successful product design, is one way to create a greater public awareness of things that matter to me and other designers. I have accepted an invitation to join the Millennium Products Panel and am excited that I will be able to encourage British creativity. I was also extremely flattered to be awarded the CBE in the 1998 New Year Honours List.

In the last year many talented and creative people have joined Dyson. The workforce has doubled to 950 and the company has experienced compound growth of 300%. Success has brought rewards, but also many challenges in running such a rapidly expanding international business. Looking to the future, Dyson is investing £15 million in a new 65,000 sq ft R&D facility adjacent to our existing factory, which will employ 200 young people generating ideas and developing new product designs. It will be opened by Tony Blair in July. Dyson may be growing up, but we're not growing old. We have an adolescent zeal for good design and a belief that we can promote it.

index

With thanks to Kay Harford, Amanda Huish, Stephanie Whitham, Dawn Gallagher, Gillian Pearce, Lavinia Collison, Kathy Underhill, Arlene Williams, Jon Crumblehulme, John Radley, Anna Langston, Debby Stokes, Patricia Woolford, Paul Kellow, Andrew Hughes, Gregory Lloyd Pryce, Dale Irving, Joanna Clark, Catherine Rainbow, Mary Hay, Martin Aldham Haigh, Paul Cowdall, Neil Musgrave, Pauline Henly, Steven Healey, Lesley Elcock, Sylvia O'Leary, Alix Dewhirst, Melanie Batt, Angela Cavaciuti, Wendy Marselle, Kevin Pearce, Simon Elliott, Jane Bateman, Lorraine Scott, Karen Ballantyne, Judith Barham, Nicolas Beckwith, Beryl Henly, Marilyn Williams, Ingrid Tomlinson, Don Falcone, Martin Williams, Joy Smyth, John Marshall, Alan Mower, Tracey Murphy, Justin Robert Watts, Deborah Bendle, Melanie Townsend, Janet Barley, Graeme Clark, Derek Headon, Julie Sarah Remington, Jason Phillip Tindal, Kevin Bennett, Elaine Harper, Tony Mellors, Barrie Ashford, Dawn Dukes, Suzanne Burgess, Jayne Plackett, Nicky Mallinder, Tracy Ellis, Laura Smith, Tina Glen, Nicola Manning, Tracey Scully, Elizabeth Morris, Kevin Russinger, Nicholas Broughall, Janice Jennings, James Millar, Jamie Carter, Richard Cottis, Jane White, Nick Barnes, Stephen Gittins, Colin Irvin, Elizabeth Black, Roger Parry, Ian Ryles, Trevor Walker, Claire Conley, Graham Minshaw, Paul Holmes, Robin Jaques, Peter Hodsoll, Stephen Jukes, Andy White, Geraldine Seager, Jon Rowley, Michael Hamill, Sarah Stevens, Andrew Boulton, Kenneth Gateley, Harold Tomlinson, Jackie Jones, Helen Arnold, Diane Gillett, Michele Wall, Emma Westgarth, Caroline Errington, Helen Say, Magali Hamon, Sarah Breckenridge, Julie Downing, Timothy Jensen, Peter Melbourne, Sarah Wrann, Jennie Griffiths, Bella Roberts, Mary Collins, Sally Champion, Anne Broadbent, Sam Tracy, Marlene Frizzel, Sue Joce, Sharon Young, Edward McGeady, Annabelle O'Connell, Rosemary Cooke, Eunice Noonan, Michelle Heap, Heather Minishaw, Fabrice Bourat, Nathalie Comte, Isabelle Gallouin, Dennis De Roos, John Clark, Charles Hampson, Michelle Hands, Mark Bickerstaffe, Philip Dix, Gail Lydall, Steven Challes, Joanne Humphrey, Rachel Catling, Faye Coombes, Lynda Cusdin, Timothy Julian Sexton, Jim Turner, Anna Money, Paul Dymond, Denise Ann Norcott, Cherry Goddard, Alistair Nash, Jeremy Whiting, Johnathon Porter, Guy Goddard, Simon Killane, Sidney Shield, Graeme Lock, David Thomas, Peter David Thomas, Martin Pope, Kenneth Lee, Walter Spicer, Richard Palmer, Bob Gomez, James Gore, John Briffit, Shawn House, Steve Randall, Pam Cook, Herbert Magri-Overend, Lisa Briggs, Robert Bunting, Brett Conway, Graham Carter, Gary Gardo, Anthony Ireland, Timothy Newton, Ruby Betts, Alan Briggs, Richard Needham, Adam Tucker, Nick Pearch, Neil Edwards, Glen Leakey, Malcolm McFarlane, Rebecca Trentham, Jonathan Snell, Jackie Johnson, Julie Evans, Marilyn Merchant, George Smith, Anita Leighton, Adam Taylor, Michael Whatmore, Damian Merchant, John Morgan, Christopher Young, Carol Caygill, Lenor Mustoe, Deborah Thomas, Ali Lahcen, Wayne Carpenter, Bruce Bates, Margaret Glass, Audrey Topsom, David Clarke, Marion Hicks, Patricia Skull, William Hoare, Kevin Peet, Robert Baldwin, Louise

Chadbourne, Peter Thomas, Jamie Luckett, Gary Clifford, Marcia Chadbourne, Kieron Amos, George Kordula, Nigel Caines, Johnathan Stapleford, Malcolm Cooper, Jacqueline Smith, Teresa Triggs, Micheal Crawford, Patrick Reid, Marcus Reeve, Frederick Brown, Alexander Connell, Edward Pascal, Marie Scott, David Foster, Brian Bird, Chris Elkins, Marion Watts, Marie Palmer, Angela Boswell, Shirley Norton, Christine Maloney, Jacqueline Kinzel, Pamela Woodward, William Pinchin, Steve Briffitt, Richard Howard, Michelle Priestner, Pauline Woodward, Terence Woodward, John Broom, Geoffrey Castle, Mark Clifford, John Howles, Philip Buckland, Jean McCaffrey, Jonathan Aplin, Stuart Jago, David Catley, Jenny Jordan, Lewis Dunlop, Brian Block, Ian Cook, Toby Rivett, Rodney Young, Neil John Soutar, Mike Minihan, Danny Cotter, Christopher Harmen, Mark Moore, Collette Clayton, Keith Knowles, Malcolm Chambers, Michele Falcone, Lee Scarth, Paul Damon Ford, Roger Moore, Jill Trudgian, Paul Rosser, Scott Constable, David West, Lisa Porter, Alan Blakeborough, Simon Winter, Christopher Steward, Richard Crawford, Colin Treweke, Graham Sutherland, Leonard O'Connell, Mariusz Podraza, Kevin Rack, Tracey Homeswood, Susan Chivers, Alan Doman, Paul Lucas, Jennifer Hares, Fiona West, Valerie Morgan, Michael Morgan, Peter Hill, Dean Brown, Edward Harris, Barrie Hawkins, Stephen Hanks, Collis Aneita Dawkins, Clarence McLeod, Tracy Pierce, Linda Pierce, Lynda Moss, Catherine Mitchell, Stuart Belt, Stanley Wynter, Diane Wood, Alexander Leckie, Gary Mason, Tara Davies, May Harford, Richard Turner, Adrian Stowe, David Holland, Louise Webb, Raymond Potter, Anthony Bain, Malcolm Perrett, Susan King, Susan Simmons, Louise Burke, Rosemarie Stalker, Robert Meadows, Stephen Boardman, Aleya Diab, Robert Matthews, Gary Rundle, Louise Boswell, Gordon Willshire, Angela Wigman, Regan Garlick, Max Buckley, Andrew Murphy, Darron Dooley, Nicholas Edwards, Jacqueline King, Jonathon Hatter, Haydn Briggs, Gareth Treweke, Glyn Price-Brind, Jason Bull, Lisa Chadbourne, Christina Kinzel, Jean Hodsoll, Roger Timbrell, Laura McGuire, Joanne Slade, Andrew Jones, Marcus Hall, David Bishop, Simon Blake, Jacqueline Gibbon, Brian Dixon, David Binstead, Helen Petie, Helen Drew, Colin Samphire, Susan Joce, Jonathan Bird, Valerie Satchell, Clive King, Tanya Genever, Philip Whittaker, Karen Preece, Jennifer McPherson, Michaela Griffiths, John Farrell, Alexandra Riby, Elaine Gale, Timothy Spicer, Sara Crewe, Philip Blythe, Shirley Davies, Elizabeth Tanner, Lisa Kent, Richard Mickish, Wendie Mayl, Stella Rumers, Tracey Ball, Edna Miles, Jamie Bennett, Jacob Wardle, Julie Allen, Gillian Eatock, Geoffrey Fortune, Alan Coates, Kathleen Carter, Keith Appleton, Christine Trowbridge, Robert Andrew, Alan Lambert, Martin Tostevin, Noel Caffrey, Sharon Tamplin, Elizabeth Hooper, Rita Connell, Shayne Walker, Craig Dicker, Helen Spencer, Wayne Kibble, Claire Reynolds, Paul O'Connell, Paul Stevenson, Neil Young, Greg Kilmurray, Nigel Henly, Julie Edgell, Patrick Wicks, Susan Paisey, Brian Lawford, Jagpal Singh, Dennis Phillips, Tammy Paisey, Victoria Davies, Julie Ireland, Ronald Haines, Robert Ponting, Susan

Bridge, Caroline Chadbourne, Paul Edwards, Mark Jago, Terance Cowan, Celia Timbrell, Luke Harding, Greg Prowting, Stephen Casey, Paul Sanderson, Tracy Cook, Paul Pattinson, Tracy Mead, Leslie John Green, Peter Knighton, Leanne Cabell, Caroline Ryan, Simon Thomas, Donna Chivers, Annabelle Phillips, Anthony Townsend, Jabir Ahmed, Paul Simpson, Trevor Bull, Rita Henly, Rachel Hobbs, John Wheeler, Tracey Phillips, Georgina White, Anthony Bishop, Linda Forster, Nigel Skinner, Roger Parker, Joseph Headland, James Taylor, Timothy Hughes, David Castle, Gavin Tate, Theresa Stapleton, Sara Beckett, Alan Sheppard, Sandra King, Stephen Naylor, Joan Payne, Sue Glachan, John Hedges, Andrew Fergusson, Terence Gilbert, Graham Smith, Donna Yorke, Stuart Goswell, Jeremy Gahagan, Angela Watts, Rebecca Hamilton, Kevin Barber, David Benford, David Higgins, Jackie Edge, Margaret White, Timothy Brownsell, Marie O'Connell, Hazel Hunt, Christopher Hehir, Emma Gobey, Elaine Bushrod, Alvin Beaven, Christine Temple, Matthew Allard, Peter Arnold, Alexander Bommer, James Braithwaite, Matthew Childe, Jason Clark, Keith Curtis, Deirdre Dyson, Jacob Dyson, Samuel Dyson, Nicholas Fitton, Thomas Ford, Michael Ganderton, Michael Gay, James Gill, Christopher Hodgson, Judith Hughes, Alexander Knox, Wouter Konings, James Lamb, Andrew MacLeod, Michael Merrington, Richard Nighy, Lee Pearson, Chris Perrin, Neil Phillips, Jonathan Porter, Chris Procter, Miles Quance, Daniel Reynolds, Alexander Riley, Robert Seaman, Kevin Simmons, John Sissons, Allison Spiller, Evan Stevens, Mark Storer, Robert Stringer, Andrew Thompson, Mike White, Pat Young, Ernest Smith, Joann Gardner, Adrian Cole, Sharon Cole, Michael A Morgan, Krysia Lawrence, Stuart Galbraith, Daniel Fitzsimons, James Wright, Michael Rea, Keith Howell, Raymond Dyke, Yasmin Mckenzie, Shaun Garrett, Patrick Brundell, Raymond Woodruff, Matthew Baskerville, Andrew Lang, Kevin Warner, Kevin Pike, John Reynolds, Edward Thomas, Sean Chaplin, Andrew Drew, Kevin Hatherall, Adrian Mings, Keith Drew, Colin Fletcher, Matthew Brotherton, Michael Holmes, Peter Cooke, Peter Jones, Michael Gavaghan, Simon Kuchczynski, Jeffrey Hawkins, Michael Fischer, David Fletcher, John Mitchell, John Deacon, Adrian Richards, Jeff Olsen, Anthony Dolman, Jason Alba, Mary Kordula, Robert Williams, Mike Deacon, Stuart Williams, Jason Carey, Barry Joce, Michael Suter, Ray Waters, Jeremy Garlick, Andrea Coggins, Nicholas Foster, Robin Brown, Allan Millman, Norman Soles, Ian McLeod, Tony Murauka, Gill Smith, Dick Baxter, Dick Fischer, Mike Rootes, Ken Mullen, Mike Burlington, Gareth Jones, Simeon Jupp, Peter Gammack, Graham Clark, Sháá Wasmund, Clare Harmen, Harriet Rodgers, Kathyn Carter, Scott Constable